UNDERSTANDING THE TIMES SERIES

A Biblical Worldview and Apologetics Curriculum for Grades 9–12

FOUNDATIONS

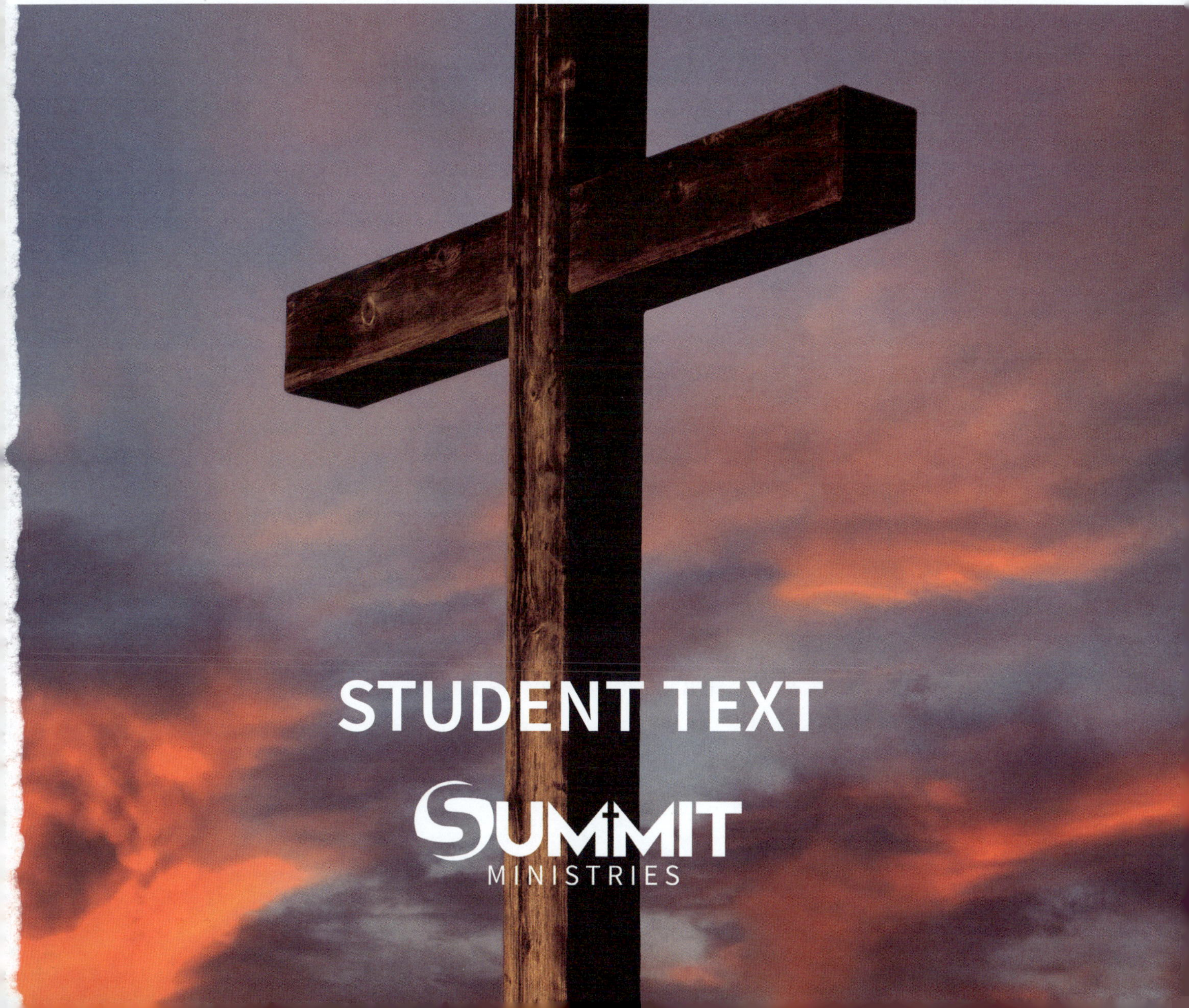

STUDENT TEXT

SUMMIT MINISTRIES

Acknowledgements

Director of Publishing and Content:

Aaron Klemm

Manager of Curriculum and Instructional Design:

Macki Jones, MA Curriculum & Instruction

Authors

Ben Keiser, MATS Biblical Studies
Julie Smyth, MA Biblical Studies
Kim Pettit, MA Communications
Macki Jones, MA Curriculum & Instruction
Mike Hamel
Robin Dembicki, MEd Educational Leadership

Editorial Team

Avrie Roberts
Beth Robinson
John Conaway
Julie Smyth, MA Biblical Studies
Kim Pettit, MA Communications
Lorraine Wadman
Macki Jones, MA Curriculum & Instruction
Robin Dembicki, MEd Educational Leadership
Sabrina-Page Bernardi, MLIS

Design Team

Peter A. Schmidt
Scot McDonald
Claire Coleman
Mike Riester

Foundations, Book I of the Understanding the Times Series
Student Textbook

Published by Summit Ministries
P.O. Box 207
Manitou Springs, CO 80829

The Foundations Student Textbook adapts and expands on *Understanding the Faith: A Survey of Christian Apologetics* by Jeff Myers, copyright © 2016 David C. Cook
Foundations is published with the permission of David C Cook.

ISBN: 978-1-957406-36-7

Printed in India
First Printing, 2024

Table of Contents

1 Introduction

1. How Can I Find Direction in Life?

▸ **OBJECTIVE: You will be able to describe what a worldview is and give examples of worldviews observed in the world today.**

Suppose you find yourself lost and alone in the city of San Francisco, California. In order to get unlost, what would you do? The first thing you would probably do is reach for your phone. Suppose your phone battery is dead. What then? To find your way, you would need to get a map or ask someone for directions. But what you need is not just *any* map or set of directions. After all, if you're lost in San Francisco and someone gives you a map of Detroit, you're not going to make much progress. What you need is a clear map of San Francisco or directions from someone who knows the city well.

Life is similar. At some point most of us find ourselves a little bit lost and in need of directions. We ask ourselves questions like: "Who am I?" "Where did I come from?" "Why am I here?" "Whom can I trust?" and "How should I live?" If we know the answers to these questions, we will have a better chance of navigating the world in a way that is purposeful and meaningful. But finding directions for life is not easy. After all, there are hundreds of voices that all claim to offer direction and answers to life's biggest questions. These diverse voices all represent worldviews. A **worldview** is *a pattern of ideas and beliefs that helps us make sense of the world and that guides our decisions and actions.*

Christianity, Islam, secularism, Marxism, new spirituality, and postmodernism are just a few of the worldviews in the world today. Each of these claims to accurately explain the world and help people find direction and purpose for life. But some worldviews fail to accurately describe reality. They are like having a map of Detroit when you're lost in San Francisco. Following a faulty worldview can get you even more lost and may result in disastrous consequences. So, how can you know which worldview is right?

Finding the right path requires careful study. Summit Ministries' Understanding the Times Series is designed to aid you on this journey. This series is written from the conviction that the Christian worldview best explains the world and helps us to live in it with meaning and purpose. It is designed to help you find your way through life using the lens of Christianity. Along the way, we'll also explore objections to Christianity and consider the answers that other worldviews give to life's big questions. This series consists of four books.

1. **Foundations:** This volume introduces the foundational building blocks of the Christian worldview. These include God (Father, Son, and Holy Spirit), the Bible and its metanarrative or grand storyline, what it means to love God and neighbor, and how to practice your faith in Christ.
2. **Apologetics:** This volume provides guidance for defending and commending the Christian faith to others. It also demonstrates how the Christian worldview stands up to common objections to it in society today.
3. **Worldviews:** This volume considers the Christian worldview in comparison to five other worldviews while examining the answers they each give to life's biggest questions in areas like theology, philosophy, politics, biology, and more.

4. **Culture:** This final volume shows how the Christian worldview has the resources to engage with the most challenging and controversial issues of our day, and it provides a model for faithful Christian engagement with the world.

2. What Does It Mean to Be a Christian?

▸ **OBJECTIVE: You will be able to explain what it means to be Christian, as well as three common misconceptions about being a Christian.**

The book in your hands, *Foundations*, seeks to help you understand what Christianity is all about. In this first chapter, we'll introduce you to some of the foundational ideas on which the Christian worldview is built. In the chapters that follow, we'll unpack those ideas in greater detail. Let's begin with a question: "What does it mean to be a Christian?" If you were to ask 100 different people this question, you might get 100 different answers. However, not all answers are equal, and there are many misconceptions about Christianity.

One of the most common misconceptions is that Christianity is about following a set of rules. Here's what this view sometimes sounds like: "Christians are not supposed to swear, drink, use drugs, or have sex outside of marriage. By obeying these rules, they earn God's favor and are rewarded with heaven, but everyone else is condemned to hell." Christians who have this view are sometimes harshly critical of anyone who does not live up to their moral standard, while non-Christians think being a Christian means being judgmental and never having any fun.

Other people have the misconception that Christianity is an otherworldly religion that doesn't have much to do with the here and now. We might state this view like this: "This world is going to hell in a handbasket, but one day Christians will escape to heaven. In the meantime, it's our job to make sure we get as many people saved as possible. Nothing else really matters." Christians who have this misconception sometimes fail to show much concern for the natural world or earthly problems like poverty and injustice, while non-Christians think Christians are so obsessed with going to heaven that they neglect everything else.

Another common misconception is the idea that you are automatically a Christian if your parents were, that Christianity is something that you are born into, a part of your family or cultural heritage. People with this idea may have respect for Jesus and the Bible, but they may not be inclined to take either very seriously. Meanwhile, devout followers of other religions sometimes wonder why these "Christians" don't seem to care very much about their faith.

Despite the popularity of these views, they do not help us understand that Christianity is about what God has done, is doing, and will do. It's about participating in the great story that God is telling, that finds its climax in Jesus. In fact, the word *Christian* refers to *a person who follows Christ.* The word is derived from *Christ*, a title for Jesus which means *Messiah*. Jesus' followers were first called *Christians* in Antioch during the first century.[1] It is possible that the

title was invented by non-Christians and used in a derogatory way to describe those who followed Jesus.[2] In any case, the name has stuck. Christianity is centered on the person of Jesus Christ and focuses its understanding of the world through the teachings of the Holy Bible.

To be a Christian is to be a Jesus-follower (Luke 18:22); it is to believe that what he said about himself is true, place one's trust in him, and commit to following his ways. Christians believe Jesus is more than just a good moral teacher. Christians believe Jesus is God, and that he came to save us from our sins by dying on the cross and rising again so we can experience true life. He is the only One worthy of our ultimate allegiance and has commissioned us to bring and participate in Jesus' good news of salvation, healing, and hope to the world. This is what Christianity is all about.

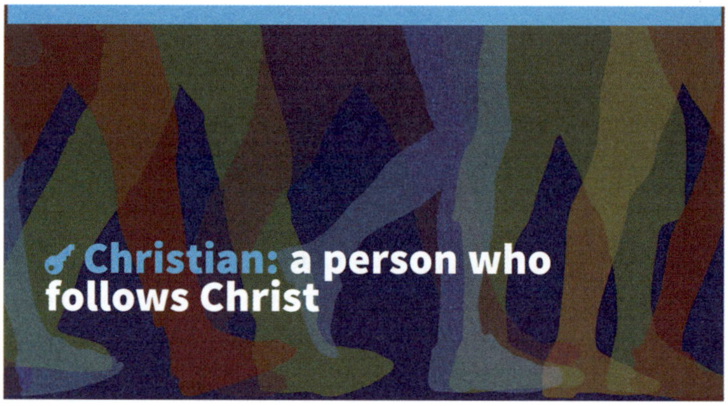
Christian: a person who follows Christ

3. What Is the Bible, and What Is Its Place in a Christian's Life?

▸ **OBJECTIVE: You will be able to articulate why the Bible is foundational for Christians.**

The description of Christianity that we have offered above comes from a careful reading of its foundational book—the Bible. For Christians, the Bible plays a central role in shaping and informing our thoughts, values, decisions, and actions. It is foundational to our worldview. If you've spent any amount of time among Christians, you've probably heard things like, "The Bible says," "According to Scripture," or "We want to have a biblical worldview." But why all the fuss? What's the big deal about the Bible anyway? Isn't it just an old book?

Yes, the Bible is a really old book, written *by* people who were inspired by God and *to* people who have long since been dead. However, Christians value the Bible and place themselves under its authority because they believe that in it, God reveals himself to us. He does this so that we can enter into a personal and eternal relationship with him and live meaningfully and purposefully. While the Bible was not written directly *to* us, it has been written *for* us. God speaks through it, even today, to communicate his will and help us live in ways that are pleasing to him.

The Bible consists of sixty-six diverse books, which collectively tell the great story of God, the world, and our place in the world. These books have been divided into chapters and then portions, called *verses,* which are all numbered. Christians often reference a Bible passage by stating a book's name followed by the chapter and verse, and you will see such references throughout this book. (You'll learn more about what the Bible is in Chapter 2).

It may sound naïve to live your life with reference to a book that is almost 2,000 years old (and most of it is much older). Yet, it is only in modern times that people have come to think of older things as less valuable or reliable. The Christian writer C. S. Lewis identified this modern error as *chronological snobbery*. He argued that it's a mistake to assume that we today are necessarily smarter or more enlightened than our ancestors.[3]

Chronological snobbery fails in at least two ways. First, while it's certainly true that humans have made great strides in learning, this hasn't necessarily made us better people. For example, we now have incredible technology, which can be harnessed to do wonderful things. But this same technology can also be, and often is, used to harm people. Think of all the weapons now available for killing people on a mass scale! Second, if you're looking for directions in San Francisco, would you rather take them from someone who's been around and knows the city well, or someone who just moved there? We can ask the same question when it comes to finding directions in life. While age doesn't guarantee that something is true, an idea that has stood the test of time and transformed the lives of millions of people for good should not simply be shoved aside in favor of the latest, most fashionable idea.

So, the Bible should not be dismissed simply because it is old. We must look deeper. Both old ideas and new ideas must be carefully considered. Ultimately, all of us look to someone or something to give us direction in life. The question is not if we will submit to an authority, but to whom or to what we will submit. That's why, in Chapter 3, we'll consider some evidence from history and archeology that supports the Bible's claim to be a reliable guide for life.

4. How Are We Supposed to Read the Bible?

▸ OBJECTIVE: You will be able to explain two common mistakes that people make in reading the Bible.

The Bible is God's revelation to us, so we should treat it with reverence and learn well how to use it. We should approach it with humility, listen to it, and be ready to learn from it, rather than to impose our own ideas upon it. To say that the Bible is God's Word is *not* to say that it simply dropped out of heaven as a rule book to be followed, ready-made with answers to all of our questions. It is not as simple as following a GPS with easy instructions—stop, turn right, reverse, etc. In fact, there are many mistakes to avoid when reading the Bible, two of which are described here. (We'll look at five more in Chapter 4.)

The first mistake to avoid is called *proof texting*. It is what happens when Bible readers assume that finding God's will on a particular topic is as simple as locating a verse in Scripture or when they string together dozens of random verses to prove a particular point. The main problem with this approach is that it totally ignores the context and storyline of the Bible.[4] By proof texting, you can make the Bible say pretty much anything you want. For example, did you know that the Bible says *there is no God*?

Yes, these very words are in the Bible; but if you look at the context, you will discover that far from denying the existence of God, the author is actually making the claim that God *does* exist: "The fool says in his heart, 'There is no God'" (Psalm 14:1).

Of course, we need to gather verses together to discover what the Bible actually says, but we need to do this in a responsible way. The difference is between starting with a belief and then trying to make the Bible fit that belief (proof texting), or starting with an open mind and letting the Bible shape our beliefs. In Chapter 4, we'll learn seven steps that can help us become better Bible readers.

The second mistake is pursuing the Bible as the end goal rather than the pursuit of God. In others words, do not place the importance of the Bible above God, the Person who wrote it. Ultimately, the Bible's authority is authority that comes from God. When people forget this, the Bible can become a rigid rule book or a weapon with which to condemn others or to support our own agendas.

To read the Bible well, we need to understand its content in context. This requires discernment. In the end, however, reading the Bible isn't just about getting the right interpretation, but about getting in on what God is doing.[5] As we'll see in Chapter 5, the Bible is a grand story, in which we are invited to be participants. By calling it a story, we're not saying that the Bible is a made-up fairy tale. Rather, the Bible tells the *true* story of the world. It is a story that helps us make sense of all our individual stories. In reading the Bible, we discover who God is, how much we are loved, what his plan for the world is, and how we can be a part of what God is doing. It is in this grand story that we begin to find answers to life's biggest questions.

5. Where Have We Been? Creation to Israel

▸ **OBJECTIVE: You will be able to briefly describe what happened in the first three acts and the interlude of the biblical story.**

Those who pick up a Bible for the first time encounter all sorts of odd things—a human being made out of dirt, another taken out of him, a mysterious talking serpent, long stories about a seemingly small and insignificant group of people, strange laws, miracles, violence, and prophecies. If you think the Bible is a collection of nice moral tales, you're in for a shock. To make sense of the Bible, it is helpful to think of its overall story like the acts or movements in a play. In this book, we'll discuss the biblical story in six acts with an intermission or interlude.[6] Here is an overview of the first three acts and the interlude:

Act 1: Creation. The Bible begins with God. Out of nothing, God speaks all of creation into existence. The Bible gives us two brief chapters to describe this, and many details we would like to know are left out. But these two chapters want us to get at least one thing absolutely clear: God's creation is good. They also describe the creation of human beings, who are made in the image of God. Humans are to fill the earth with their descendants

and partner with God in bringing abundance out of creation. At the beginning of the Bible's story, humans have life-giving and harmonious relationships with God, themselves, other people, and nature. This is the subject of Chapter 6.

Tapestry, Bible scenes, 16th-century Italy

Act 2: The Fall. This blissful situation sadly doesn't last. God gives the first humans one rule: don't eat from the Tree of Knowledge of Good and Evil. But a mysterious serpent appears and essentially tells the humans that God is holding out on them, that if they disobey his command and eat the fruit, they will be gods themselves. Surrendering to the temptation, they eat the fruit, and it isn't long before the world is plunged into chaos. Violence spreads on the earth. Humans no longer trust God or one another; they become internally broken and nature becomes a threat. All of this is the result of what the Bible calls sin, and it will occupy our attention in Chapter 7.

Act 3: Redemption Initiated. The good news is that God isn't the sort to withdraw when things go wrong. Instead, he stays involved and chooses a single family, through which he intends to bless the whole world. This is the family of Abraham, whose descendants became the nation of Israel. The majority of the Old Testament (the first part of the Bible) is taken up with their story and so is Chapter 8 of this book. It is a story of struggle, failure, and unfaithfulness to God, interspersed with blips of faithfulness and hope. Through Israel's history, God reveals his true character and demonstrates his refusal to give up on the world he created.

Interlude: The Second Temple Period. The Old Testament ends with Israel scattered and awaiting God's redemption. During a period of almost 400 years after the last book of the Old Testament, there is no direct revelation from God. But this time was anything but silent. In Chapter 9, we'll survey this important period to discover what happened to God's people during this trying time. For both Jews and Christians, these three acts and the interlude describe our history. This is where we have been.

6. Where Are We Now? Jesus to New Creation

▸ **OBJECTIVE: You will be able to summarize the final three acts of the biblical story.**

Unless we understand the first parts of the biblical story—creation, fall, and redemption initiated—we will have a very difficult time making any sense of the rest of the story,

which continues with the New Testament (the second section of the Bible).[7] The New Testament portrays Jesus as the climax of Israel's story. Because of Jesus, a whole new world has come into being, not only for Israel, but for all people. This is what the next three acts of the biblical story are all about.

Act 4: Redemption Accomplished. According to the Bible, Jesus is more than just a good teacher or a spiritual sage. He is God in the flesh. In fact, being free from sin, Jesus models for us everything that humans were meant to be. Jesus is also the long-awaited Messiah, the one who fulfills all the hopes and expectations of Israel. Jesus came to Earth to announce that the kingdom of God was arriving in his life and ministry. He claimed to be the true Lord of this kingdom, and he demonstrated his authority by teaching and healing.

Yet, Jesus was not the Messiah everyone expected. The Jews were hoping for a political messiah who would overthrow their conquerors and defeat their enemies. Jesus, however, came peacefully and preached a message of forgiveness and reconciliation. Eventually, he was put to death by jealous religious leaders colluding with political authorities. Surprisingly, the New Testament writers portray Jesus' death not as a defeat, but as his victory over sin and death. Three days after his crucifixion, Jesus arose from the grave and soon after ascended to God's throne to claim his rulership over the whole world. We'll learn more about what all this means in Chapter 10.

Act 5: Restoration Initiated. The subject of Chapter 11 is the church. After the ascension of Jesus, the Holy Spirit descended on Jesus' followers, empowering them to proclaim the good news about Jesus throughout all the world. Soon they began gathering in small communities to worship Jesus and follow his teaching. The church was born. The church lives in an *already, not yet* time. In other words, the kingdom of God has already arrived in Jesus, but it has not yet been fully implemented. The church is tasked with proclaiming the good news of God's kingdom and showing how it makes a difference in every relationship. This good news is not just about individual salvation, but about healing and hope for all of creation.

Resurrection of Christ, All Saints Church, Zagreb, Croatia

Act 6: Restoration Accomplished. In Chapter 12, we'll see how the story of the Bible ends. The story that began in a garden ends in a magnificent city, where God is worshipped and evil is banished forever. Before that end, the church must learn what it means to be faithful to Jesus and suffer for his name by resisting the forces of evil in the world. One day, Jesus will return to Earth, bringing judgment. Then, all things will be made new and God's kingdom will be fully implemented. We will be transformed so that we can live as the people we were created to be.

These last three acts help us see where we are now, and what is coming in the future. They show us how we can find meaning for our stories by participating in God's story.

7. Who Is God? Who Am I?

▸ OBJECTIVE: You will be able to discuss the importance of knowing God and ourselves.

The Protestant reformer John Calvin once said that all true wisdom consists of knowledge about God and knowledge about ourselves.[8] Theologians and philosophers have studied both of these things in great depth under the headings of theology (study of God) and anthropology (study of humans). However, truths about God and ourselves are not systematically laid out, but given directly and indirectly throughout Scripture. We learn about God through the way he reveals himself in the biblical story. We learn about ourselves by listening to what God says about people and observing the lives of various biblical characters. In Chapters 13–14, we'll take a deeper, more focused dive into what the biblical story reveals about who God is and who humans are.

The Trinity, detail, Church of Santa Maria dell,Anima, Rome, Italy

Proverbs 9:10 says, "The fear of the LORD is the beginning of wisdom, and the knowledge of the Holy One is insight." Many people view God primarily as a police officer who keeps people in line or as a court judge who passes sentences on criminals. Others see God as a nice old man who is pretty much fine with whatever we do. Still others believe that God is a bitter and angry tyrant, an egotistical madman obsessed with his own power and glory. Because what we believe about God will affect the way we live, it's important that we have true knowledge of God as he is revealed in Scripture.

That said, the goal of theology is not to get God figured out. God is infinite, we are finite, and so our knowledge of him will always be limited. However, in Chapter 13, we'll see that God has revealed enough of himself so that we may know him and entrust ourselves to him. We'll learn that God reveals himself as self-existent, spirit, personal, eternal, all-knowing, all-powerful, present, unchanging, holy, wise, righteous, and loving. We'll also take a look at what it means that God is a Trinity and why this doctrine is at the heart of the Christian faith.

Knowledge of ourselves is the subject of Chapter 14. Self-discovery is an important part of personal growth. Of course, self-discovery can be dangerous when it becomes a quest for independence from God and others or a pathway to indulging sinful desires. However, the kind of self-discovery we're talking about here has to do with growing into the individual people God created us to be—people who love God and others. This involves learning more about our unique personalities, how God has designed us, and what he says about us.

Sadly, for many Christians, their identity is defined by sin, and they view themselves as worthless. While the Bible is clear that we are trapped and embroiled in sin from that we cannot escape on our own, "sinner" is not our true identity. That is not who we were created to be. God created us out of love and he longs for us to be all that he created us to be. We are called to imitate Christ as image-bearers; it is when we are transformed to be more like Christ that we become the best version of ourselves. When we live out of our new identity as God's beloved children, we are living as the people God created us to be.

8. How Can I Become Like Jesus?

▸ **OBJECTIVE:** You will be able to conclude that becoming like Christ is a lifelong process.

The goal of the Christian life is to become like Christ. However, having a Christian worldview will not necessarily make you more like Jesus. We might think that if we get our beliefs straightened out, our behavior will necessarily follow the right course. Though our beliefs do influence our behavior, they do not determine it. For example, if I really believe that people are made in God's image, then I have motivation and a responsibility to treat them with dignity and respect. However, just because I believe people are made in the image of God doesn't mean that I will always treat them that way.

Our behavior may influence our beliefs just as much as our beliefs influence our behavior. For example, consider the people who are addicted to pornography, which is readily accessible in many formats. Yet, if people are made in God's image, as Christianity teaches, then pornography is wrong. It treats people as objects to be used and abused for one's own selfish pleasure instead of as human beings worthy of respect. Someone who wants to keep looking at pornography may adopt a worldview to justify that behavior.[9]

It is said that you will become like whatever you worship. To worship someone or something is to show your devotion and adoration. If you worship money, you likely will become cold, callused, and greedy. If you worship power, you may become arrogant and domineering. So then, becoming like Christ requires more than simply having correct beliefs. It requires that we learn to worship him with the whole of our lives. As one Christian philosopher puts it, "We don't need less than knowledge; we need more. We need to recognize the power of habit."[10] We need habits that help train us to be followers of Jesus. However, following Jesus is not only about having good habits any more than it is only about having right beliefs. Becoming like Christ also means that our affections, desires, and motivations will be aligned with Christ. This only happens through the transforming power of the Holy Spirit.

Throughout the centuries, Christians have engaged in numerous habits and spiritual practices—prayer, meditating on Scripture, solitude, giving, and more—all with the intended goal of helping us to become more like Christ. These are often called *spiritual disciplines*. This term can be somewhat misleading, as it suggests that these habits are dull drudgery. However, spiritual disciplines are not about just doing religious stuff but about practicing our faith and opening ourselves up to God's work in us. They are about what Christ does in us to transform us to be like him.

Becoming like Christ is a lifelong process, but this is not a process that occurs in isolation. We learn to be like Jesus in the company of others. We need other believers to encourage us and help us practice the habits that open us to God's Spirit. We'll learn more about all this in Chapters 15–16.

9. What Does It Look Like to Be a Disciple of Jesus?

▸ **OBJECTIVE: You will be able to express why love is a Christian's primary calling.**

What people think Christianity is all about often has something to do with their experience of Christians. For some people, Christians are the biggest turnoff to Christianity. Sadly, some people have only ever experienced Christianity from Christians who are judgmental, mean-spirited, or unconcerned about the world. If you've experienced this yourself, you know how damaging it can be. While this is a disappointing reality, we cannot judge Christianity only on the basis of our experience (as important as that is). There are two primary reasons for this.

First, as we will see in Chapter 7, Christianity teaches that all human beings have fallen into sin. And trusting in Jesus doesn't make sin disappear. Though sin no longer has power over the Christian, every day Christians must say *no* to sin and *yes* to the Holy Spirit. Every Christian is still on the journey of being transformed into Christlikeness. So, in one sense, it is no surprise that Christians can be just as sinful as anyone else. The second reason that we cannot judge Christianity only on our experience of Christians is this: we cannot blame Jesus when Christians live in a way that is opposite to what he taught.

At the heart of Jesus' teaching is the idea that God is love. Jesus showed us how much God loves us by giving of himself. He willingly surrendered his own life on the cross so that we could be saved from sin and death and experience true life. This life is above all to be characterized by love—that is, love is a Christian's primary calling. That may sound trite to you. After all, people use the word *love* for many things. People talk about loving pizza and loving their family; they say things such as "love is blind" or "all you need is love." There is much confusion about what the word *love* actually means. For many people today, loving someone is to be accepting of whatever they do as right and good for them.

But this is not love. God's love accepts us as we are, but it does not leave us there. It does not rest until we have been transformed. The love that Jesus showed is totally self-giving, sacrificial, and for our good. Christian love is giving of ourselves for others. It means honoring people as God's image-bearers and seeking their welfare before our own. To be a Christian is to learn how to love in this way. It is to follow the example of Jesus, who showed love in all his actions (more about this in Chapter 17).

If there is no love in a Christian community, something is clearly wrong. However, there are no perfect Christian communities. Learning to love like Jesus takes time. It is not natural for us to love in this way. We do not easily love our friends and neighbors, let alone our enemies. Yet, over and over again throughout the centuries, the gospel has transformed people, changing them from self-centered individuals to generous and loving human beings. The love of Jesus, displayed through his followers both individually and in

community, has had a tremendously positive impact on the world. Having received God's love for themselves, Christians are empowered by God's Spirit to demonstrate to the world that God is love.

10. Conclusion

We believe the Christian worldview best explains the world we live in and helps us to live in it with meaning and purpose. Like a good map, it helps us navigate the many decisions we face and circumstances we encounter. This book is our attempt to help you learn how to read that map. Of course, this book doesn't claim to have all the answers or address every concern you may have. It is also written from a Protestant perspective, and it does not engage in theological debates between the various branches of the Christian faith.

Perhaps you have been a Christian for a while and are looking to deepen your faith, or maybe you are still unsure of how Christianity is relevant to your life. Perhaps you are a new Christian who is seeking to understand what it means to be a follower of Jesus for the first time. Or perhaps you do not call yourself a Christian at all but are still curious about Christianity. Wherever you are in your journey, this book is for you.

We hope that in these pages, those who have been Christian for a long time will discover fresh ways in which to understand Scripture and God's plan for them; that new Christians will receive clear explanations of what the Christian story is all about; and that those who are curious or skeptical will hear the good news of the gospel and be invited to follow Jesus.

As you begin this book, we invite you to do four things:

1. Think about where you are in relationship to the Christian faith. Take some time to write down your experience with Christianity, your doubts about it, and any feelings or perceptions you have about Jesus, yourself, the world, the Bible, or anything else related to Christianity. Knowing where you are will help you better engage with the material in this book.

2. Be open to learning new things and thinking about things in a different way. Growth in any area requires humility and hard work. You must first recognize that you don't have it all figured out. And neither do we! That's why it's important to carefully evaluate what you are reading in this book and to be open to discovering new ways of thinking about Christianity.

3. Discuss what you are learning with your classmates. Sometimes talking it out is the best way to gain understanding. Share with your classmates what you are learning, as well as your questions, and see what they have to say. Be curious about the thoughts of others and gracious when you disagree.

4. Pray about what you are learning. Ultimately, the Holy Spirit is the one who illuminates us and convinces us of the truth. That's why we must continually pray for his guidance. Even if you are not a Christian, you can pray a prayer that invites God to help you—something like, "God, if you are really there, please reveal yourself to me and help me to learn about you."

By the end of this book, we hope that you will have a solid understanding of the basics of the Christian worldview. Ultimately, the Christian worldview is not merely about understanding, but about getting involved in what God is doing. As you read, think about how God is inviting you to respond and participate in his kingdom. Let's dive in!

ENDNOTES

[1] "And in Antioch the disciples were first called Christians" (Acts 11:26).

[2] Justin Taylor, "Why Were the Disciples First Called 'Christians' at Antioch? (Acts 11, 26)," *Revue Biblique* 101, no. 1 (1994): 78.

[3] C. S. Lewis, *Surprised by Joy: The Shape of My Early Life* (Orlando, FL: Harcourt Brace & Company, 1955), 207. Lewis defines chronological snobbery as "the uncritical acceptance of the intellectual climate common to our own age and the assumption that whatever has gone out of date is on that account discredited."

[4] "Proof Texting," Theopedia.com, https://www.theopedia.com/proof-texting

[5] Eugene H. Peterson, *Eat This Book: A Conversation in the Art of Spiritual Reading* (Grand Rapids, MI: Eerdmans, 2006).

[6] The outline of the biblical metanarrative used in this book is adapted from Craig G. Bartholomew and Michael Goheen, *The Drama of Scripture: Finding Our Place in the Biblical Story*, 2nd ed. (Grand Rapids: MI, Baker, 2014). *The Drama of Scripture* is an excellent text for understanding the biblical metanarrative in greater depth. We highly recommend it for those looking for a deeper dive on what is presented in Chapters 6–12 of this book.

[7] Scot McKnight, *The King Jesus Gospel: The Original Good News Revisited* (Grand Rapids, MI: Zondervan, 2011), 34–44.

[8] John Calvin, *Institutes of the Christian Religion*, trans. by Henry Beveridge (Peabody, MA: Hendrickson Publishers, 2008), Book 1.1, 4.

[9] The Bible invites us to bring all our sins and burdens to Jesus (1 John 1:9, Matthew 11:28–29). He can heal and transform our desires (1 John 1:7, Titus 2:14, 2 Corinthians 5:17).

[10] James K. A. Smith, *You Are What You Love: The Spiritual Power of Habit* (Grand Rapids, MI: Brazos Press, 2016), 6.

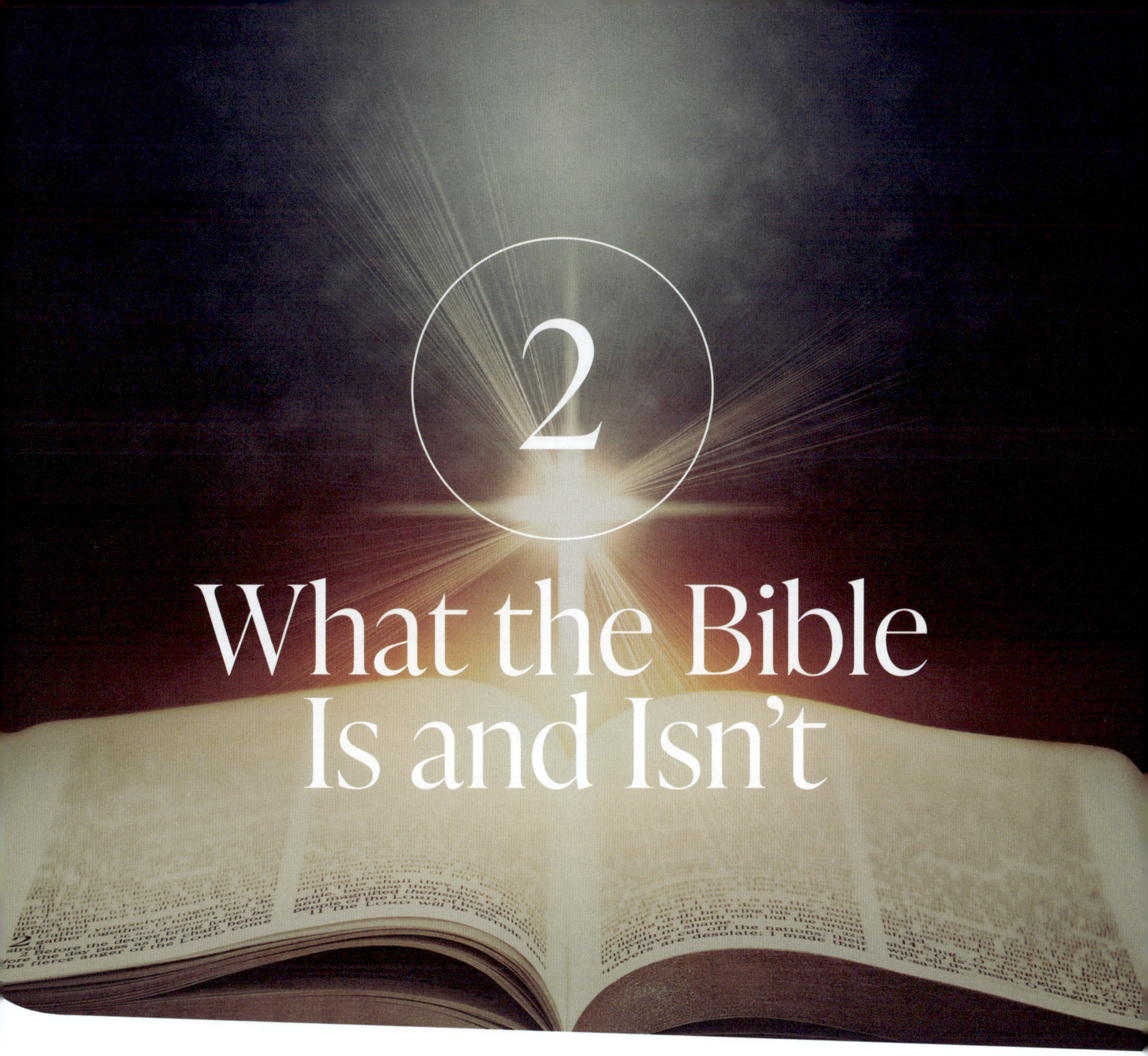

2

What the Bible Is and Isn't

1. The Importance of the Bible in History

▸ **OBJECTIVE:** You will be able to articulate four ways the Bible has influenced the world.

The Bible is the best-selling book of all time. It is printed, in part or in whole, in more than 3,400 languages.[1] There has never been another book like it. In this chapter we'll explore what the Bible is and is not. We will look at concepts such as revelation and truth that can help us grasp the place of the Bible in our lives. Hopefully, we will gain a better understanding of why and how this one book has changed the world.

"The Bible is the single most important book ever written," says the founder of the Historical Bible Society. "It is an eyewitness account of historical events of such magnitude that they have literally shaped the world in which we live. Without this book, the Western world and a good deal of the Eastern world would be completely different today."[2]

Creation of Adam by Michelangelo

Biblica, also known as *The International Bible Society*, likewise explains what is so important about the Bible:

> The Bible . . . tells the story of the Creator and his creation. It shares how humans are capable of great things, but also terrible things. It shows us how much the Creator cares for his wayward creation and what he has done to rescue it. . . . The Bible tells the story of Jesus' life, death, resurrection, and ascension, and how he came to save [us] from an eternity apart from God.[3]

The impact of the Bible can be seen in many different areas. Summit Ministries' founder, David A. Noebel, gives several examples:[4]

The Bible is part of world literature. There are more quotations in *Bartlett's Familiar Quotations* from the Bible than from any other source. Even atheist Richard Dawkins, who abhors the Bible as a source of morality, said, "A native speaker of English who has never read a word of the King James Bible is verging on the barbarian."[5]

The Bible had a significant influence on our nation. Many of the founding fathers of the United States relied upon the Bible. John Adams, the nation's second president, wrote: "The Bible is the best book in the world." His son John Quincy Adams, who became the sixth US president, wrote: "The Bible is the book [above] all others, to be read to all ages, and in all conditions of human life . . . every day."[6]

The Bible changed Western civilization. The Bible's moral guidance influenced many aspects such as the abolition of slavery, freedom and dignity for women, the formation of hospitals and schools, the promotion of liberty and justice, the advancement of science, the development of great art and architecture, and the sanctity of human life.[7]

Knowledge of the Bible is the mark of an educated person. As one Yale University professor famously wrote, "Everyone who has a thorough knowledge of the Bible may truly be called educated; and no other learning or culture, no matter how extensive or elegant, can, among Europeans and Americans, form a proper substitute."[8]

Learning about the impact of the Bible is good, but people have different ideas about what the Bible actually is and how to read and apply it.

2. How People Read the Bible Today

▸ **OBJECTIVE: You will be able to identify and explain four common ways people approach and read the Bible today.**

There are four common ways people approach and read the Bible today.

Skeptic: The skeptic approaches the Bible with hesitancy, unsure that what the Bible teaches is true or relevant. Skeptics tend to read with a critical eye and have a heightened awareness of perceived injustice or contradictions in the Bible. They ask hard questions of the text that casual readers may not be comfortable asking.

Some skeptics consider the Bible as a purely human invention. They may argue that it was written by prescientific people to explain things in nature they could not otherwise explain. Skeptics often say that the Bible contains outdated morals, customs, and myths of an ancient culture and should therefore be ignored. Some believe the Bible is full of errors and harmful teachings and speak out against its use in schools or society.[9] Many skeptics are atheists, materialists, or humanists.

Scholar: The scholar does more than simply read the Bible; the scholar studies it as deeply as a doctor studies medicine or a lawyer studies law. The skeptical scholar handles the Bible as a human book of great literary worth— a book that contains a lot of history, wisdom, and poetry, which has served as an inspiration for major works of literature and art. It is a book that has shaped whole countries through its influence on laws and culture.

Of course, there are also Christian scholars. Many are professors, theologians, and philosophers who have learned the original languages and study the Bible to learn more about God, his creation, and how to live out the Christian faith. Christian scholars seek to open up Scripture to regular readers in ways that make God's Word come alive. They treat the Bible with reverence, believing, "All Scripture is breathed out by God and profitable for teaching, for reproof, for correction, and for training in righteousness, that the man of God may be complete, equipped for every good work" (2 Timothy 3:16–17).

Seeker: The seeker reads the Bible looking for answers to life's big questions. He or she sees the Bible as *a* holy book, though not necessarily *the* Holy Book. According to a Gallup poll, 71 percent of respondents said the Bible was a holy book, though most don't accept everything it says. In fact, only 24 percent said the Bible is "the actual word of God."[10] Many seekers do not believe the Bible is the final word on spiritual matters. In other words, the Bible contains religious truth but it is not unique. They think competing works, such as the Quran for those of the Islamic faith and the Vedas for those of the Hindu faith, also contain religious truth.

Other seekers drawn to the Bible approach it with expectations more in line with Hebrews 4:12, which says, "For the word of God is living and active, sharper than any two-edged sword, piercing to the division of soul and of spirit, of joints and of marrow, and discerning the thoughts and intentions of the heart." Such individuals are open to the idea that the Bible alone is God's Word to humanity. They are looking for truth, meaning, purpose, and fulfillment.

Saint: The word *saint* is used more than 60 times in the New Testament to describe believers (for example, in Acts 26:10, Romans 1:7, 1 Corinthians 1:2). The word means *holy one*, signifying that believers are set apart by God. Scripture refers to all Christians as saints.

Four Evangelists, Saint Catherine Church, Stabroek, Belgium

Saints do more than read the Bible; they study it diligently—often with the help of Christian scholars—in order to understand it and apply it to life. They strive to obey the admonition of 2 Timothy 2:15, "Do your best to present yourself to God as one approved, a worker who has no need to be ashamed, rightly handling the word of truth." They do not read the Bible simply for information, but to grow in their relationship with God so they can better love him and other people.

These four ways of reading Scripture are not all mutually exclusive. A person can approach the Bible in different ways at different times. A skeptic can become a scholar, a seeker can become a saint, and a saint can be a scholar, too. Such shifts depend on seeing the Bible for what it actually is.

3. What the Bible Is

▸ OBJECTIVE: You will be able to describe the different components of the Bible and how it is arranged.

The Bible is a coherent book made up of 66 separate works written over the course of 1,500 years by at least 40 different writers. Some were kings and philosophers; others were fishermen and tentmakers. As one scholar put it, "They lived in diverse cultures and wrote in a variety of literary styles. But the message of the Bible is one great drama in which all of the parts fit together."[11]

The Bible is divided into two sections, the Old Testament and the New Testament. What Christians call *the Old Testament*, Jews refer to as *the Tanakh*. This portion of the Bible contains 39 books of history, poetry, and prophecy. The first five books (Genesis, Exodus, Leviticus, Numbers, and Deuteronomy) are known as *the Torah*. The Old Testament also includes Joshua, Judges, 1 and 2 Samuel, 1 and 2 Kings, as well as the Prophets (the three major prophets Isaiah, Jeremiah, and Ezekiel; and 12 minor prophets). The rest of the Old Testament is called *the Writings* and it includes everything else.

The New Testament contains 27 books. The first four books of the New Testament are called *the Gospels*. These historical accounts are biographies of Jesus' life. The Gospels are followed by the book of Acts, which tells the history of the early church. Next come letters, or epistles, to the churches and other Christians. The New Testament ends with the apocalyptic book of Revelation.

The Old Testament narrative covers a period that begins with Genesis and ends with Malachi around 400 years before Christ. However, the individual books are not all arranged according to when they were written or what happened first. Similarly, the New Testament begins with the four Gospels, although these weren't the earliest written books that are part of the New Testament. That distinction goes to some of the epistles.

In between the Old and New Testaments was a period of 400 years called the intertestamental period. The **Apocrypha** is *Jewish literature written during the intertestamental period and included in the Bible by some branches of Christianity.* It includes additions to the works of Esther and Daniel as well as other books. Some of these books are found in versions of the Septuagint, the Greek translation of the Old Testament used in Jesus' time. Which books make up the Apocrypha is a matter of debate and varies between Protestant, Roman Catholic, Orthodox, and Coptic churches. Though these works provide insight into ancient Jewish thought and culture, most Protestants do not consider them authoritative.

Tobit Catches a Fish (Book of Tobit 6, Apocrypha). Copperplate engraving by Carl Schuler, published c. 1850.

Besides the books found in the Old Testament, the New Testament, and the Apocrypha, there is another category of works that should be discussed here. There are quite a few books that scholars collectively refer to as the *pseudepigrapha*. The term comes from the Greek words *pseudo*, meaning *false*, and *epigraphein*, meaning *to inscribe*. None of these books are part of Protestant or Catholic Bibles, but some Orthodox and Coptic churches include one or two of the more famous books.

Some of these works are anonymous but most claim to have been written by a prominent religious figure. Quite a few claim to have been written by prophets or apostles. Four of the most well-known today are *The Gospel of Peter*, *The Gospel of Thomas*, *The Gospel of Mary*, and *The Gospel of Judas*. Besides the fact that they were written many years after the deaths of Peter, Thomas, Mary, and Judas, the main problem with these works is their theology. The Jesus they depict doesn't match the Jesus we see in the New Testament Gospels. Also, their teachings on sin, the nature of God, ethics, redemption, and other vital topics are contrary to what we find throughout the Scriptures.[12]

4. Not Merely a Book of Instructions

▸ **OBJECTIVE:** You will be able to explain why the Bible is like a map and how it is like a compass.

Many people, including some Christians, think of the Bible as just a list of instructions or rules to obey. A common acronym says that "Bible" stands for "'*B*asic *I*nstructions *B*efore *L*eaving *E*arth." In this view, the Bible's value is like that of a checklist. It tells us what we need to get done on Earth before we go to heaven.

However, while there certainly are some instructions and rules in the Bible, the Bible doesn't look like a rule book. It is something else altogether. It is full of stories, poems, wisdom, and prophecy. They are about who God is and what he has done, is doing, and will do in the world and for all eternity. The Bible is from God and for humans. Studying it orients us to the world God both created and redeemed. This allows us to live wisely.

Pastor Rick Warren gives four reasons why we should consult the Bible:

- **To help us know God:** God reveals himself through his Word.
- **To teach us the truth:** God's Word contains eternal truth.
- **To show us how to live:** The Bible has practical wisdom for everyday life.
- **To give us spiritual strength:** The Bible teaches us how to mature in the faith.[13]

In Chapter 1, we said a worldview is like a map that helps us understand the world and guides our decisions and actions. A good map will provide a sense of perspective so you can orient yourself to the world. It shows you the way to your intended destination and helps you find the right path when you are lost. In a similar way, studying the Bible shows how to get your bearings so you can find your way and live well in God's world. It tells you which way to go, enabling you to navigate the world with wisdom.

Perhaps an even better analogy for the Bible is that of a compass. A compass does its job by showing you magnetic north—a point that you can use to find out which direction you are actually going. It offers a reference point outside of yourself. Deviating from it, even a little, means that the longer you travel, the more lost you'll become. The same is true with the Bible. The Bible-compass analogy helps us see God's Word less as a to-do list and more as a guide to wise living in this fallen world, where beauty and ugliness, safety and danger exist side by side. Good interpretation of Scripture always points you in the right direction and shows you how to use wisdom even when the way is unclear.

Many religions and philosophies offer direction. Why trust the Bible? This question brings us to a significant point in this book: Christianity is a revealed religion. It claims the existence of a God who has the authority to speak into our lives. If the Bible's revelation about God is accurate, then what it says is authoritative. This is serious and warrants a closer look at the idea of revelation.

5. What Does It Mean to Call the Bible "Revelation"?

▸ **OBJECTIVE:** You will be able to distinguish between general and special revelation.

The word *revelation* means *to make something known that was previously unknown*. The Hebrew word *gālâ* and the Greek word *apokalypto* "express the idea of uncovering what was concealed."[14]

Christianity claims that God is infinite, beyond what we can fully comprehend. Yet God wants to be known. As one theology professor put it:

> God created people fundamentally for relationship with himself. This relationship depends on knowing who he is as he has revealed himself. God is personal, which means he has a mind, will, emotions, relational ability, and self-consciousness. Because he is personal, and not merely an impersonal object, God must personally reveal himself to us.[15]

Would people know about God even if they did not have the Bible? To a certain extent, yes. There are many aspects of his character they would not understand, but through his creation many things about him would be clear. Psalm 19:1–4 says, "The heavens declare the glory of God, and the sky above proclaims his handiwork. Day to day pours out speech, and night to night reveals knowledge. There is no speech, nor are there words, whose voice is not heard. Their voice goes out through all the earth, and their words to the end of the world."

General revelation is *God's universal revelation about himself and morality from nature and our conscience.* Like the unveiling of a famous painting, general revelation is an unveiling in which God's work speaks for itself. Because it is clear, ignorance of reality is no excuse. Romans 1:19–20 says, "For what can be known about God is plain to them, because God has shown it to them. For his invisible attributes, namely, his eternal power and divine nature, have been clearly perceived, ever since the creation of the world, in the things that have been made. So they are without excuse."

General revelation is not only evident in creation, but is written on our hearts as well. That is why our conscience bothers us when we do something we know is wrong. Romans 2:14–15 says, "For when Gentiles, who do not have the law, by nature do what the law requires, they . . . show that the work of the law is written on their hearts, while their conscience also bears witness, and their conflicting thoughts accuse or even excuse them."

General revelation reveals God's work only in its broadest strokes. In other words, human beings can learn some of the basics about God from reflecting upon his creation and what their conscience shows them. For example, we can see that the intricate complexity in the world points to the existence of something beyond itself—something divine. But how do we know which god or gods exist or what God is like? How do we know what God's plan for the world is or what happens after we die? For this we need another kind of revelation.

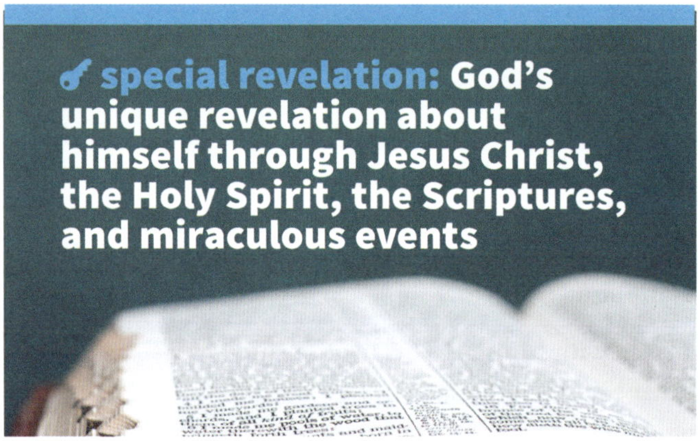

Special revelation is *God's unique revelation about himself through Jesus Christ, the Holy Spirit, the Scriptures, and miraculous events.* God reveals himself personally to us. Jesus reveals what God is truly like, and Scripture reveals who Jesus truly is (John 1:1–18).

When we call Christianity a *revealed* religion, we affirm something more than the existence of a Creator God. We proclaim God's special revelation to human beings. God has revealed himself through the Holy Spirit (John 14:26), the Scriptures (Psalm 19:7–11, 2 Timothy 3:14–17), and miraculous events such as dreams, visions, and prophecy. God continues to speak to us through the Bible today. It is God's Word, but what exactly this means and how we know it to be true requires closer examination.

6. How We Got the Bible

▸ **OBJECTIVE:** You will be able to determine how the canon of Scripture was selected.

▸ **OBJECTIVE:** You will be able to describe the three criteria used to select the books of the New Testament.

As previously noted, the Bible is a collection of 66 books and letters written over 1,500 years by many different writers. But many other works were written during this time period. How do we know which books are God's revelation? Why aren't some of those other works included in our Bible? How did Christians decide upon these 66 books?

In the first centuries of church history, certain books stood out to believers as being divinely inspired. These books make up what scholars call the **canon** of Scripture, *the collection of biblical writings commonly acknowledged as genuine and authoritative.* Canon comes from the Greek *kanón*, meaning *a rule or standard for testing straightness.* Likewise, the term came to be applied to the catalog of sacred books held to be God's inspired Word since it is the authoritative standard for morality and guide for our lives.

The Old Testament canon had mostly been established by the time of Jesus. It contained the majority of books that are in our Old Testament today. The New Testament canon of 27 books was ratified at the Third Council of Carthage (AD 397).[16] However, the books of the Bible weren't made canonical by any council. They were simply recognized as such, meaning the Council recognized which books were being used and considered authoritative by most Christians in the early church.

In regard to the New Testament canon, two prominent seminary professors give some helpful background:

> We have good historical reasons to think that the concept of a New Testament canon was relatively well established and perhaps even a widespread reality by the turn of the [second] century. Although the borders of the canon were not yet solidified by this time, there is no doubt that the early church understood that God had given a new set of authoritative . . . documents that testified to the redemptive work of Jesus Christ and that those documents were the beginning of the New Testament canon.[17]

Generally speaking, there were three criteria used to decide which New Testament documents were received as inspired and authoritative—that is, as Scripture.

1. Apostolicity: Was the book written by an apostle or an associate of an apostle? The Gospel of Mark passes this test because Mark was an associate of Peter; the Gospel of Luke and the book of Acts were accepted because Luke was a close traveling companion of Paul.

2. Orthodoxy: Did the book conform to the teachings of the apostles and the theology in the writings of early church leaders?

3. Pedigree: Was the book accepted early on in the life of the church and by the majority of churches across the region? It was important that a book wasn't just accepted in one location but that lots of Christians in different cities and regions accepted it.[18]

Guided by the Holy Spirit, the early church recognized which books were God's revelation. Taken together, Christians see these books as comprising the canon of Scripture—the very Word of God.

Ruins of the City of Carthage near Tunis, Tunisia

7. What Does It Mean to Say the Bible Is the "Word of God"?

▸ **OBJECTIVE:** You will be able to explain why it is false to say the Bible contains God's words.

▸ **OBJECTIVE:** You will be able to give three reasons to be confident that the entire Bible is God's Word.

There is growing confusion today over what people mean when they say the Bible is God's Word. Some people say the Bible *contains* God's words, which is a very different thing from saying it *is* God's Word. To say the Bible merely contains God's words implies that it contains some other things too, but who is to decide which parts of the Bible are God's words and which are not?

Claiming that the Bible *contains* God's words places the decision of what is true in human hands, meaning God's Word is what we say it is. If we don't like something in the Bible, we could claim, "God would never say or do that." Instead of listening to God's revelation, we can cut up the text to satisfy our preconceived notions about God. This is contrary to the whole point of biblical revelation, which is to help us know and be in relationship with the true God.

Here are some reasons to be confident that the entire Bible is God's Word:

inspiration: the doctrine that God enabled people to write the words of Scripture

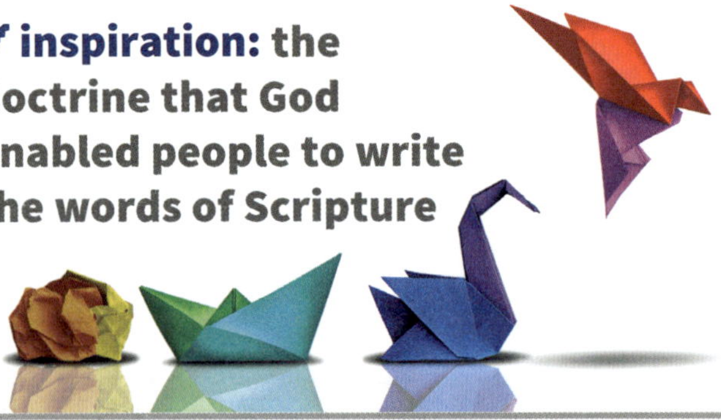

The Bible is inspired by God. The literal meaning of the term *inspired* is *to breathe.* It comes from the Greek word *pneuma* used in 2 Timothy 3:16, "All Scripture is breathed out by God and profitable for teaching, for reproof, for correction, and for training in righteousness." **Inspiration** is *the doctrine that God enabled people to write the words of Scripture*; it is why we call the Bible *God's Word.*

To say that the Bible is inspired is to say that the Holy Spirit motivated its authors to write it. The Holy Spirit spoke through human beings to communicate God's revelation. As 2 Peter 1:20–21 says, "Knowing this first of all, that no prophecy of Scripture comes from someone's own interpretation. For no prophecy was ever produced by the will of man, but men spoke from God as they were carried along by the Holy Spirit."

More than 3,000 times, the writers of the Bible claim to have received messages from the Holy Spirit.[19] They clearly believed they were led by God's Spirit to write what they did. The Holy Spirit breathed God's intentions into their minds and hearts so that what they wrote accurately displayed his nature and character.

The Bible is rooted in history. The Bible isn't just a random holy book proceeding from the imagination of a spiritual person. It is based on actual events in history. As philosopher William Lane Craig says:

> Christianity . . . is rooted in real events of history. To some people this is scandalous because it means that the truth of Christianity is inexplicably bound up with the truth of certain historical facts, such that if those facts should be disproved, so would Christianity. But at the same time, this makes Christianity unique because, unlike most other world religions, we now have a means of verifying its truth by historical evidence.[20]

What this means is the Bible can be debated. As Christians, we can confidently argue for its truth. We do not have to take God's revelation on blind faith. God has revealed himself in history! We'll learn more about the historical accuracy of the Bible in Chapter 3.

The Bible is inerrant. Many people go beyond inspiration to say the Bible is inerrant—that is, without error. **Inerrancy** is *the doctrine that the Bible is without error in the original writings.* This does not mean there have been no errors in transmitting the text through time. But we can say that the essential doctrines of the faith have been transmitted reliably, and the best translations today will not mislead us.[21]

The doctrine of inerrancy says the Bible is totally trustworthy and reliable in all that it teaches. As one author put it, "There are no statements in the Bible which are falsely reported and no teachings which are inaccurate. Every statement, every event, is recorded for us truthfully. There are no deceptions or inaccuracies . . . in the pages of Scripture."[22]

8. Does the Bible Actually Claim to Be True?

▸ OBJECTIVE: You will be able to express what the correspondence theory of truth is and how it relates to the Bible.

The Bible records a conversation between the Roman leader of Jerusalem, Pontius Pilate, and Jesus, as part of Jesus' trial: "Then Pilate said to him, 'So you are a king?' Jesus answered, 'You say that I am a king. For this purpose I was born and for this purpose I have come into the world—to bear witness to the truth. Everyone who is of the truth listens to my voice.' Pilate said to him, 'What is truth?' " (John 18:37–38)

The question, "What is truth?" hangs in the air even today. It is likely that Pilate was familiar with the intellectual contortions ancient philosophers had performed around the question of truth. Aristotle, for example, had come up with this head-scratcher: "To say of what is that it is not, or of what is not that it is, is false, while to say of what is that it is, and of what is not that it is not, is true; so that he who says of anything that it is, or that it is not, will say either what is true or what is false; but neither what is nor what is not said to be or not to be."[23]

Most people feel confused when they hear definitions like Aristotle's. But at the root, Aristotle is saying something fairly self-evident: *a belief, thought, or statement is true if it corresponds to reality.* This is called *the correspondence theory of truth.*

Here's an example of how this theory works: While not everyone agrees on what is wrong with the world, most people recognize there *is* something wrong with it. People lie, cheat, and steal. Why is this the case? According to the Bible, humans fell into evil when they rejected God's plan in the garden of Eden. The fall in Genesis 3 corresponds to the way the world actually is; it helps us understand reality. It also explains why our attempts to fix the world have not succeeded. On our own, human beings can never put the world back together and create a utopia. Only Christ can restore all things; only Christ can set the world right again.

According to one Christian philosopher, the Bible implicitly advances the correspondence view of truth—that truth is that which corresponds to reality. He lists many examples:

> The Hebrew and Greek words for *truth* are rich in meaning but have at their core the idea of conformity to fact. Scripture also emphasizes that God is true to his truth, meaning that he is faithful and will not lie (Hebrews 6:18). God is a God of truth, whose word is truth (John 17:17). The Holy Spirit is "the Spirit of truth" (John 14:17, 15:26, 16:13) and so will teach us true things. Jesus, the Son of God, is "full of grace and truth" (John 1:14), and declared himself to be "the way and the truth and the life" and that no one could come to the Father apart from him (John 14:6). The prophets (Jeremiah 8:8), Jesus (Matthew 24:24), and the apostles (1 John 4:1–6) warn of those who pervert the truth of God through errors and lies. Hence, all of Scripture puts God's revealed objective truth at the solid center of spiritual and ethical life and faithfulness.[24]

The Bible claims that truth about reality can be known, even if we cannot have perfect knowledge. The Bible puts a mirror up to our world and helps us see ourselves for who we truly are.

9. Why Truth Matters

▸ OBJECTIVE: You will be able to explain why relativism is a false belief and why truth matters.

The idea that there is truth we can actually know is largely lost today. Spend just a few minutes discussing issues like politics and religion, and you'll hear someone say, "There is no truth!" or "That may be true for you, but it is not true for me." This view holds that truth is relative to each individual person or culture. **Relativism** is *the belief that truth, knowledge, or morality is relative to the individual, society, or historical context.*

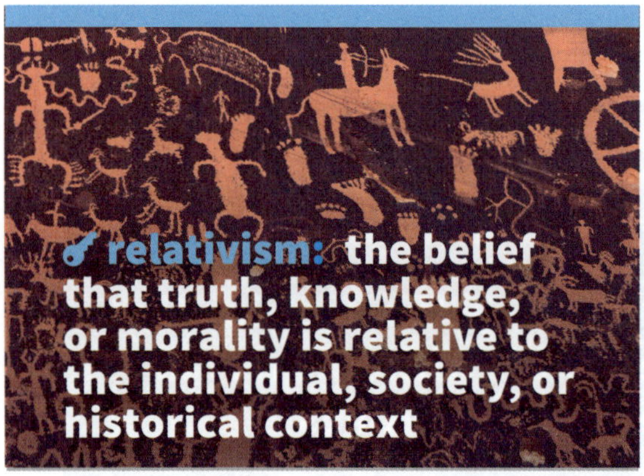

There are several reasons people believe in relativism. They might believe there are no moral absolutes or eternal truths that apply to all people at all times in all settings. Or they might think that even if those standards exist, they can't be known with certainty. Consider how many religions claim they have the truth, but their versions of truth are contradictory. How can we be certain which one is right? Or someone might be honest and simply say, "I don't care if there are moral absolutes; I'm going to live the way I want to."

This last reason is particularly striking. "Relativism is not a coherent philosophical system," asserts one theologian. "It is riddled with contradictions—both logical and experiential. . . . People don't embrace relativism because it is philosophically satisfying.

They embrace it because it is physically and emotionally gratifying. It provides the cover that they need to do what they want."[25]

If someone tells you, "There is no truth," ask, "Is that statement true?" If they say, "Yes," they have just made a self-refuting claim. If there really is no truth, then the statement "There is no truth" is false, because there would be at least one truth (that there is no truth). The same logic applies to the statement, "The truth cannot be known." If so, then how do we *know* this claim is true?

In fact, truth can be known, and it is the only foundation on which to build a life. As one Christian apologist puts it:

> Truth yields life. If we are sailors lost at sea, we need true north. If we're branches on a tree hoping to bear fruit, which we are, we need a connection to a true vine. Truth tells us where we are, who we are, to whom we belong, and the real story in which we can fully live. It seems to me that our American culture, in its present condition, is both lost and starving for truth, and therefore vulnerable to the deception of power politics, marketing schemes, and politically correct slogans of professors, politicians, and media that often lead to the death of the soul and the body. Lies lead to death and a culture of death, but the truth sets people free for life.[26]

The world is desperate for truth, but without knowing God's Word, through which he reveals his nature and character, our attempts to communicate truth will be nothing more than the offering of an opinion.

10. Conclusion

Let's review. Christianity says the Bible is the inspired Word of God in both the Old and New Testaments. Through it, the almighty God, the Creator of the universe, speaks to humankind. The Bible is God's revelation, not a rule book or checklist of instructions. As one theologian says:

> The Bible is not a book like any other. It makes a claim that God spoke and speaks through its message. It argues that as his creatures, we are accountable to him for what he has revealed. The trustworthiness of Scripture points to its authority as well. Scripture is far more than a history book, as good and trustworthy as that history is. It is a book that calls us to examine our lives and relationship to God. Beyond the fascinating history, it contains vital and life-transforming truths about God and us.[27]

These claims are revolutionary and, as you can imagine, controversial, because if the Bible's claims to reveal God are authoritative, then the Bible's authority extends to every area of life, and to everyone in the world, at all times.

In the next chapter we'll wade right into the middle of the controversy and consider whether the Bible is actually authoritative for our lives today.

ENDNOTES

[1]As of 2021, the full Bible is available in 704 different languages. The New Testament is available in another 1,582 languages. Selections and stories are available in a further 1,196 other languages, "Our Impact," Wycliffe Bible Translators, https://www.wycliffe.org.uk/about/our-impact/.

[2]Dan P. Buttafuoco, "Five Reasons Why the Bible Is the Most Important Book on Earth," The Pocket Testament League, 2013, https://members.ptl.org/alive/whyscripture.php.

[3]"Why Is the Bible Important?" Biblica: The International Bible Society, https://www.biblica.com/resources/bible-faqs/why-is-the-bible-important/.

[4]David A. Noebel, "5 Reasons to Study the Bible," Summit Ministries, February 24, 2016, https://www.summit.org/resources/articles/5-reasons-to-study-the-bible/.

[5]Richard Dawkins, "Why I Want All Our Children to Read the King James Bible," The Guardian, May 19, 2012, https://www.guardian.co.uk/science/2012/may/19/richard-dawkins-king-james-bible.

[6]John Adams and John Quincy Adams cited in "What Leading Americans Have Said about the Bible," Houston Baptist University, https://hbu.edu/museums/dunham-bible-museum/influence-in-history-and-culture/what-leading-americans-have-said-about-the-bible/.

[7]Alvin J. Schmidt, How Christianity Changed the World (Grand Rapids: Zondervan, 2004).

[8]William Lyon Phelps, Human Nature in the Bible (New York: Charles Scribner's Sons, 1922), ix.

[9]Joseph C. Sommer, "Some Reasons Why Humanists Reject the Bible," American Humanist Association, https://americanhumanist.org/what-is-humanism/reasons-humanists-reject-bible/.

[10]Lydia Saad, "Record Few Americans Believe Bible Is Literal Word of God," Gallup, May 15, 2017, https://news.gallup.com/poll/210704/record-few-americans-believe-bible-literal-word-god.aspx.

[11]Robert Saucy, Scripture: Its Power, Authority, and Relevance (Nashville: Word Publishing, 2001), 78. See also Carl F. H. Henry's, "The Lost Unity of the Bible," in God, Revelation, and Authority, vol. 4, God Who Speaks and Shows: Fifteen Theses, Part Three, 2nd ed. (Wheaton, IL: Crossway, 1999).

[12]Sheri Bell, "Why the Lost Gospels Don't Belong in the Bible," Josh McDowell, A Cru Ministry, February 28, 2018, https://www.josh.org/lost-gospels-dont-belong-bible/.

[13]Rick Warren, "The Bible: God's Owner's Manual for Life," PastorRick.com, April 24, 2020, https://pastorrick.com/the-bible-gods-owners-manual-for-life/.

[14]Millard J. Erickson, Christian Theology, 2nd ed. (Grand Rapids: Baker Academic, 2001), 201.

[15]Erik Thoennes, Life's Biggest Questions: What the Bible Says about the Things that Matter Most (Wheaton, IL: Crossway), 41–42.

[16]William Smith, "The Canon of Scripture," Smith's Bible Dictionary, Bible Study Tools, https://www.biblestudytools.com/dictionary/canon-of-scripture-the/.

[17]Andreas J. Köstenberger and Michael J. Kruger, The Heresy of Orthodoxy: How Contemporary Culture's Fascination with Diversity Has Reshaped Our Understanding of Early Christianity (Wheaton, IL: Crossway, 2010), 149–50.

[18]This is summarized from Jonathan Morrow's article, "How Do We Know the Bible Includes the Right Books?", in Apologetics Study Bible for Students, ed. Sean McDowell (Nashville: Holman Bible Publishers, 2010), 1230.

[19]Gordon R. Lewis, "What Does It Mean that God Inspired the Bible?", in *The Apologetics Study Bible*, ed. J. P. Moreland, Paul Copan, and Ted Cabal (Nashville: Holman Bible Publishers, 2017), 1516.

[20]William Lane Craig, Reasonable Faith: Christian Truth and Apologetics, 3rd ed. (Wheaton, IL: Crossway Books, 2008), 207.

[21]See John R. W. Stott, The Authority of the Bible (Downers Grove, IL: InterVarsity Press, 1974).

[22]Don Stewart, "What Is the Doctrine of Biblical Inerrancy?" Blue Letter Bible, https://www.blueletterbible.org/Comm/stewart_don/faq/bible-difficulties/question1-what-is-the-doctrine-of-biblical-inerrancy.cfm.

[23]Aristotle, Metaphysics, ed. Roger Bishop Jones, trans. W. D. Ross, 58–59. Available online at http://texts.rbjones.com/rbjpub/philos/classics/aristotl/mbook_draft.pdf.

[24]Douglas Groothuis, Christian Apologetics: A Comprehensive Case for Biblical Faith (Downers Grove, IL: IVP Academics, 2011), 126.

[25]John Piper, "The Challenge of Relativism," Desiring God, March 16, 2007, https://www.desiringgod.org/messages/the-challenge-of-relativism.

[26]Kelly Monroe Kullberg, quoted in Jonathan Morrow, Think Christianly: Looking at the Intersection of Faith and Culture (Grand Rapids: Zondervan, 2011), 50.

[27]Darrell L. Bock, Can I Trust the Bible?: Defending the Bible's Reliability (Norcross, GA: RZIM, 2001), 52.

3

Does the Bible Have Authority?

1. Who's in Charge?

▸ **OBJECTIVE: You will be able to articulate what authority is and what it means to submit to God's authority.**

The poem on the following page, *Invictus*, is Latin for *unconquered*. This is one of the most quoted poems ever written. Oddly enough, it was the favorite poem of statesman Nelson Mandela and also mass murderer Timothy McVeigh. While it is a statement of human endurance, it is also an arrogant assertion that we are our own authority. We answer to no one.

Invictus

Out of the night that covers me,
Black as the pit from pole to pole,
I thank whatever gods may be
For my unconquerable soul.

In the fell clutch of circumstance
I have not winced nor cried aloud.
Under the bludgeonings of chance
My head is bloody, but unbowed.

Beyond this place of wrath and tears
Looms but the horror of the shade,
And yet the menace of the years
Finds and shall find me unafraid.

It matters not how strait the gate,
How charged with punishments the scroll,
I am the master of my fate,
I am the captain of my soul.

— William Ernest Henley[1]

The word *authority* comes from a Latin word meaning *influence* or *command*. It answers the question, "Who's in charge?"

Have you ever seen the statement "Question Authority" on a bumper sticker? There is, of course, a valid democratic sentiment to it. Don't believe everything you hear, especially from the government. Today, however, "Question Authority" usually expresses *radical individualism*. "No one has the right to tell me what to do," people say. Few enjoy being told what to do or how to think. Yet the rejection of authority tosses out the baby with the bathwater. It removes both illegitimate and legitimate forms of authority. When all authority is banished, civil society becomes impossible. But as the iconic musician Bob Dylan sang, "You're gonna have to serve somebody." How can we know when to submit to authority and when to oppose it?

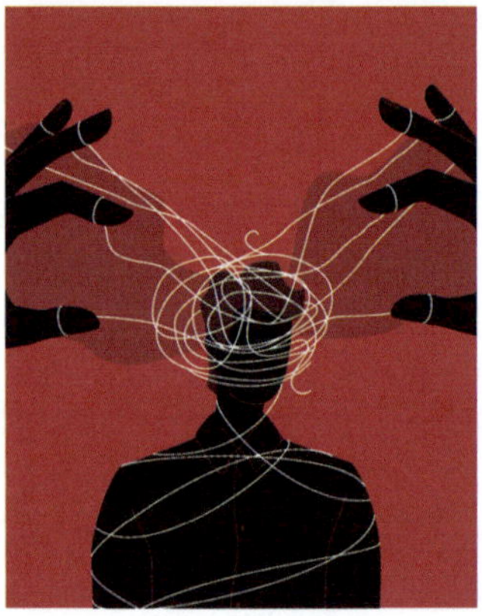

For Christians, the lines of authority are clear. To confess "Jesus is Lord" is to proclaim one's submission to his authority. The New Testament word for *obey* comes from two Greek words meaning *hear* and *under* (that is, to place oneself under authority). Embracing Jesus' worldview—believing what he taught and obeying his teaching—is an invitation to "a long obedience in the same direction," a journey toward conformity to Christ.[2] Romans 8:29 says, "For those whom he foreknew he also predestined to be conformed to the image of his Son."

But what does it look like to place ourselves under God's authority? How do we know what he wants? Christians maintain that what God wants is not unknowably mysterious. We believe that God makes himself known and conveys his authority most clearly through Scripture. In this chapter we'll explore the evidence for the Bible's authority and accurate preservation, as well as answer common objections that people have about the Bible's authority. In the end, we'll see that the Bible is a trustworthy book that has implications for all of life.

Let's begin with what the Bible says about itself.

2. Internal Evidence for the Bible's Authority: Old Testament

▸ **OBJECTIVE: You will be able to use internal evidence from the Bible to defend the Old Testament's authority.**

▸ **OBJECTIVE: You will be able to give specific examples of how Jesus confirmed his trust in the Old Testament.**

Internal evidence is *evidence from Scripture that supports the claims of the Bible.* The Bible claims authority for itself. Throughout the Old Testament, phrases like "Thus says the Lord" and "The Word of the Lord came to me" occur more than 3,000 times. The writers claimed that they were sharing God's authoritative revelation.[3] God not only spoke *to* the prophets, he also spoke *through* the prophets as Hebrews 1:1–2 affirms: "Long ago, at many times and in many ways, God spoke to our fathers by the prophets."

The writers also claimed that God's revelation is perfect, right, and flawless:

> The law of the Lord is perfect, reviving the soul; the testimony of the Lord is sure, making wise the simple; the precepts of the Lord are right, rejoicing the heart; the commandment of the Lord is pure, enlightening the eyes. –Psalm 19:7–8

> Every word of God proves true; he is a shield to those who take refuge in him. Do not add to his words, lest he rebuke you and you be found a liar. –Proverbs 30:5–6

The Old Testament writers clearly thought they were communicating God's authoritative revelation, but what did Jesus think? How did he view the Old Testament? According to Christian apologist Josh McDowell, Jesus viewed it "as the authoritative word of God:"

As God in human flesh, Jesus speaks with final authority. And his testimony regarding the Old Testament is loud and clear. Jesus believed that the Old Testament was divinely inspired, the veritable Word of God. He said, 'The Scripture cannot be broken' (John 10:35). He referred to Scripture as 'the commandment of God' (Matthew 15:3) and as the 'Word of God' (Mark 7:13). He also indicated that it was indestructible: 'Until Heaven and earth pass away, not the smallest letter or stroke shall pass away from the law, until all is accomplished' (Matthew 5:18).[4]

In his teaching, Jesus treated stories in the Old Testament as true and authoritative. Examples include the story of Cain and Abel (Genesis 4:1–16, Luke 11:51), the destruction of Sodom and Gomorrah and Lot's wife (Genesis 19:23–26; Luke 17:29, 32), Moses at the burning bush (Exodus 3, Mark 12:26), the provision of manna for Israel (Exodus 16, John 6:31–51), and Jonah and Nineveh (Jonah, Matthew 12:38–41).

Moses and the Stone Tablets

After his resurrection, Jesus told his disciples that the Old Testament pointed to him: "These are my words that I spoke to you while I was still with you, that everything written about me in the Law of Moses and the Prophets and the Psalms must be fulfilled" (Luke 24:44).

One pastor summarizes Jesus' trust in the Old Testament this way:

- Jesus consistently refers to the Old Testament as the present and eternal truth of God.
- Jesus always assumes Scripture is final in authority and that all parts are of equal authority.
- Jesus always assumes Old Testament prophecies must be fulfilled as given.
- Jesus always treats the miraculous events of the Old Testament as if they occurred exactly as written.
- Jesus leans on the Old Testament in his spiritual anguish (Matthew 4:1–10, 27:46).
- Jesus never hesitates to confront error, but he says absolutely nothing about problems in the Scriptures. Apparently, Jesus found nothing to confront in the Old Testament.
- Jesus builds on the foundation of the Old Testament by clarifying the profound extent to which its teachings must be applied (Matthew 5:27–28).[5]

3. Internal Evidence for the Bible's Authority: New Testament

▸ **OBJECTIVE: You will be able to describe the apostles' intent and authority for writing the New Testament.**

What about the New Testament? Is it also authoritative? Yes! Jesus gave authority to the apostles to bear witness about him (Matthew 28:16–20). He promised that the Holy Spirit would help them to do this (John 14:26). The Holy Spirit, who spoke through the prophets in the Old Testament, inspired the apostles to share the gospel of Jesus Christ in the New Testament.

The apostle John spoke with the authority Jesus gave him by reiterating old commands and offering new commands:

> Beloved, I am writing you no new commandment, but an old commandment that you had from the beginning. The old commandment is the word that you have heard. At the same time, it is a new commandment that I am writing to you, which is true in him and in you, because the darkness is passing away and the true light is already shining. –1 John 2:7–8

The apostle Peter referred to the writings of Paul, who was not present during the earthly ministry of Jesus, as also having the authority of Scripture:

> And count the patience of our Lord as salvation, just as our beloved brother Paul also wrote to you according to the wisdom given him, as he does in all his letters when he speaks in them of these matters. There are some things in them that are hard to understand, which the ignorant and unstable twist to their own destruction, as they do the other Scriptures. –2 Peter 3:15–16

Paul himself also shared the view that his teaching had authority as God's Word:

> If anyone thinks that he is a prophet, or spiritual, he should acknowledge that the things I am writing to you are a command of the Lord. If anyone does not recognize this, he is not recognized. –1 Corinthians 14:37–38

> And we also thank God constantly for this, that when you received the word of God, which you heard from us, you accepted it not as the word of men but as what it really is, the word of God, which is at work in you believers. –1 Thessalonians 2:13

It is important to understand that the internal evidence in Scripture does not, by itself, prove that the Bible is true. After all, anyone could pick up a pen and claim to be writing a message from God. What the internal evidence shows is that the writers of the Bible did not intend to simply offer advice or tell some good stories. Instead, they claimed that they were communicating God's authoritative revelation. If they had not believed this, there would very little reason for Christians today to believe that the Bible is God's authoritative Word. Also, the fact that all the biblical authors (writing in different times and places) manage to teach a consistent message makes their claims to be speaking God's Word much more believable. Let's now turn to the external evidence for Scripture that supports its authority, accuracy, and reliability.

4. External Evidence for the Reliability of the Old Testament

▸ **OBJECTIVE: You will be able to identify specific examples of external evidence that support the Old Testament's reliability.**

Remember, internal evidence is evidence from Scripture that supports the claims of the Bible. In contrast, *external evidence* is *evidence from outside the Bible that confirms the historical reliability of Scripture*. Christians' trust in the authority of Scripture is not blind. It is based on sound reasoning supported by historical confirmation, archaeological evidence, and fulfilled prophecy. Let's first consider evidence for the reliability of the Old Testament.

Ancient bas-relief from Persepolis, previously ruled by Darius and Xerxes, in Shiraz, Iran

Historical events recorded in the Old Testament can be confirmed in ancient nonbiblical sources. Such events include:

- The campaign into Israel by Pharaoh Shishak (1 Kings 14:25–26, 2 Chronicles 12:1–9)
- The revolt of Moab against Israel (2 Kings 1:1, 3:5)
- The defeat of Ashdod by Sargon II (Isaiah 20:1)
- The campaign of Sennacherib against Judah (2 Kings 18:13)
- The siege of Lachish by Sennacherib (2 Chronicles 32:9)
- The assassination of Sennacherib by his own sons (2 Kings 19:36–37)
- The fall of Nineveh and other Assyrian cities as predicted by the prophets (Nahum 1:1–3:19, Isaiah 10:5–19)
- The fall of Jerusalem to Nebuchadnezzar (2 Kings 24:1–2; Jeremiah 21:7, 22:5)
- The captivity of Jehoiachin, king of Judah, in Babylon (2 Kings 24:15, Esther 2:6)[6]

Archaeological discoveries also verify the accuracy of the Old Testament.[7] One scholar identified over 50 figures from the Bible who have been confirmed archaeologically. These include Israelite kings, Mesopotamian monarchs, and lesser-known figures.[8] Here are a few other important discoveries:

- **Eleventh century BC:** Most of the cities mentioned from Genesis through the book of Joshua have been discovered.
- **Tenth century BC:** Some of the building projects of Solomon have been unearthed at Megiddo and Gezer.[9]
- **Ninth century BC:** The monolith inscription of Shalmaneser III mentions "Ahab the Israelite" as having the most powerful military elements in the Israelite and Syrian coalition.[10]
- **Eighth century BC:** The Khorsabad Annals give the account of Sargon II's captivity of Samaria in 722 BC.[11]
- **Seventh century BC:** The tunnel Hezekiah built to bring water into Jerusalem has been found (2 Kings 20:20; 2 Chronicles 32:30).[12]

Then, there is the matter of fulfilled prophecies. Many predictions recorded in the Old Testament actually came to pass,[13] including:

- Babylon ruling over Judah for 70 years (predicted in Jeremiah 25:11–12, fulfilled in 2 Chronicles 36:20–21)
- The Jews surviving Babylonian rule and returning to the Promised Land (predicted in Jeremiah 32:36–37, fulfilled in Ezra 1:5, Nehemiah 2:16–17)
- Babylon's kingdom being overthrown and reduced to swampland (predicted in Isaiah 13:19, 14:23; fulfilled gradually through the work of Darius, Cyrus, Xerxes, and other conquerors)[14]
- Tyre being attacked by many nations and its stones, timber, and soil being cast into the sea (predicted in Ezekiel 26:3–12; fulfilled in attacks by Babylon and by Alexander the Great)[15]
- Edom being toppled and humbled, (predicted in Jeremiah 49:17; fulfilled after the city was conquered by the Nabateans)[16]

The Black Obelisk, originally found in Nineveh: King Jehu of Israel bows before King Shalmaneser III of Assyria

The Old Testament predicts the coming Messiah in more than 300+ prophecies. Many are so specific that the probability of fulfilling even a handful is stageringly improbable; the odds of fulfilling just eight were once estimated to be one in 10^{17} (one in 100,000 trillion). The Jesus Film Project published a list of 55 prophecies that Jesus fulfilled relating to his birth, ministry, death, resurrection, and role in the church.[17] Prophecies related to Jesus' second coming are yet to be fulfilled.

5. External Evidence for the Reliability of the New Testament

▸ **OBJECTIVE: You will be able to list ancient nonbiblical writings that confirm the historicity of Jesus and the teaching of the early Christians.**

▸ **OBJECTIVE: You will be able to describe the role of eyewitness testimony and the church fathers in affirming the accuracy of the Gospels.**

The reliability of the New Testament is also supported by external evidence. Historical writings outside of the New Testament affirm basic facts about Jesus and his disciples, as historian Edwin Yamauchi observes:

> Even if we did not have the New Testament or Christian writings, we would be able to conclude from such non-Christian writings as Josephus, the Talmud, Tacitus, and Pliny the Younger [that] Jesus was a Jewish teacher; many people believed he performed healings and exorcisms; he was rejected by the Jewish leaders; he was crucified under Pontius Pilate in the reign of Tiberius; [and that] despite this shameful death, his followers, who believed that he was still alive, spread beyond Palestine so that there were multitudes of them in Rome by AD 64.[18]

The book of Acts gives a number of historical details for which we can find archaeological evidence. Scholars have affirmed several details of Luke's accounts, providing evidence that Paul's journeys took place the way the author says they did. These findings, along with many others, validate the accuracy of the only history book of the early church accepted in the biblical canon.[19]

There is much more evidence affirming the basic historical truthfulness of the Bible. Consider the Gospels. Liberal scholar John P. Meier, from the University of Notre Dame, rigorously studied the miracles in the Gospels. Even he found that almost half of them included enough detail to conclude that the historical scene they described could have occurred as reported. [20]

First, we can trust that the Gospels are authoritative and accurate accounts of the life and ministry of Jesus because they were written based on eyewitness testimony. "This is the disciple who is testifying to these things and wrote these things, and we know that his testimony is true" (John 21:24). Elsewhere John insists that he was proclaiming what he and others "have heard, which we have seen with our eyes, which we have looked upon and have touched with our hands, concerning the word of life" (1 John 1:1).

This means the Gospels were written early enough to be affirmed or denied by other eyewitnesses and by those who heard the Gospel message from eyewitnesses. This next generation included church fathers like Ignatius, Polycarp, and Clement. **Church fathers** were *theologians and writers who established the foundations of Christianity.* The apostle Paul had described himself as a father of those who believed the good news he preached about Jesus (1 Corinthians 4:15), and this title was later applied more broadly to the leaders of the church in the first centuries after it began.

The teachings of the church fathers closely mirror what we read in the New Testament. A former detective who researched the Gospels describes the value of the church fathers for reinforcing the apostolic writings:

> Early Church Fathers sat at the feet of the apostles and learned from the apostolic eyewitness accounts. These secondary leaders then wrote letters and documents of their own, repeating the claims of their teachers. . . . The Early Church Fathers did confirm enough of the New Testament claims to validate and authenticate the writings of the apostles.[21]

This external evidence points to the reliability and truthfulness of Scripture.

the Dead Sea Scrolls: the oldest surviving collection of Jewish canonical texts written 300–400 years before the birth of Christ

6. Accurate Preservation of the Bible

▸ OBJECTIVE: You will be able to explain how the Dead Sea Scrolls and many early New Testament manuscripts confirm the accurate preservation of the biblical writings.

We have seen that there is both internal and external evidence for the Bible's authority; but how do we know that the Bible has been accurately preserved over time? How do we know that the words in the Bible today are the words that the original authors wrote down?

From the beginning, those charged with transmitting God's Word sensed the need to conduct their work with great care. This can be seen with the discovery of the Dead Sea Scrolls in a cave at Qumran, in Israel. The **Dead Sea Scrolls** are *the oldest surviving collection of Jewish canonical texts written 300–400 years before the birth of Christ.* One stunning scroll contained almost the complete text of the book of Isaiah. This scroll was nearly one thousand years older than the next oldest copy of Isaiah known at that time. The book of Isaiah was probably copied hundreds of times, yet the copy of Isaiah found among the Dead Sea Scrolls is virtually the same as newer copies. Between the manuscripts there was a variation of less than 5 percent, most of which consisted of spelling variations.[22]

The people of Israel understood their holy books were God's Word and took great care to accurately preserve them.[23] Former detective J. Warner Wallace details how later scribes known as *the Masoretes* (in the Middle Ages) developed strict measures to guarantee every new copy of Scripture was an exact reproduction of the original. For example:

- Nothing could be written from memory; each line was to be copied letter for letter from a reliable predecessor.

- Scribes and copyists also kept detailed statistics to guard against error. As an example, Leviticus 8:8 (in the Hebrew structure of the Bible) was identified as the middle verse of the Torah. A single word in Leviticus 10:16 was identified as the middle word of the Torah and a single letter in Leviticus 10:42 was identified as the middle letter of the Torah.
- Scribes and copyists listed important statistics at the end of each book. As an example, the total number of verses in Deuteronomy is 955, the total in the entire Torah is 5,845; the total number of words is 97,856, and the total number of letters is 400,945. By assembling statistics such as these, each book could be measured mathematically to see if there were any copyist errors.[24]

The New Testament documents were also carefully preserved from the outset. As apologist Teri Dugan notes:

- The writings of the New Testament were immediately copied and widely dispersed throughout the Roman Empire and beyond (see the book of Acts), thus eliminating time for changes, forgeries, or embellishments.
- We have over 25,000 early New Testament manuscripts and fragments from *five different document families* from ancient Christian communities, dating as early as the second century AD.
- Scholars find a 99.5 percent agreement between these early manuscripts with variations stemming mainly from differences in spelling, grammar, word order, and minor deletions or additions (noted in modern Bible footnotes)—none of which [affect] any doctrine of the Christian faith.[25]

Though we do not have the original manuscripts of the New Testament, there is still enough evidence to reconstruct the original text. Josh McDowell explains:

> As scholars do not have the original documents of the Scriptures, they have had to determine if the existing (extant) copies of the originals are reliable. The greater the number of copies, and the earlier their dating, the easier it is to reconstruct a text closer to the original and identify errors or discrepancies in subsequent copies. Scholars believe the New Testament manuscripts to be the most frequently copied and widely distributed books of antiquity. The abundance of Scriptural manuscript copies have made it possible to reconstruct the original text with virtually complete accuracy. The authenticity of the New Testament text we have today rests on the foundation of a massive amount of historical documentation.[26]

Church fathers mural, St. George Church, Kurbinovo, Macedonia

Such evidence provides good reason to acknowledge the basic authority and reliability of the Bible.

7. Answering Objections to the Authority of the Bible

▸ **OBJECTIVE:** You will be able to appraise and formulate responses to three common objections to the reliability and authority of the Bible.

Despite the evidence, many people have questions about the Bible. They ask: How could the Bible, written by fallible human, claim to be authoritative over our lives? Wasn't the Bible corrupted over time? What about other "gospels" and ancient texts that were excluded from the Bible? Let's take a look at each of these objections.

textual variants: **differences between particular words, phrases, or passages within multiple copies of the same ancient manuscript**

Objection 1: The Bible was written by human beings. To answer this objection, we must first decide whether people are capable of saying or writing *anything* that is true. If so, would they not be capable of truthfully writing down what God told them to? Apologist Greg Koukl makes this point through a series of questions:

> "Do you have any books in your library? Were those books written by humans? Do you find any truth in them? Is there a reason you think the Bible is less truthful or reliable than other books you own? Do people always make mistakes in what they write? Do you think that if God did exist, he would be capable of using humans to write down exactly what he wants? If not, why not?"[27]

The Bible describes the origin of Scripture as a process that is both human and divine. Except in cases where God gave specific messages to the writers, God did not dictate what they wrote (overriding their personalities), nor did the authors write their own personal ideas about God. Instead, God inspired the authors, who then communicated God's truth using their own writing styles:

> 2 Samuel 23:2: "The Spirit of the Lord speaks by me; his word is on my tongue."
>
> 2 Peter 1:20–21: "Knowing this first of all, that no prophecy of Scripture comes from someone's own interpretation. For no prophecy was ever produced by the will of man, but men spoke from God as they were carried along by the Holy Spirit."

Objection 2: The Bible has been corrupted. If the biblical material was copied over and over again, wouldn't mistakes add up over time, corrupting the text? To answer this question, we must understand the nature of copy mistakes. When scholars examine multiple manuscripts, they compare them word by word, sentence by sentence. Often **textual variants** arise, which are *differences between particular words, phrases, or passages within multiple copies of the same ancient manuscript.* Because we have so many manuscripts, the number of textual variants between the manuscripts is quite high.

The majority of textual variants are spelling errors, unclear readings, and obviously questionable alterations in manuscripts.

If a variant of an ancient manuscript includes spelling differences, changes in word order, and the use of synonyms, then it doesn't affect the meaning of the text and is not of major concern. Variants in manuscripts that affect the meaning of the text are considered more serious. In the end, fewer than 4,000 of the original 400,000 variants have any real significance at all for the meaning of the text, and none affect any core doctrines.[28]

Objection 3: Important books have been left out of the Bible. In 1945, the **lost gospels**, *gnostic texts written sometime between AD 200 and 400*, were discovered in Egypt. Some of these texts had the word *gospel* in the title. *The Da Vinci Code* and similar fiction and nonfiction works have popularized the myth that the church unfairly suppressed these so-called lost gospels.

Why were these lost gospels excluded from the biblical canon? The lost gospels fail all three necessary criteria—apostolicity, orthodoxy, and pedigree—making them inferior to the canonical writings in the New Testament. Most of these documents were written in the second through fourth centuries, meaning that none were written by apostles (apostolicity); nor were they widely accepted in the early church (pedigree). The theology of many of the lost gospels is inconsistent with the teachings of earliest Christianity (orthodoxy). Instead, the lost gospels are strongly influenced by gnosticism.[29] **Gnosticism** is *a heresy that affected the early church and that taught the material world was inherently evil.* It also taught that salvation can be obtained only through self-denial and esoteric knowledge of divine reality. Because they believed that Jesus appearing in a body would have corrupted his ministry, some gnostics taught that Jesus was merely a spirit who *appeared* to be human. For these and other reasons, the lost gospels were ultimately left out of the biblical canon.[30]

8. How Far Does God's Authority Extend?

▸ **OBJECTIVE:** You will be able to summarize five areas of life that are under God's authority.

We've seen that the Bible is supported by internal and external evidence, has been carefully preserved, and can stand up to objections. But how far does the Bible's authority extend? Ultimately, the Bible derives its authority from God. So, if the Bible is God's Word, *nothing* escapes its authority, just as nothing escapes God's authority. Let's look at just a few areas that are subject to God's authority as revealed in Scripture:

God has authority over culture. Time and again, the Bible shows believers are tempted to embrace the values and morals of the surrounding cultures—whether they were the Canaanites in the Old Testament or Corinthians in the New Testament. Child sacrifice and sex slavery were openly practiced in many ancient cultures. The prophets and apostles regularly confronted these and other evil practices within their own cultures. These practices cannot be legitimized as "true for the culture that practiced them." Instead, God's standards of right and wrong are true for *all* cultures at *all* times.

God has authority over governments. Even the authority of nations is derived from and dependent upon God, whether that authority is acknowledged or not. The Bible says the nations will accomplish God's purposes. In response to Pilate, Jesus said, "You would have no authority over me at all unless it had been given you from above" (John 19:11). Romans 13:1 says there is no authority except that which is from God. When governing authorities conflict with the authority of God, Christians must obey God first (Acts 5:29).

God has authority over knowledge. It is common for people to say, "I won't believe something unless it can be proven scientifically." They assume science to be the most reliable means of knowing truth. But to believe only what science can prove excludes anything that cannot be empirically demonstrated, including the underlying principles of science itself. The truth is, biblical writers were enabled by the Holy Spirit to write more than they knew and understood about science.

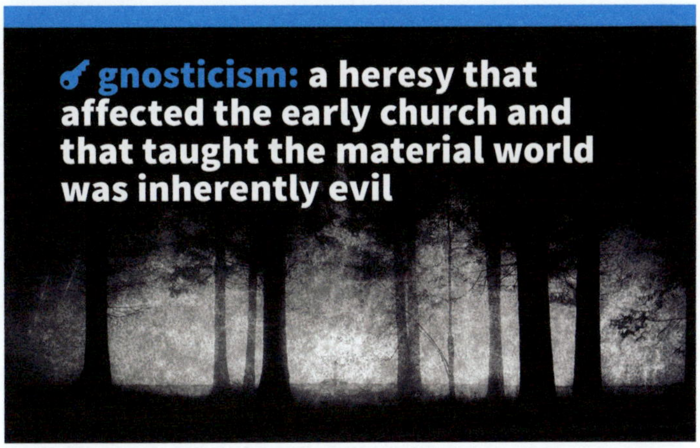

God has authority over our emotions. God commands that we love him and love others (Luke 10:27). He even commands that we love our enemies and pray for them (Matthew 5:44). Truth is not determined by our feelings. Truth is not defined by what makes us comfortable. Truth does not depend on how many people agree with it. Feelings can guide us to truth, but they can also mislead us. We may feel good about things that are untrue and bad about things that are true. In the end, we are called to accept God's authority about what is true over how we might feel about it at any given moment.

God has authority over entertainment. Entertainers often speak about such wide-ranging issues as abortion, the environment, and spirituality, and are considered authoritative simply because millions of people listen to them. But fame is not the same as authority. The popularity of an idea is not, in itself, an indication of the idea's truth. God claims authority over the voices we listen to. He insists that we filter out what is not true or not worth thinking about (Philippians 4:8).

9. Why Should We Submit to God's Authority?

▸ **OBJECTIVE:** You will be able to describe the importance of examining and evaluating all truth claims for accuracy.

▸ **OBJECTIVE:** You will be able to explain why God wants people to obey him.

Submitting to God's authority, as revealed in the Bible, is a weighty matter. Some people have no problem doing it. Others know they should obey God but struggle to do so. Still others reject God's authority entirely. These different responses usually have something to do with a person's early experiences of authority.

Our earliest experience with authority is one in which we tend to believe or obey our parents, teachers, and pastors. At first, it doesn't even occur to us to doubt them. However, over time we gradually learn that they are not expert authorities on everything. They can be wrong. If we are rebellious, we might think this gives us the right to disobey or ignore them entirely.

Some of us may have experienced abuse from those in authority. We know firsthand how abusive authorities can seriously damage people's lives, so we reject or avoid authorities. We may even be hesitant to accept God's authority.

Of course, in turning away from or disobeying our parents, teachers, and pastors, we choose to obey someone else—usually our peers or popular cultural icons. We're selective, often unreasonably so. We refuse our parents' "Because I said so" but unquestioningly obey a rock star whose best argument is "Because I said so."

Accepting someone else's claims without question is merely to exchange one authority for another. Instead, we should carefully evaluate their claims to see if they are true. We must carefully examine the evidence for the Bible's authority for ourselves, rather than simply accepting the views of skeptics. At the start of this chapter, we said many people have questions about the Bible and its authority. Asking questions is a good thing. It helps us to grow intellectually, as we think for ourselves. But it must be done with a spirit of humility and genuine openness to learning.

Of course, even if there is good evidence for God's authority, not everyone will want to accept it. We may not always want to obey him. We might find that his authority upsets our agenda. Many see God as power-hungry and domineering, but God is not like that. God is good! He does not use his authority to abuse or manipulate us. God's authority is not about controlling us or spoiling our fun. Instead, he wants us to give him authority over our lives because he knows that we can only find true life in him.

God's authority extends to the whole of our lives. We are told in Scripture to be stewards of our minds (Romans 12:2; Ephesians 4:23; Colossians 3:2, 10), and our physical bodies (1 Corinthians 6:12–20). We are told to be truthful, loving, generous, and hospitable (Ephesians 4:15, 25; Romans 12:9–21). Obeying God leads to a life of flourishing. With God, we can become all that he created us to be.

10. Conclusion

Submitting to authority requires faith in that authority. We must decide where we will place our faith. Someone who boards an airplane puts his or her faith in physics, engineering, the pilots, the air traffic control system, the maintenance crew, and an endless number of other people and factors. This is not blind faith. People who fly trust the system designed to put airplanes safely in the air. Is it possible their faith is misplaced? Yes. But no one can live apart from ongoing faith in the systems and truths we have come to trust as reliable or true.

Trust in God's authority is like trust in the airline system. It is not blind. In this chapter, we have seen that God expresses his authority in Scripture, which is both internally and externally trustworthy. Jesus claimed authority, and the accuracy of biblical documents lends credence to his claim. Jesus also showed trust in the Old Testament revelation and lent his authority to those who would later write the New Testament. The authority of Scripture has been transmitted to us by careful copying over the centuries. Finally, Scripture can stand up to the toughest scrutiny.

We have come full circle. Bob Dylan, a famous musician, was right: "You're gonna have to serve somebody." But whom? Some find they have a problem with God's authority because they're not sure if he's good. Others don't want to accept what the Bible says is best for human flourishing. Others honestly search, but they doubt whether anyone can properly understand God's message as given through his Word. To grapple with these difficulties, we will next study how to read the Bible.

ENDNOTES

[1] William Ernest Henley, "Invictus," in *Poems* (London: David Nutt, 1907), 119.

[2] The phrase "long obedience in the same direction" comes, ironically, from Friedrich Nietzsche, *Beyond Good and Evil* (New York: Millennium Publications, 2014), 46. For his usage see *The Selected Writings of Friedrich Nietzsche* (Radford, VA: Wilder, 2008), 471. Eugene Peterson appropriates the term in his book *A Long Obedience in the Same Direction: Discipleship in an Instant Society* (Downers Grove, IL: InterVarsity Press, 2000) as a figure of speech for following Christ.

[3] Gordon R. Lewis, "What Does It Mean that God Inspired the Bible?", in *The Apologetics Study Bible*, ed. J. P. Moreland, Paul Copan, and Ted Cabal (Nashville: Holman Bible Publishers, 2017), 1516.

[4] Josh McDowell Ministry, "How Did Jesus View the Old Testament?", bethinking.org, https://www.bethinking.org/bible/q-how-did-jesus-view-the-old-testament.

[5] W. Gary Phillips, research provided to Jeff Myers, April 16, 2013.

[6] J. Warner Wallace, "The Case for the Reliability of the Old Testament (Downloadable Bible Insert)," Cold-Case Christianity with J. Warner Wallace and Jimmy Wallace, May 2, 2018, https://coldcasechristianity.com/writings/the-case-for-the-reliability-of-the-old-testament-bible-insert/.

[7] Jeffrey Sheler, *Is the Bible True? How Modern Debates and Discoveries Affirm the Essence of the Scriptures* (San Francisco: Harper Collins, 1999), 254.

[8] Lawrence Mykytiuk, "53 People in the Bible Confirmed Archaeologically," Biblical Archaeology Society, September 14, 2001, https://www.biblicalarchaeology.org/daily/people-cultures-in-the-bible/people-in-the-bible/50-people-in-the-bible-confirmed-archaeologically/.

[9] R. K. Harrison, *Introduction to the Old Testament* (Peabody, MA: Hendrickson, 2004), 125.

[10] Harrison, *Introduction to the Old Testament*, 127.

[11] Harrison, *Introduction to the Old Testament* 128. See also Victor Matthews, *Old Testament Parallels: Laws and Stories from the Ancient Near East*, 3rd ed. (Mahwah, NJ: Paulist Press, 2007), 137–38.

[12] Harrison, *Introduction to the Old Testament*, 128. See also Matthews, *Old Testament Parallels*, 137–38.

[13] J. Warner Wallace, "From Reliable to Divine: Fulfilled Prophecy in the Old Testament," Cold-Case Christianity with J. Warner Wallace and Jimmy Wallace, April 11, 2018, https://coldcasechristianity.com/writings/from-reliable-to-divine-fulfilled-prophecy-in-the-old-testament/.

[14] *Barnes' Notes on the Bible*, BibleHub.com, https://biblehub.com/commentaries/barnes/Isaiah/13.htm.

[15] "Tyre would be attacked by many nations," AboutBibleProphecy.com, aboutbibleprophecy.com/Ezekiel_26_3.htm.

[16] Edom would be toppled and humbled," AboutBibleProphecy.com, aboutbibleprophecy.com/Jeremiah_49_16htm.

[17] Jesus Film Project, "55 Old Testament Prophecies about Jesus," Jesus Film Project, January 4, 2018, https://www.jesusfilm.org/blog-and-stories/old-testament-prophecies.html.

[18] Quoted in Michael J. Wilkens and J. P. Moreland, *Jesus under Fire: Modern Scholarship Reinvents the Historical Jesus* (Grand Rapids: Zondervan, 1996), 221–22.

[19] F. F. Bruce, *The New Testament Documents: Are They Reliable?* (Grand Rapids: Eerdmans, 1981). Other examples from Acts include: (1) Acts 13:7—Cyprus became a senatorial province (as opposed to *imperial* province) in 22 BC, and thus the governor was rightly called *proconsul* Sergius Paullus; (2) Acts 16:12, 20, 35—*praetors* (magistrates of Philippi) were attended by *lictors* (sergeants, who beat Paul and Silas with rods—these titles are confirmed by the Roman writer Cicero); (3) Acts 17:6, 9—at Thessalonica, the term *politarchs* (found in no other city) was corroborated by an inscription discovered there; (4) Acts 18:12—Achaia had been a senatorial province only since AD 44, so the term *proconsul* for Gallio, who had arrived in July of AD 51, is entirely accurate.

[20] John P. Meier, *A Marginal Jew: Rethinking the Historical Jesus*, vol. 2, *Mentor, Message, and Miracles* (New York: Doubleday, 1994).

[21] J. Warner Wallace, "Can We Construct The Entire New Testament from the Writings of the Church Fathers?" Cold-Case Christianity with J. Warner Wallace and Jimmy Wallace, June 13, 2016, https://coldcasechristianity.com/writings/can-we-construct-the-entire-new-testament-from-the-writings-of-the-church-fathers/.

[22] Garry K. Brantley, "The Dead Sea Scrolls and the Biblical Integrity," *Apologetics Press*, https://www.apologeticspress.org/apcontent.aspx?category=13&article=357.

[23] J. Wallace, "Can the Reliability of the Old Testament: A Trustworthy Process of Transmission," Cold-Case Christianity with J. Warner Wallace and Jimmy Wallace, April 27, 2018, https://coldcasechristianity.com/writings/establishing-the-reliability-of-the-old-testament-a-trustworthy-process-of-transmission/.

[24] Warner Wallace, "Establishing the Reliability of the Old Testament."

[25] Teri Dugan, "A Case for the Bible 101: Manuscript Evidence Part 3 – How did we get the New Testament?" Truth, Faith, and Reason, March 16, 2018, https://truthfaithandreason.com/a-case-for-the-bible-101-manuscript-evidence-part-3-how-did-we-get-the-new-testament/.

[26] JMM Team, "Testing the Historical Reliability of the New Testament," Josh McDowell Ministry, January 10, 2018, https://www.josh.org/historical-reliability-new-testament/.

[27] Gregory Koukl, *Tactics: A Game Plan for Discussing Your Christian Convictions* (Grand Rapids: Zondervan, 2009), 44.

[28] Darrell L. Bock and Daniel B. Wallace, *Dethroning Jesus: Exposing Popular Culture's Quest to Unseat the Biblical Christ* (Nashville: Thomas Nelson, 2007), 60–72.

[29] See Marvin Meyer, *The Gnostic Gospels of Jesus: The Definitive Collection of Mystical Gospels and Secret Books about Jesus of Nazareth* (New York: HarperOne, 2005).

[30] The writings of many of the church fathers are still widely available. For example, see *Against Heresies* by St. Irenaeus of Lyons, Project Gutenberg, http://self.gutenberg.org/article/WHEBN0000015414/Irenaeus#Scripture.v.

4 How to Read the Bible

1. A Bible Study Gone Wrong

▸ **OBJECTIVE:** You will be able to determine how not to do a Bible study.

Sophia: “Guys, I was reading the book of Jeremiah and came across the most amazing passage in chapter 29. It says, ‘For I know the plans I have for you, declares the Lord, plans for welfare and not for evil, to give you a future and a hope. Then you will call upon me and come and pray to me, and I will hear you. You will seek me and find me, when you seek me with all your heart.’”

Mason: “Wow, that’s cool!”

Sophia: "Yeah, I think I'm going to make this my life verse. It gives me hope because it shows that God wants to bless me and give me a good job and an awesome husband someday."

Noah: "Are you sure that is what it means? I don't think we're supposed to read it in such a personal way—"

Sophia: "Who are you to say what it means to me? This is what God is telling me. If he's telling you something different, that's cool."

Susannah: "I don't think we need to argue. We can all be right. Maybe we should just pray about it."

Sophia: "What good will that do? It means what it means to me, and it means what it means to you. There's no point in praying about it."

Chloe: "Well, I hate to interrupt, but even if we don't all agree, God has still met us here today. You know, the Bible says, 'Where two or three are gathered together, I am there with them.'"

Jacob: "I love having studies like this. It's like God is showing us things from the Bible that no one has ever noticed before!"

Noah: "I have this strange feeling we're making it about us and how we feel rather than about God."

Jacob: "Well isn't it about us? I mean, God loves us, so isn't that the whole point?"

Most of these students want to know God personally, and that's good. But rather than try to understand a text's true meaning, they're reading it through the filter of their own desires and cultural understandings. Since they are not paying attention to context, they are in danger of misunderstanding and misapplying Scripture.

It's hard to blame them, though. After all, the Bible can be a hard book to understand. It was written to people who have been dead for thousands of years, in a cultural context and ancient languages that are totally foreign to most individuals in the West. Yet, we are often told in our churches the Bible is the most important book of all time and that we should be reading and studying it every day. But if the Bible was not written specifically to us, why even bother reading it? Is it possible to understand it? And how could a book that is over 2,000 years old have any possible relevance to our lives today?

To answer these questions, we need to learn *how* to read Scripture. In this chapter, we'll approach the Bible as a book God intends us to read, understand, study, pray over, and live out. In a world overrun by skepticism and unbelief, as well as credulity and a lack of critical thinking, the Bible serves as a fixed point for all who want to follow Jesus. In order for us to really grasp its power, we must first learn how to read it well and truly.

2. *Tolle Lege*: Pick It Up and Read It

▶ **OBJECTIVE:** You will be able to infer the necessity of personal Bible reading.

It might surprise you to know that for most of history, very few Christians owned their own Bibles. In many parts of the world, widespread illiteracy and the expensive nature of books made them luxuries available only to the rich. But Johannes Gutenberg's printing press changed all that. One historian points out that the mass production of Martin Luther's writings (more than 300,000 copies of his books and pamphlets sold just from 1517 to 1520) is what gave life to the Protestant Reformation. It established a Christian tradition embraced by more than 600 million people today. Now, people who profess the Christian faith make up 35 percent of the world's population, about 2.5 billion people.[1]

Reproduction of Gutenberg press, Printing History Museum, Lyon, France

In this day and age, it might be hard to find a Christian in the West who doesn't own a Bible. But while there is no book so popular and available as the Bible, how many Christians actually read it on a regular basis? Sadly, for many Bible owners, the Bible is nothing more than a decoration, collecting dust on the shelf. It's like a pile of kindling without a match. Unless the kindling is lit, it can provide neither heat nor light. Even if we *can* read, the Bible will do us little good if we *won't* read it.

In 2020, Bible reading in America looked like this:

> Between early 2019 and 2020, the percentage of US adults who say they use the Bible daily dropped from 14 percent to 9 percent. . . . Overall, about a fifth (22 percent) of US adults interact with the Bible multiple times a week, not counting Scripture use at church . . . More than a third (35 percent) of Americans say they never read the Bible [and] sixty percent read the Bible four times per year or less.[2]

According to Lifeway Research:

> Less than a quarter of those who have ever read a Bible have a systematic plan for reading the Christian scriptures each day. And a third of Americans never pick it up on their own. . . . Even among worship attendees less than half read the Bible daily. The only time most Americans hear from the Bible is when someone else is reading it.[3]

Illiteracy-by-choice is not a new problem. More than 1,500 years ago, a young man complained, "We have no leisure to read. Where are we to find the books? How or when could I get ahold of them? From whom could I borrow them?"[4] Even back then, this was a false complaint. The young man's problem wasn't a lack of books. It was lack of interest.

Yet, one day he heard a child in a neighboring home chanting, "Pick it up and read it. Pick it up and read it" (in Latin: *Tolle lege, tolle lege*). Taking this as a sign from God, the young man picked up the Bible and began reading. When he encountered Romans 13:13–14, this young man, Augustine, recognized his own sinfulness. He committed his life to Christ and ultimately became one of the world's most revered and influential theologians.

We'd do well to follow Augustine's example. Bible reading isn't something that should be left to the pros. While we should certainly care about what theologians say, we should also read and study the Bible ourselves.

3. A Lifelong Journey

▸ **OBJECTIVE: You will be able to distinguish various benefits of studying God's Word.**

Studying and applying Scripture is a lifelong journey. We will not understand everything. We will make mistakes. And as we grow and mature, our thinking can change. At times we might feel like we are not getting anything out of the Bible, but we must not give up!

The apostle Paul wrote to his protégé Timothy, "Do your best to present yourself to God as one approved, a worker who has no need to be ashamed, rightly handling the word of truth" (2 Timothy 2:15). Paul didn't expect Timothy to be perfect, but he did expect him to do his best. And Paul had no illusions that he had it all figured out either. Even as an old man, Paul intended to continue studying to his dying day (as evidenced by his request for books in 2 Timothy 4:13). We should follow Paul's example by diligently studying God's Word.

Also, the Bible suggests several benefits to readers who study it:

- **Blessing:** Psalm 119 indicates that those who study Scripture will be blessed with delight, wisdom, hope, freedom from shame, and protection against doing evil.
- **Insight into how to bear spiritual fruit:** Jesus himself said that to bear spiritual fruit, we need to remain in him and have his word remain in us (John 15:1–8).
- **Freedom from spiritual bondage:** Jesus said those who abide in his word will know the truth that will set them free (John 8:31–32).
- **Direction in life:** Proverbs 3:5–6 says that God directs those who trust in and acknowledge him. Faithful reading of Scripture helps us to know God better, enabling greater trust.
- **The ability to grasp truth and defeat error:** The Scriptures expose the true condition of the human heart (Hebrews 4:12–13) and enable us to discern and defeat error (2 Corinthians 10:3–5).

4. Self-Centered Bible Reading

▸ **OBJECTIVE: You will be able to give examples of how postmodernism has affected the study of the Bible.**

If you've ever found yourself reading the Bible and asking, "What does this mean to me?" you're not alone. In some ways, this can be a good question to ask. Reading the Bible shouldn't be a mere academic exercise. We rightly want to know how it applies to our lives. We're all searching for answers to our most pressing questions. However, if we read the Bible incorrectly or self-centeredly, we might not sense its power, nor see that power at work in our lives and culture.

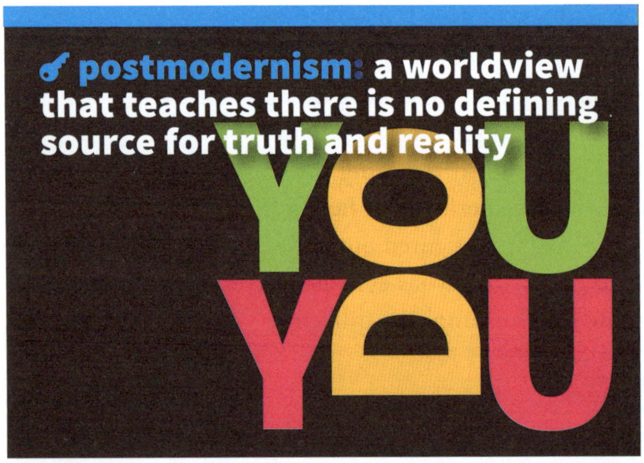

We naturally hope the Bible, like aspirin, will relieve life's everyday pains. This hope, though, has grown into a kind of narcissism—part of a larger cultural mood that promotes a hyper-personalized approach to *all* of life. This cultural mood is called **postmodernism**, *a worldview that teaches there is no defining source for truth and reality.*

Academically, postmodernism developed as scholars responded to the failure of modern science and technology to produce a utopian existence. As a response, postmodernists turned their attention away from "capital T Truth" to small, localized truths that were constructed through people's individual and cultural experiences. In other words, postmodernism says there are no universal truths that apply to all people. Instead, all you can know is your own "truth," which is determined by your experience. Postmodernism assumes the concept of relativism.

Culturally, postmodernism affects how we think about everything, including the Bible. Postmodernists say that we can only really know our descriptions of the world, not the world itself. Our talk about the world, they say, isn't really about the world at all, but about us. In 1968, Roland Barthes wrote "The Death of the Author," a short essay in which he argued that we should not value the origin of a text (the author's intentions) as much as its destination (the reader's experience). Readers should free themselves from the author's single intended meaning and invent new meanings.[5]

If we cannot really know the world, then we certainly cannot learn anything about the world from a written book. According to postmodernism, there is no truth in the Bible to be discovered, only our own interpretations. Postmodernism assumes that what you think is true, may be true for you, but that doesn't mean it is true for anyone else.

If we accept the assumptions of postmodernism, we can basically make the Bible say anything we want it to say; we don't have to concern ourselves with what God actually wants to communicate to us. According to postmodernism, we can invent our own meanings and use the Bible in any way we want.

Let's consider a few examples of this self-centered approach to the Bible: Ignoring passages that speak about suffering, some people have taught that the Bible is all about how to gain health and wealth and live a prosperous life. Dangerous cult leaders have used portions of Scripture to lead people to support evil causes. Slave traders used the Bible to justify slavery.

These are all tragic examples of people taking Scripture out of context to suit their own personal desires. Though not all faulty interpretations reflect postmodern thinking, postmodernism provides no grounds for us to say an interpretation is wrong; it holds that every single interpretation is equally valid.

All of us inevitably read the Bible through our own cultural lens, experience, or sometimes self-centered motives. However, we must try to be aware of these things and not allow them to determine what the Bible means. If we don't, we not only miss what God wants to communicate to us, but we are also in danger of misapplying Scripture. To guard against this danger, we must learn how to read Scripture correctly. To get started, let's look at some common mistakes and see how we might avoid them.

5. Common Mistakes in Bible Reading, Part 1

▸ **OBJECTIVE: You will be able to identify three common mistakes that people make when reading the Bible.**

The mistakes people make when reading Scripture can be corrected through a little intellectual discipline. This begins with a strong *hermeneutic*. The term **hermeneutics** (from the Greek word *hermeneuo*, meaning *to interpret*) describes *the process of devising the best methods for understanding and interpreting a text*; it is most often used with regard to interpreting Scripture. As we look at each mistake and how to correct it, we'll put in place "hermeneutic building blocks" that increase the accuracy of our interpretations, and thus our knowledge of God.

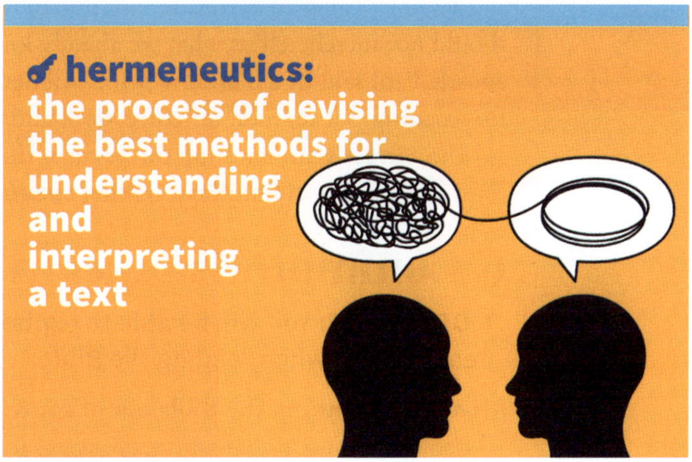

Mistake 1—Assuming the Bible doesn't need to be interpreted: We cannot escape the fact that even though the Bible is the authoritative and inspired Word of God, it still must be interpreted. As theologians Gordon Fee and Douglas Stuart point out:

> The first reason one needs to learn *how* to interpret is that, whether one likes it or not, every reader is at the same time an interpreter. That is, most of us assume as we read that we also understand what we read. We also tend to think that *our understanding* is the same thing as the Holy Spirit's or human author's *intent*. However, we invariably bring to the text all that we are, with all of our

> experiences, culture, and prior understandings of words and ideas. Sometimes what we bring to the text, unintentionally to be sure, leads us astray, or else causes us to read all kinds of foreign ideas into the text.[6]

When it comes to Scripture, if we don't have a proper interpretation, we can delude ourselves into thinking we know what God means when, in fact, we don't.

Mistake 2—Assuming the Bible applies uniquely to us: As they connect with the text, some people make the mistake of *individualizing* the text. They suppose that any or all parts apply to them in a unique way, outside of the original context.

In the Bible study gone wrong at the opening of this chapter, Sophia expresses precisely this mindset. She imagines Jeremiah 29:11 ("For I know the plans I have for you, declares the Lord, plans for welfare and not for evil, to give you a future and a hope.") to be a personal promise of blessing from God to *her*. But these words were not written to her. They served as a prophecy to Israel at a particular point in time based on the nation's particular circumstances. This does not mean that this text has no meaning for us today, only that we must first consider what it meant to the people it was written to.

Before we focus on ourselves or our current circumstances, we should focus on God—on how to deepen and enrich our understanding of him. By looking at the full context of the text, we learn more about who God shows himself to be and how he has dealt with his people in the past. From this we get insight into his unchanging nature and character and can better understand how we might more fully bear his image.

Mistake 3—ignoring passages that don't fit our theology: When people try to make sense of all of Scripture, they often create a *system*, or a sort of file cabinet into which everything neatly fits. This *systematic theology* is not bad in and of itself. But it can go awry if people choose to highlight some verses rather than others as a way to make artificial space for their developed theology.

We must value all Scripture, not just the sections that serve our agendas. The Bible should not merely tell us what we already know or only the things we want to hear. The apostle Paul said in 2 Timothy 3:16, "All Scripture is breathed out by God and profitable for teaching, for reproof, for correction, and for training in righteousness . . . "

The corrective to ignoring the parts of the Bible that don't fit our theology is simple: we must approach it in humility, making *ourselves* fit *it* rather than trying to make *it* fit *us*.

6. Common Mistakes in Bible Reading, Part 2

▸ **OBJECTIVE:** You will be able to explain two additional common mistakes people make when reading the Bible.

Mistake 4—Taking the Bible out of context: Similar to over personalizing Scripture, Christians also commonly misapply verses to their situations that were originally intended in a specific way for a specific audience. In other words, they ignore the context. The **context** is *the historical background and literary setting of a text that helps clarify its meaning.*

A prime example of taking the Bible out of context is Matthew 18:19–20: "Again I say to you, if two of you agree on earth about anything they ask, it will be done for them by my Father in heaven. For where two or three are gathered in my name, there am I among them." This is often taken as a promise that whenever believers get together to pray in the name of Jesus, God will do whatever they ask. But if we back up just four verses and look at the context, it's clear that Jesus is referring to bringing two or three witnesses in to help resolve a conflict. In fact, the phrase "two or three witnesses," is never used in Scripture except in reference to the testimony of witnesses in establishing justice.[7]

Many of the big mistakes people make when reading the Bible can be remedied by interpreting biblical texts in context. As Fee and Stuart counsel, "A text cannot mean what it never meant. Or to put it in a positive way, the true meaning of the biblical text for us is what God originally intended it to mean when it was first spoken. This is the starting point."[8]

Mistake 5—Interpreting the Bible based on contemporary standards: The Bible is *eternally relevant* in that "it speaks to all humankind, in every age and in every culture."[9] Yet the Bible was communicated in certain languages, times, and cultures. This is what we call *historical particularity*. Scripture's eternal relevance and its historical particularity are in tension. This tension is good, like the tension we experience when we exercise, yet at times it feels better to relieve the tension.

One example of this tension is due to the nature of the English language. In the past, the words *man* and *men* were understood to include both men and women. Today, we generally do not use *man* and *men* in this way, preferring terms that can apply to both men and women (such as *mail carrier* instead of *mailman*), or that include everyone (such as *people* instead of *men*). But making these changes may distort the meaning of a text. In Galatians 4, the apostle Paul uses an analogy about inheritance using the term *sons*. Some translators, wanting to be more inclusive and relieve some of the tension of this seemingly exclusive male language, have changed the wording to *children*. According to Presbyterian pastor and author Tim Keller, this is a mistake:

> Many take offense at using the masculine word "sons" to refer to all Christians, male and female. Some would prefer to translate verse 26: "You are all children of God" (as the NIV 2011 does). But if we are too quick to correct the biblical language, we miss the revolutionary (and radically egalitarian) nature of what Paul is saying. In most ancient cultures, daughters could not inherit property. Therefore "son" meant "legal heir," which was a status forbidden to women. But the gospel tells us we are *all* sons of God in Christ. We are *all* heirs. Similarly, the Bible describes all Christians together, including men, as the "bride of Christ" (Revelation 21:2). God is evenhanded in his gender-specific metaphors. Men are part of His Son's bride; and women are his sons. His heirs. If we don't let Paul call Christian women "sons of God," we miss how radical and wonderful a claim this is.[10]

As you can see, we must be very careful not to distort the meaning of Scripture in an attempt to make it more relevant to our culture. Instead, we must carefully study the meaning of the text to see how it applies to our lives today.

7. Steps to Reading the Bible Well, Part 1

▸ **Objective: You will be able to explain the first three steps to reading the Bible well.**

The mistakes we discussed above focus on what we should *not* do. But what *should* we do? How might we read Scripture *well*? Earlier, we used the term *hermeneutics* to describe the general principles of interpreting Scripture. Good hermeneutics begins with another term theologians use, *exegesis*, from the Greek word *hegeisthai*, for *guide* or *lead*, and the prefix *ex*, meaning *out of*. **Exegesis** is *the exposition or explanation of a text based on careful study and analysis*. So, exegesis refers to the proper interpretation of a particular passage (that is, what you can fairly conclude *out of* it). Large-scale interpretation (hermeneutics) must begin with the small-scale, difficult work of wrestling with each chapter, verse, line, and word (exegesis).

According to Fee and Stuart, "The key to good exegesis, and therefore to more intelligent reading of the Bible, is to learn to read the text carefully and to ask the right questions of the text."[11] Attention must be paid to both the details and the big picture. To make interpreting Scripture easier, let's take a look at a seven-step process.

Step 1: Choose a good translation. Since most of us cannot read in Hebrew, Aramaic, or Greek (the original languages the Bible was written in), we will need a solid translation to study God's Word. There are three types of Bible translations according to Fee and Stuart:

1. *Formal equivalence translations:* These translations "attempt to keep as close to the 'form' of the Hebrew or Greek, both words and grammar, as can be conveniently put into understandable English." Examples are the King James Version (KJV), the New King James Version (NKJV), the New American Standard Bible (NASB), and the English Standard Version (ESV).

2. *Functional (dynamic) equivalence translations:* These translations "attempt to keep the meaning of the Hebrew or Greek but to put their words and idioms into what would be the normal way of saying the same thing in English." Examples are the New American Bible (NAB), the New Living Translation (NLT), and the New International Version (NIV).

3. *Free translations or paraphrases:* These translations "attempt to translate the ideas from one language to another, with less concern about using the exact words of the original. A free translation . . . tries to eliminate as much of the historical distance as possible and still be faithful to the text." Examples are the New English Bible (NEB), the Living Bible (LB), and The Message (MSG).[12]

So, which type should you choose? You may want to use several and note where they differ. This is fairly easy with online Bible programs that offer several translations at the click of a mouse. For example, contrast the first part of Psalm 36:5 in the King James Version ("Thy mercy, O LORD, is in the heavens"), the New Living Translation ("Your unfailing love, O LORD, is as vast as the heavens"), and The Message ("God's love is meteoric, his loyalty astronomic"). Comparing translations demands close attention, especially when you're going over a familiar passage.

Step 2: Understand the content. The term *content* refers to the meaning of words or the subject matter of a work. Ask what you would ask of any material you read: *What does it say? Who is saying it? To whom? Where? When? Why? How?* The answers may not all be in the passage; some may be in the surrounding material. Never content yourself with reading a single verse. Verses belong to paragraphs, paragraphs belong to chapters, chapters belong to books, and books fit into the Bible as a whole. (Note: The current chapter and verse divisions in the Bible weren't developed until over 1,000 years after the New Testament was written!)

historical context: the time, place, culture, and audience of a text

Step 3: Understand the historical context. The historical context considers *the time, place, culture, and audience of a text.* It is what the author and audience would have assumed to be true about life and the world.

The historical context of any verse, book, or passage you read needs to be a factor in how you interpret what you are reading. Every word of the Bible was written at a certain point in history, in the midst of a certain set of circumstances. Often, this outside information will give you a lot of insight as to the purpose of what has been written. The why, when, and where details of the passage will be connected to the historical context.[13]

Historical context also includes the geographical, topographical, and political factors that are relevant to the author's setting. Ask: "What were the events or reasons that caused the author to write?" and "What is the purpose of the writing?"

8. Steps to Reading the Bible Well, Part 2

▶ **OBJECTIVE: You will be able to describe the four remaining steps to reading the Bible well.**

Step 4: Understand the literary context. The literary context includes things like *the genre, structure, and grammar of a text.* Just as there are musical genres such as country, hip hop, and classical, there are different genres in literature. The Bible includes poetry, historical narratives, laws, prophecies, psalms, proverbs, parables, epistles, and apocalyptic literature. It also "employs many literary devices, such as euphemisms, allusion, imagery, and foreshadowing."[14]

Understanding the genre helps us determine how to interpret a passage properly. For example, the Psalms are poetry full of figurative and symbolic language. We understand, for example, that Psalm 17:8, "Keep me as the apple of your eye; hide me in the shadow of your wings" does not literally mean God's eye has an apple in it or that he has wings. Similarly, we understand Exodus is a historical narrative, and that the passages about manna falling from heaven (Exodus 16) or the Ten Commandments (Exodus 20) are not figurative but intended as historical accounts. Each genre comes with its own set of interpretive principles. A proverb, by definition, is not a prophecy or a promise. A parable is not a poem. Understanding genre helps us to know not only what a passage says, but to what extent we might apply it to our own lives.

Step 5: Look for relationships. If you look closely, you will see many interesting parallels in Scripture. For example, Matthew describes Jesus being led into the wilderness, where he fasted for 40 days and nights. He was then tempted by the devil to turn stones into bread. Jesus answered, "It is written, 'Man shall not live by bread alone, but by every word that comes from the mouth of God'" (Matthew 4:4). If we look at Deuteronomy 8, the passage Jesus quoted, we find this is where Moses gave instructions to Israel. By comparing and contrasting Jesus' 40 days with the Israelites' 40 years in the wilderness, we see stunning parallels. God's Word is full of recurring themes and symbols. Identifying such connections helps us have a fuller understanding of what God is communicating to us.

Step 6: Use Bible helps. Bible commentaries are helpful tools to understand both the *context* and the *content* of Scripture. According to Fee and Stuart, a good commentary should supply three things: "(1) helps on sources and information about the historical context, (2) answers to [many] content questions, and (3) thorough discussions of difficult texts as to the possibilities of meaning, along with the supporting arguments."[15]

A good commentary, or set of commentaries, digs into the theological issues rather than merely sharing the author's experiences. It offers balanced discussions of possible meanings of the text rather than proposing only what the author prefers. The best commentaries also give insights into the culture and historical background of each biblical book, as well as points of interest regarding the Hebrew and Greek words used.

Step 7: Courageously pursue a response. We are to be "doers" of the word, not hearers only (James 1:22). That said, not every passage is meant as a command or point we must act upon. Most of the Bible is descriptive in nature. It tells of past events, explores the lives of our ancestors, and provides a record of God's plan of redemption. A *descriptive* passage describes what happened and teaches us through inference and example. It gives us a sense of where the people of God have been so that we might discern how to live in our present situation more faithfully.

A *prescriptive* passage, on the other hand, provides specific hallmarks of how we ought to live. There are many prescriptive passages in the Bible. They reflect something of God's nature and the created order and thus give commands to be obeyed or values to be adopted. Examples include the Ten Commandments (Exodus 20:2–17), the Sermon on the Mount (Matthew 5:1–16), and the Great Commission (Matthew 28:16–20).

9. Practicing What We Learn

▸ **OBJECTIVE:** You will be able to list three ways to apply what you learn in Bible study.

God can speak to us in many ways: through our own reading of Scripture, a sermon, a small group Bible study, the counsel of a friend, in the beauty of nature, and sometimes even in dreams or visions. Regardless of the channel, what God says will always be consistent with the great story of Scripture and applied to our heart by his Holy Spirit. "When the Spirit of truth comes," Jesus promised his disciples, "he will guide you into all the truth, for he will not speak on his own authority, but whatever he hears he will speak, and he will declare to you the things that are to come" (John 16:13). As Christians, we, too, are led by the Spirit. As Paul reminds us, "For all who are led by the Spirit of God are sons of God" (Romans 8:14).

It is the Holy Spirit, then, who guides us to truth and prompts us to apply it to our lives. Our job is to study Scripture faithfully and listen to the Holy Spirit's promptings to put what we have learned into practice. The key is acting on what we know. Jesus said in John 13:17, "If you know these things, blessed are you if you do them."

So how do we go about being "doers of the word" (James 1:22)? What specific actions can we take to apply what we learn in Scripture? We suggest three things, for starters:

1. Journal what you're learning. You can buy inexpensive paper journals at any discount store. It's great to get off-line for a bit and actually write things down. Writing your thoughts in a journal can help you stay focused while you study. It is also a good way to chronicle what you are learning.

2. Share what you're learning. It's easy to get stuck in your own head when reading Scripture. A good way to avoid this problem is to talk to others about what you are reading in the Bible. Try finding a trusted friend or mentor, or a Bible study where you can regularly share what you learn and hear what others are learning.

3. Live what you're learning. God's Word is powerful and often God meets us with specific promptings about how we should live differently. Pray for courage and commit to putting God's Word into practice!

10. Conclusion

Some people read Scripture and steadily increase in faith. Others read and grow doubtful because of difficult passages or perhaps because they encounter a God in Scripture they didn't quite expect. If you experience doubt, you're not alone. Very godly people have had doubts. John the Baptist experienced doubt that Jesus was actually the Messiah (Matthew 11:2–3). Peter doubted when he was walking on the water to Jesus (Matthew 14:22–33). Thomas wouldn't believe Jesus had risen until he placed his hands in Jesus' wounds (John 20:24–29).

One of the most celebrated figures of the Protestant Reformation, Martin Luther, also experienced grave doubts. Ten years after posting his 95 theses on the church door at Wittenberg, Luther wrote of an agonizing experience of doubt: "For more than a week I was close to the gates of death and hell. I trembled in all my members. Christ was wholly lost. I was shaken by desperation and blasphemy of God."[16]

Reflecting on the experience, Luther emphasized the importance of being anchored in truth in the middle of such experiences: "All this is written for our comfort that we should see how deeply God hides his face and how we must not go by our feeling but only by his Word."[17]

In the moment, doubt can feel paralyzing, causing worry and fear; but the truth is that doubt is actually a healthy part of spiritual growth. If we handle it properly, we can grow in greater understanding and confidence by asking good questions and courageously pursuing answers. Ultimately, like Luther, we can find confidence if we are anchored in Scripture—Scripture which we have carefully studied and explored, as we are guided by the Holy Spirit.

When you experience doubts about the Bible, or have questions, don't bury them. Look for answers in commentaries and other resources. Share your thoughts with a trusted pastor, teacher, or mentor. Find a trained theologian, take him or her out for coffee, and share what's on your heart. God never intended for us to try and grow spiritually all by ourselves. Spiritual growth takes place in community. The church is a team. An army. A body. A family. A hospital. No church is perfect, and many people have been involved with one for a long time and yet not grasped what the Bible is all about. Maybe part of your role is to help them grow too.

In the end, remember this: God is shaping every believer into the image of his Son: "Now the Lord is the Spirit, and where the Spirit of the Lord is, there is freedom. And we all, with unveiled face, beholding the glory of the Lord, are being transformed into the same image from one degree of glory to another" (2 Corinthians 3:17–18). And one of the ways this happens is through "the word of God, which is at work in you believers" (1 Thessalonians 2:13). God's Word will transform us if we will read and study it carefully. Pick up the Bible. Read it! As you do, you'll learn that it carries many significant implications for understanding God and ourselves.

ENDNOTES

[1] Todd M. Johnson and Gina A. Zurlo, eds. World Christian Database (Leiden/Boston: Brill, accessed July 2019), *Status of Global Christianity, 2020, in the Context of 1900–2050.* Posted by The Center for the Study of Global Christianity at Gordon-Conwell Theological Seminary, https://www.gordonconwell.edu/center-for-global-christianity/wp-content/uploads/sites/13/2020/01/Status-of-Global-Christianity-2020.pdf.

[2] David Roach, "Bible Reading Drops During Social Distancing," *Christianity Today*, July 22, 2020, https://www.christianitytoday.com/news/2020/july/state-of-bible-reading-coronavirus-barna-abs.html.

[3] Bob Smietana, *Americans Are Fond of the Bible, Don't Actually Read It*, LifeWay Research, April 25, 2017, https://lifewayresearch.com/2017/04/25/lifeway-research-americans-are-fond-of-the-bible-dont-actually-read-it/.

[4] Saint Augustine, *Confessions of St. Augustine* (Mineola, NY: Dover Thrift Editions, 2002), 98.

[5] Glen Ward, *Teach Yourself Postmodernism* (London: Hodder Education, 2003), 162.

[6] Gordon D. Fee and Douglas Stuart, *How to Read the Bible for All Its Worth*, 3rd ed. (Grand Rapids: Zondervan, 2003), 18.

[7] See Deuteronomy 17:6, 19:15; as well as Paul's use in 2 Corinthians 13:1 and 1 Timothy 5:19. The author of Hebrews also uses the term in Hebrews 10:28.

[8] Fee and Stuart, *How to Read the Bible for All Its Worth*, 30.

[9] Fee and Stuart, *How to Read the Bible for All Its Worth*, 21.

[10] Timothy Keller, *Galatians for You: For Reading, for Feeding, for Leading*, God's Word for You series (Purcellville, VA: The Good Book Company, 2013), 90.

[11] Fee and Stuart, *How to Read the Bible for All Its Worth*, 26.

[12] Fee and Stuart, *How to Read the Bible for All Its Worth*, 41–42.

[13] Emily Kurz, "Why Is Historical Context Important When Studying God's Word?", Ethnos360 Bible Institute (blog), October 10, 2017, https://e360bible.org/blog/historical-context-important-studying-gods-word/.

[14] Emily Kurz, "Understanding Literary Context in the Bible," Ethnos360 Bible Institute (blog), October 17, 2017, https://e360bible.org/blog/understanding-literary-context-in-the-bible/.

[15] Fee and Stuart, *How to Read the Bible for All Its Worth*, 266.

[16] Quoted in Ruth A. Tucker, *Walking Away from Faith: Unraveling the Mystery of Belief and Unbelief* (Downers Grove, IL: InterVarsity Press, 2002), 91.

[17] Quoted in Ruth A. Tucker, *Walking Away from Faith: Unraveling the Mystery of Belief and Unbelief* (Downers Grove, IL: InterVarsity Press, 2002), 91.

5 The Bible as a Story

1. Tell Me a Story

▸ **OBJECTIVE: You will be able to explain the importance of stories.**

Did your parents ever read you a bedtime story? Did you ever read one to a sibling? Maybe you looked through a few titles before you picked one. Was it *Goodnight Moon*? *Llama Llama Red Pajama*? *The Chronicles of Narnia*? Do you have a favorite story?

Of course, stories aren't only for children. While not everyone likes reading stories, most people, including adults, enjoy hearing a good story. And sometimes the best stories are not in books. You see a photograph or souvenir and ask your grandma about it. She

tells you the story of that vacation she took with your grandad long ago, and how wonderful and strange and funny it was. Or, you learn something that you never suspected: Your father once broke his leg when he lost control of his sled and slid into a tree. Your mother won a race. Your uncle met someone famous.

Stories are everywhere. They shape us and how we see the world. "Human beings have been telling stories as long as there's been a language to tell them in. We think in stories, remember in stories, and turn just about everything we experience into a story, sometimes adjusting or omitting facts to make it fit."[1] One Summit student put it this way:

> It is difficult to understate the importance of story. Stories can expand our world. . . Telling and listening to stories is how we figure out who we are. For many of us, some of our earliest childhood memories are of stories we were told and how they made us feel. Do you remember the disgust you felt at the selfishness of Cinderella's stepsisters? Or the awe inspired by the courage of Sir Gawain? Do you remember that your first concepts of sacrifice, loyalty, and justice were formed from [the] substance of fairy tales? These stories gave us our first heroes, our first concept of who we wanted to be [and] our first villains, instilling within us a deep hatred of darkness, evil, and selfishness. . . . Whether fiction or nonfiction, stories are a path to self-discovery, a tool of self-examination, and a measuring stick of character. . . . The kind of characters we identify with are formative of our own self-concept. We decide who we will be based off of who we admire.[2]

Stories are how we make sense of reality. They guide us through life just as the stars and constellations guided ancient explorers across uncharted lands and seas.

"Story is a metaphor for life," says award-winning author and storyteller Robert McKee. He explains that "Story is not only our most prolific art form but rivals all activities—work, play, eating, exercise—for our waking hours. We tell and take stories as much as we sleep—and even then, we dream. Why? Why is so much of our life spent inside stories? Because . . . stories are equipment for living."[3] Stories clearly have power to influence our lives. Let's take a closer look at how stories work.

2. Elements of a Story

▸ **OBJECTIVE: You will be able to list the different components of well-formed narratives.**

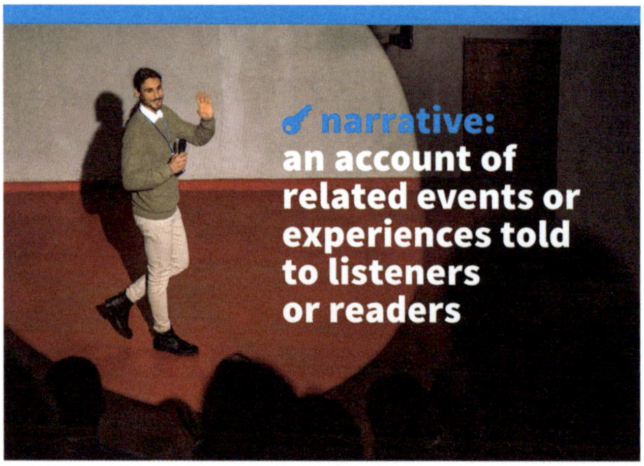

Stories are conveyed in various forms: fables and fairytales, poems and songs, epics and essays, plays and movies, limericks and jokes. They can be fiction or nonfiction, oral or written, long or short, simple or complex, funny or sad. Another word for story is a narrative.

A **narrative** is *an account of related events or experiences told to listeners or readers.*

Just as there are certain rules for constructing buildings that are safe and enjoyable to see and inhabit, so there are rules for constructing good stories. There are many different shapes and sizes of buildings, but the good ones have certain structural elements in common. The same is true of stories. The main components of well-written stories, or narratives, are:

- **Setting:** a time and a place
- **Characters:** a protagonist (hero), an antagonist (villain), and a supporting cast
- **Conflict:** a problem to solve or a challenge to overcome
- **Theme:** the message or idea the author is interested in communicating
- **Plot:** the storyline, with a beginning, middle, and end
- **Point of view:** who is telling the story and in what tense (past, present, future)[4]

The plot of a story is especially important. Most stories have a three-act structure that begins with a setup—introducing us to the characters, setting up the location and time of the story, giving us a feel for the story's universe. This is also the part where some kind of conflict is introduced. In the second act, the protagonist confronts the conflict and deals with various obstacles in the way of the goal. Sometimes, around the midpoint of the story, something happens that increases the drama or sets the story on a new trajectory. In the third and final act, the conflict builds to the climax and then ultimately resolves either happily or tragically.[5]

How an author chooses to tell a story is a part of the story too. The meaning of a story is partly communicated by the author's tone and style. Compare the different tones and styles of Dr. Seuss and J. R. R. Tolkien. Both are great storytellers, though their styles are radically different. Dr. Seuss' style involves a lot of rhyming and his tone is whimsical. Tolkien's style is epic, while his tone is usually quite serious.

A story can also have diversity within unity. Like the blending of colors in a painting, unity is a coming together of a multitude of details. In a good story, the reader eventually sees how all of the details fit together. That's why a series of random events does not constitute a story. There needs to be a connecting thread that helps us see how the events work together to form a narrative.

If you think about it, each of our lives is a story. They have a plot—a beginning, a middle, and an end, with lots of interesting characters and conflict along the way. The problem for us is that we don't know how exactly our stories are going to end or even what's going to be in tomorrow's chapter. Sometimes, our lives can feel like a series of random events. And what is the tone of our stories? Is life basically comic, tragic, or something in between? How can we make sense of our individual stories if we don't even know where they are going? To answer these questions, we need a metanarrative.

3. What Is a Metanarrative?

▸ **OBJECTIVE: You will be able to discuss the relationship between metanarratives, worldviews, and the meaning of life.**

What's a metanarrative? Narrative means *story*, and *meta* means *beyond*. A **metanarrative** is *the story beyond the story; an overarching narrative that makes sense of the world.*

A metanarrative provides a single, overarching interpretation, or grand story, showing how different stories make sense within a larger story. For example, in the musical *Into the Woods*, the stories of Little Red Riding Hood, Rapunzel, Cinderella, and Jack and the Beanstalk are incorporated into the larger story of a couple's quest to have a child.[6] This quest provides the metanarrative within which all the other stories fit together and make sense.

metanarrative: the story beyond the story; an overarching narrative that makes sense of the world

Not all metanarratives are fiction; there are nonfiction metanarratives as well. The history of the United States, for example, can be seen as a collection of related immigration stories. From the European traders who met the Native Americans already here, to the Pilgrims and Puritans who sought religious freedom; from the plight of enslaved Africans to that of Irish people fleeing the Great Famine in the mid 1800s; from Germans seeking farmland to Chinese building railroads, the story of America can be told as a great metanarrative encompassing the ways its diverse people sought freedom and opportunity.[7]

One of the most popular metanarratives in our culture today is the Marvel Cinematic Universe (MCU). As one pastor and movie critic explains:

> Every human being is hungry for a single overarching storyline that ties all of our smaller stories together. Since 2008, evidence for this hunger has been as close as your nearest cinema. That's when the release of *Iron Man* marked the genesis of the Marvel Cinematic Universe. . . . The MCU includes a multiplicity of individual narratives. Taken together, these storylines form a master narrative—a metanarrative—that turns out to be as vast as the universe itself.[8]

Suppose you knew nothing about the Marvel Cinematic Universe and the first movie you watched was *Captain America: Civil War*. You might have a hard time understanding exactly what was going on. But if you had watched all of the movies that came before it, you would be able to make much more sense of that particular movie. The Marvel Cinematic Universe provides the metanarrative that gives meaning to, and explains, how all of the individual movies fit together.

Before the MCU, there was the *Star Wars* metanarrative created by George Lucas. With *Star Wars*, Lucas wanted to tell "an old myth in a new way."[9] A myth is similar in many ways to a metanarrative. In ancient times, mythical stories about gods and heroes helped people to explain the world and the origin and history of a people. In *Star Wars*, Lucas uses the mythical story of the hero's journey (in which a hero character sets out on a quest, confronts a challenge, and returns changed), to highlight the struggle between good and evil in the galaxy. Each character in the *Star Wars* universe has such a journey, but their stories all come together in the great battle between good and evil in the galaxy.[10]

Lucas believes that this mythical story, or metanarrative, can help us make sense of our own world. Lucas sees "*Star Wars* as taking all the issues that religion represents and trying to distill them down into a more modern and easily accessible construct."[11]

The concept of metanarrative is fundamentally wrapped up with the meaning of life. In *Star Wars*, the initially selfish Han Solo finds meaning and purpose outside of making money when he realizes that he has become part of a bigger story—resistance to the evil empire. Young Jakku scavenger Rey discovers her "destiny" when she realizes that she is an heir to the ancient Jedi tradition.

In the same way, we can see our own stories as part of a bigger story—a metanarrative that gives meaning and purpose to the seemingly random events of our lives.

4. Worldviews as Metanarratives

▸ **OBJECTIVE:** You will be able to describe and critique the postmodern view of metanarratives.

▸ **OBJECTIVE:** You will be able to compare and contrast common non-Christian worldviews.

However, not everyone thinks that metanarratives can provide meaning to our lives. The term *metanarrative* was made popular by a 1979 book[12] on postmodernism, which argued that religious metanarratives can't be trusted:

> [Postmodernists] generally do not accept any overarching story that gives meaning to all of life. Instead, they focus on small, individual narratives that give meaning to their own lives. A metanarrative speaks of absolute, universal truth. An individual narrative speaks of what is "true for me" and "gives meaning to my life." Postmodern thinking rejects . . . universal truth.[13]

According to the postmodernist, there is no big story that makes sense of all the other stories. We can only find meaning and purpose in our own story. But we don't even know what will happen in the next chapter of our lives. Stuck in the middle of our story, it's hard to know how we should live it.[14]

It turns out that all people, even postmodernists, need a metanarrative to make sense of their lives. The postmodern metanarrative claims that there is no universal truth, and that someone who makes a truth claim is usually oppressing others. Do you see how this itself is a metanarrative that helps postmodernists to explain and make sense of the world?

Another way of talking about metanarratives is to talk about worldview. As you may remember from Chapter 1, a worldview is "a pattern of ideas and beliefs that help us make sense of the world and that guide our decisions and actions." All worldviews offer a metanarrative that claims to explain or give meaning to life and the events in it. Worldviews provide answers to the biggest questions we ask, such as: Where did I come from? Who am I? What is my purpose in life? What is wrong with this world? What is the solution? Where am I going after I die? and How should I live?

Here are some of the most popular worldviews today:

- **Secularism:** An atheistic/agnostic worldview that puts its faith in human ability and progress to make the world a better place
- **New spirituality:** A worldview that teaches that everything is god and that peace and harmony come from getting in touch with divine consciousness
- **Postmodernism:** A worldview that tends to be skeptical of all truth claims and rejects the idea that metanarratives can provide meaning to life
- **Marxism:** A worldview that sees all of history as class warfare and that aims for a future utopian, atheistic state where everything is held in common by the people
- **Islam:** A theistic worldview, centered on the life of the prophet Muhammad, that derives its understanding of the world from the teachings of the Quran, Hadith, and Sunnah

While there are many different worldviews, all worldviews are not equally valid. Each provides its own answers to the big questions of life, and they can't all be true. How can we know which worldview is best? We don't just want a worldview that sounds nice or helps us to get by. We need a worldview that is rooted in reality, in the way things actually are—a worldview that helps us to live meaningful and fulfilling lives. We believe that the Christian worldview offers a metanarrative that helps to explain the world as it really is and provides meaningful answers to the biggest questions of life.

5. The Bible as a Metanarrative

▸ **OBJECTIVE: You will be able to summarize the metanarrative of the Bible.**

As you learned in previous chapters, the Bible is a diverse collection of writings by many different authors. Even a quick glance shows that it doesn't resemble a textbook, encyclopedia, or other books whose primary purpose is to list facts. The Bible's various books were written over 1,500 years. They address distinct audiences and historical circumstances. Yet the Bible is not a random jumble of disconnected stories. Rather, its many stories tell one big story, or metanarrative, centered on God's working in and through his people. The story's climax is reached with the fully divine and fully human Jesus Christ: his birth, life, death, resurrection, ascension, and coming return.

About half of the Bible can be classified as **historical narrative**, which is *a historical account told in story form.*[15] To be clear, though, the Bible is not just a report of facts about the past; it is a story based on history, on reality. It tells us about life in the world as it actually is. And as we saw in Chapter 3, there is good evidence for the Bible's historical accuracy.

There are other parts of the Bible that aren't strictly historical narrative, such as wisdom literature, poetry, prophecies, and letters. But these parts were written within the historical narrative. The historical narrative establishes a trajectory from the beginning of God's story to the end. The Bible tells a story that is diverse but unified, with conflict and resolution, and an overarching plot that holds the story together.

If God is the ultimate author of Scripture, it makes sense that the details and subplots of the Bible come together in one coherent story, by the inspiration of the Holy Spirit. As theologian John Piper reminds us:

> In profound ways, the whole Bible—the whole of redemptive history—exists to create a place and time and meaning where particular, individual, finite humans can encounter its stunning parts. The parts make up the whole, and so serve the whole. They would have no meaning and no beauty without the whole. But it is just as important to say that the whole exists to give place and time and meaning to the parts so that the parts can be known and experienced and enjoyed.[16]

By engaging with the metanarrative of Scripture, we can find individual meaning for our own stories as we learn about who God is, how he works with his people, and what his ultimate plan is for us.

The Bible tells the story of the world, where God's very existence is the prelude. The world it describes is God's world—a world he created out of love, a world flooded with his creative majesty. As one poet put it, "the world is charged with the grandeur of God."[17] God speaks first in Genesis 1:3: "Let there be light." A simple sentence. No hammering, no sawing. Just the sound of God's voice turning *nothing* into *something*.

When God commanded it to, impenetrable murkiness became brilliantly illuminated. Plants and animals came to life. And then God created human beings, his image-bearers, and told them: "'Be fruitful and multiply and fill the earth and subdue it and have dominion. . . .' And God saw everything that he had made, and behold, it was very good" (Genesis 1:28–31).

In Hebrew, the phrase *very good* is *towb me'od.* It means exceedingly, heartbreakingly, abundantly, richly, loudly, immeasurably good in a festive, generous, happy, intelligent, charming, splendid way.[18]

And yet humanity has fallen under evil's assault and has been catapulted into vast spiritual and moral darkness. But, like in *The Hobbit*, when daylight broke just in time to turn the trolls into stone, Paul tells us that hope broke through into our world—just in time. "When the fullness of time had come, God sent forth his Son" (Galatians 4:4).

We know this story because it was written down. And we know how this grand story turns out. We know that God is, in Christ, "making all things new" (Revelation 21:5).

6. Comprehensive, Coherent, and Normative

▸ **OBJECTIVE:** You will be able to defend the Bible as a historical metanarrative.

As we have said, the Bible is not a pleasant fiction. It is a true story, a metanarrative grounded in history. In addition to its narrative structure and historical basis, theologians also speak of the Bible as being *comprehensive*, *coherent*, and *normative.*[19] Let's take a look at what each of these words means in relation to the Bible.

First, the Bible is **comprehensive,** which means *to be complete, including everything that is necessary or relevant.* This does not mean the Bible addresses everything we would like it to, nor does it satisfy all our curiosities. For example, while the Bible speaks of the reality of a tempter (the serpent in Genesis 3) in the garden of Eden, it does not tell us where this tempter came from (except that God created him) or why the tempter is in the garden. The Bible does not tell us all we would like to know about science or history. The Bible also does not tell us where or if we should go to college or whom we should marry (or if we should get married). What the Bible does tell us is all we need to know about God to live meaningfully and faithfully in his world.

Second, despite its diversity, the Bible is coherent. To be **coherent** means *to be orderly, logical, and consistent throughout.* It means the parts stick together and don't clash or contradict each other. The many individual stories in the Bible, from different authors, cultures, countries, and centuries, can be pieced together like a jigsaw puzzle. The pieces themselves may have rough edges and might seem incompatible with each other, but put together in the right way, they form one coherent picture.

It is remarkable how the Bible is coherent, given that it was written over such a long period of time by many authors who often didn't even know each other. Imagine a group of strangers trying to write a story over 1,000 years. With all the changes that happen in culture combined with the different styles of each author, it would be hard to keep things consistent throughout. And yet the Bible is miraculously coherent, pointing to its divine inspiration, the Holy Spirit, guiding the hands of so many authors to tell one coherent story!

coherent: to be orderly, logical, and consistent throughout

A norm is the accepted standard by which we judge something. An inch is an inch because it complies with an agreed-upon unit of measurement. Therefore, the Bible is normative.

To say the Bible is **normative** means that it is *setting norms or standards, especially when it comes to behavior.*

The Bible being normative means that it reveals the God-given standard for how people should live. Because the biblical metanarrative gives us a true picture of reality, it cuts through our false notions, exposes our sinfulness, and calls for a response from everyone who interacts with it. As Scripture puts it: "The word of God is living and active, sharper than any two-edged sword, piercing to the division of soul and of spirit, of joints and of marrow, and discerning the thoughts and intentions of the heart. And no creature is hidden from his sight, but all are naked and exposed to the eyes of him to whom we must give account" (Hebrews 4:12–13).

The historical metanarrative of Scripture is comprehensive, coherent, and normative. But how could the biblical authors write such a coherent book?

7. Caught Up in a Bigger Story

▸ **OBJECTIVE:** You will be able to identify biblical characters who were aware they were part of God's larger story.

The internal coherence of the Bible is primarily due to divine inspiration. However, it is also worth observing that the biblical authors, though they may not have known or understood the details of the whole story, seem overwhelmingly conscious of the fact they were operating within a larger narrative.

The people who spoke and eventually wrote down what became the Old Testament were aware they were part of God's story. In several instances God spoke directly to them and told them the part they had to play. The phrase, "Thus says the Lord" occurs more than 400 times in the English Standard Version of the Old Testament. Other phrases also convey the same idea. The human authors knew the story didn't originate with them or end with them. Prophets like Isaiah and Jeremiah spoke of a future day when God would return to rule the world with justice and righteousness, giving his people new hearts so they might truly love God and neighbor.

The same awareness can be seen in the New Testament. The people in Jesus' life knew they were part of something special. Mary, his mother, sensing her part in a bigger story, sang a song we now know as *the Magnificat*, a beautiful statement about God's faithfulness and deliverance (Luke 1:46–55). Zechariah, the father of Jesus' cousin John the Baptist, was skeptical at first; however, he later realized the events he witnessed were a part of God's grand narrative (Luke 1:67–79). Simeon and Anna, prophets in the temple, also sensed God's grand story when they spoke blessings over the infant Jesus (Luke 2:29–38).

Mark 1:14–15 records the beginning of Jesus' ministry: "Now after John was arrested, Jesus came into Galilee, proclaiming the gospel of God, and saying, 'The time is fulfilled, and the kingdom of God is at hand; repent and believe in the gospel.'" By recording Jesus' words that "The time is fulfilled," Mark demonstrated his awareness that the story of Jesus is part of a larger story—a story that began all the way back in Genesis and is reaching its climax in the ministry of Jesus.

In Romans 1:1–5 we learn that Paul saw his own ministry in light of the big story that began with God's promises to Israel and extended to all nations. Peter also recognized that those who believe in Christ are part of a larger story (1 Peter 1:3–13).

All throughout Scripture, God's servants are people who sense they are part of something bigger than themselves, something God is doing all over the world and throughout the ages. Each of them was caught up in a bigger story. As believers, we too are invited to play our part in the great story that God is telling. But how does that bigger story play out?

8. Outline of the Biblical Story

▸ **OBJECTIVE:** **You will be able to describe the six main acts in the biblical metanarrative and their corresponding Scriptures.**

There are several ways to understand the metanarrative of Scripture. Numerous theologians have developed charts and maps for helping people understand the outline of Scripture. In this textbook, we have chosen to follow the outline presented by Craig Bartholomew and Michael Goheen in their book *The Drama of Scripture*.[20] This outline describes the biblical metanarrative in a six-act structure, with an interlude between act three and four. You can think of each act as an act in a play. The chart on the next page (figure 5.a) allows us to see the Bible as one great metanarrative, which tells the story of the world beginning with God's creation and leading all the way up to the final restoration of all things.

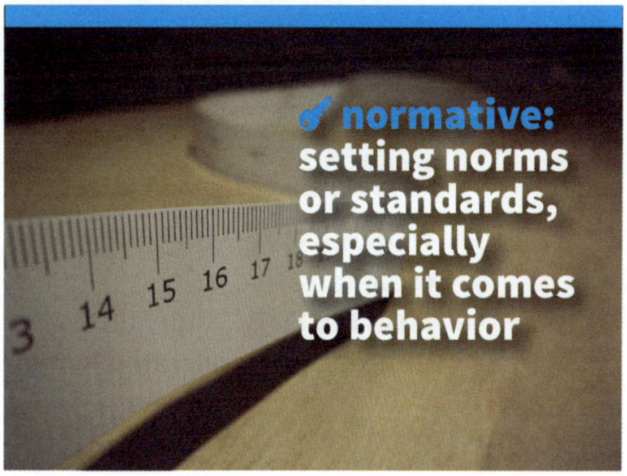

In Chapters 6–12, we'll unpack this metanarrative in greater detail. As we do, we'll see that it is not just a story about the past and the future, but a story about God, humans, the world, and everything in it—a story in which we find meaning and purpose for our lives now. We are characters in this great drama. We have a part to play!

One theologian summarizes the biblical metanarrative like this: "'God the Father has reconciled his created but fallen world through the death of his Son, and renews it into a Kingdom of God by his Spirit.' Note the [terms] *created*, *fallen*, *reconciled*, *renews*, and *Kingdom of God*. Each of these terms applies to the whole cosmos and not just to individuals."[21] So, while the great story provides meaning and purpose for our individual lives, it also offers meaning and purpose for the whole world. Through this great metanarrative, we have been invited into something bigger than ourselves.

Acts in the Biblical Metanarrative	Description	Primary Texts
Act 1: Creation—God's Good World	God creates a good world where humans, made in God's image, can live in harmony with him, themselves, others, and creation.	Genesis 1–2
Act 2: The Fall—Sin and Its Consequences	Sin corrupts God's world, leading to evil, the breakdown of relationships, and death.	Genesis 3–11
Act 3: Israel—Redemption Initiated	God chooses Abraham's family to be a blessing to the whole world by making them a kingdom of priests and a holy people.	Torah, Prophets, Writings
Interlude: The Second Temple Period	After their failure to be faithful to God, subsequent exile, and return to Israel, the people of God wait for a Messiah as they strive to obey God in the midst of foreign empires.	Ezra, Nehemiah, Esther, Daniel; Second Temple literature
Act 4: Redemption Initiated—Jesus	Jesus comes to Earth to announce the kingdom of God. He lives a sinless life, is crucified, and rises from the dead in triumph over evil, sin, and death. He makes reconciliation possible.	Gospels
Act 5: Restoration Initiated—The Church	Jesus ascends and the Holy Spirit empowers God's people, the church, to spread the good news through their proclamation and practice as they await the full restoration of all things.	Acts, Epistles
Act 6: Restoration Accomplished—New Creation	Jesus returns to Earth at the end of history to judge everyone and establish the kingdom of God. Sin is banished forever, and all things are made new.	Revelation

figure 5.a

9. Meeting the Author

▸ **OBJECTIVE:** You will be able to express what God's role in the biblical metanarrative is.

▸ **OBJECTIVE:** You will be able to articulate the importance of knowing that the Bible is a metanarrative when interpreting difficult passages.

Reading the Bible as a metanarrative has important implications for how we understand God. God reveals himself, not by giving us a few facts about himself, but rather through the way he acts in the world and interacts with human beings. From Genesis to Revelation, God is active in his story, like a director who is also acting in a movie he wrote. He does not sit by and watch history unfold from the sidelines. He gets involved.

We see this in his faithfulness to Israel, in his commitment to his creation, and ultimately in Jesus' sacrifice on the cross—all done because God loves the world and all the people he created.

However, as you read through the Bible, you will likely find passages that are troubling and confusing, or that lead to difficult questions, such as "If God loves everyone, why was slavery permitted in the Old Testament?" or "Why did God command the Israelites to invade the land of Canaan?" Isolated from the big story, troubling texts can make God seem petty or vindictive. This is why it is so important to understand the metanarrative. Over time, we will begin to see how troubling passages fit within the whole. This is not to explain them away or minimize the difficulties. It is to say that through the careful reading of Scripture and the illumination of the Holy Spirit, we can see that God is good, wise, and knowledgeable.

God patiently instructs, chastens, protects, delivers, and restores his people. He is faithful. As the Creator of this world, he is absolutely committed to us, and his commitment knows no bounds. As C. S. Lewis once said of Jesus:

> The great thing to remember is that, though our feelings come and go, His love for us does not. It is not wearied by our sins, or our indifference; and, therefore, it is quite relentless in its determination that we shall be cured of those sins, at whatever cost to us, at whatever cost to Him.[22]

God will always pursue redemption for his creation. Understanding the way God's love undergirds his every action provides a strong counterpoint to the common impression that God is brooding, grumpy, mean, and distant.

There is much to learn, and we must not assume our finite minds can understand everything. Knowing God through Scripture is a lifelong endeavor. One of the reasons the Bible is so rich as a literary work, apart from its value as God's Word, is there is so much to discover in each of its books—and even more to be learned as the whole grand story unfolds.

10. Conclusion

Understanding the metanarrative of Scripture will help us understand ourselves and the part we play in this cosmic drama. We are image-bearers of God, made for a relationship with our Creator. From Genesis onward, we learn that the sovereign Creator has chosen human beings to share this life—and eternity—with him. We learn that we are broken by sin and unable to save ourselves or set the world right. We also learn that we are so loved by God that he sent Jesus to give his life for us! The Father's plan of redemption and restoration, promised in the garden of Eden and previewed in Israel, finds its fulfillment in Jesus and will one day be complete.

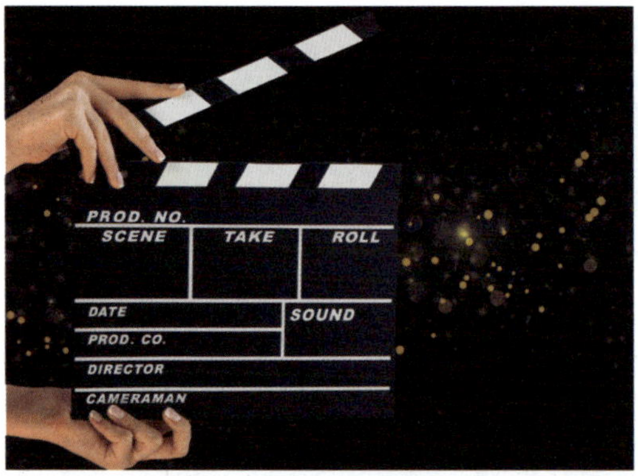

We are not mere spectators, passively watching the story unfold. We are part of the story! "The world of the Bible is our world," Bartholomew and Goheen remind us, "and its story of redemption is also our story. This story is waiting for an ending—in part because we ourselves have a role to play before all is concluded. We must therefore pay attention to the continuing biblical story of redemption."[23]

Each of our stories matters to God, and we find meaning and purpose in his great story. In the next chapter we will explore the first part of the biblical metanarrative: creation.

ENDNOTES

[1]Carl Alviani, "The Science behind Storytelling," Protagonist Studio, October 11, 2018, https://medium.com/the-protagonist/the-science-behind-storytelling-51169758b22c.

[2]Anne-Louise Cook, "Give Me a Story: A Week with Dr. Williams," Summit Ministires, October 19, 2016, https://www.summit.org/blog/semester/give-me-a-story-a-week-with-dr-williams/.

[3]Robert McKee, *Story: Substance, Structure, Style, and the Principles of Screenwriting* (New York: ReganBooks, 1997), 11.

[4]Chris Drew, "The 8 Elements of a Story – Explained for Students!," Helpful Professor.com, https://helpfulprofessor.com/story-elements/.

[5]Glen C. Strathy, "Syd Field's Model of Screenplay Structure," How To Write A Book Now, https://www.how-to-write-a-book-now.com/Syd-Field.html.

[6]"Synopsis: *Into the Woods*," Utah Shakespeare Festival, https://www.bard.org/study-guides/synopsis-into-the-woods.

[7]"U.S. Immigration Timeline," History.com, https://www.history.com/topics/immigration/immigration-united-states-timeline.

[8]Timothy Paul Jones, "Culture: The Marvel Cinematic Universe and the Metanarrative of God," November 12, 2018, TimothyPaulJones.com, https://www.timothypauljones.com/culture-the-marvel-cinematic-universe-and-humanitys-hunger-for-a-metanarrative/.

[9]"The Mythology of 'Star Wars' with George Lucas," BillMoyers.com, June 18, 1999, https://billmoyers.com/mythology-of-star-wars-george-lucas/.

[10]Gene Stansel, "Star Wars and "The Hero's Journey," February 23, 2016, Westminster Presbyterian Church, PCA, https://www.wpcgreenwood.org/blog/post/star-wars-and--the-heros-journey.

[11]BillMoyers.com, "Mythology of Star Wars."

[12]Jean-François Lyotard, *La condition postmoderne: rapport sur le savoir* (Paris: Les Éditions de Minuit, 1979), translated into English as *The Postmodern Condition: A Report on Knowledge* (Minneapolis, MN: University of Minnesota Press, 1984), xxiv, xx, 34, 37.

[13]"What Is a Metanarrative?," Got Questions, https://www.gotquestions.org/metanarrative.html.

[14]For a fuller explanation of this idea of being stuck in the middle of a story, see Iain Provan, *Seriously Dangerous Religion: What the Old Testament Really Says and Why It Matters* (Waco, TX, Baylor University Press, 2014), 1–5.

[15]Statistics vary. Robert L. Plummer, in *40 Questions about Interpreting the Bible* (Grand Rapids, MI: Kregel, 2010), 191, cites "about 60 percent" for OT and NT combined. Gordon D. Fee and Douglas Stuart, in *How to Read the Bible for All Its Worth*, 3rd ed. (Grand Rapids, MI: Zondervan, 2003), 89, suggest that "over 40 percent" of the OT is narrative.

[16]John Piper, "The Great Story and the Single Verse," Desiring God, October 24, 2012, https://www.desiringgod.org/articles/the-great-story-and-the-single-verse.

[17]See "God's Grandeur," by Gerard Manley Hopkins, Poetry Foundation, http://www.poetryfoundation.org/poem/173660

[18]See "meod" Strong's Hebrew reference number 3966, and "tob" Strong's Hebrew reference number 2896a, in Robert L. Thomas, *New American Standard Exhaustive Concordance of the Bible/Hebrew-Aramaic and Greek Dictionaries*, updated ed. (Nashville, TN: Holman Bible Publishers, 1981).

[19]The focus on comprehensive and normative is discussed in Craig G. Bartholomew and Michael W. Goheen, *The Drama of Scripture: Finding Our Place in the Biblical Story* (Grand Rapids: Baker, 2004), 20.

[20]This chart is adapted from the outline of the biblical metanarrative in Craig G. Bartholomew and Michael Goheen, *The Drama of Scripture: Finding Our Place in the Biblical Story*, 2nd ed., (Grand Rapids: Baker, 2014). The titles have been slightly modified.

[21]Art Lindsley, "Creation, Fall, Redemption," *Knowing & Doing* (Winter 2009): 1, https://www.cslewisinstitute.org/Creation_Fall_Redemption_page1. Lindley was citing the Dutch Reformed theologian Herman Bavinck.

[22]C. S. Lewis, *Mere Christianity* (New York: HarperCollins, 2017), 133.

[23]Bartholomew and Goheen, *The Drama of Scripture*, 213.

6

Act 1: Creation

1. Creation Stories

▸ **OBJECTIVE: You will be able to explain the purpose of creation myths.**

Every story has a beginning. In the ancient world, there were many stories about how everything came to be, called *creation myths*. A **creation myth** is *a story that explains the nature of reality and how the universe and human beings came about.* These myths help answer questions like: Who am I? What is my place in the world? What is my relationship to nature, other people, and the divine? and How should I live?

Not all creation myths claim to be "true" in the historical sense, but they are all intended to convey essential truths about the world. Creation myths provide an all-embracing account of the nature of reality and our place within it.

Almost every culture has some kind of creation myth. Many ancient creation myths begin with chaos or warfare between the gods; others with sexual intercourse or a seed or egg. Some include bizarre and grotesque details about how things came to be. Consider a few examples:

- **Egyptian:** Life originates in the primordial waters. The creator-god Ra creates himself and then creates other gods from his body.[1]
- **Tahitian:** The god Ta'aroa emerges from a shell and creates the world, using one half of the shell for the sky and the other half for the earth.[2]
- **Sumerian:** The god Enlil uses a hoe to separate the heavens and the earth and causes humans to "sprout" from the ground.[3]

Many people approaching the Bible for the first time find its creation story to be equally strange. In fact, a survey of the creation myths from the ancient world reveals some similarities between the Genesis creation story and pagan creation myths. These similarities have led some scholars to conclude that Genesis relies on pagan myths to create an origin story for Israel.[4]

Consider, for example, one of the most widely known creation myths from the ancient world—the *Enuma Elish*. In this myth, the god of order (Marduk) slays the goddess of chaos (Tiamat) and uses her body to create the cosmos. The account then describes the creation of the world in similar ways to the biblical story in Genesis. For example, both Genesis and the *Enuma Elish* stories begin in darkness. Both show the creation of light, the firmament, dry land, stars or luminaries, and the creation of humans. Both stories show the deity resting.[5]

But Genesis is not just another pagan myth. Christians believe it is true and that Genesis 1–2 explains the nature of reality and our place in the world. In this chapter, we'll explore how the Genesis story teaches core truths about God, humans, nature, and the universe itself. In the end, we'll see how this story challenges both pagan myths and alternative worldviews.

The gods Ra, Ta'aroa, and Enlil

2. Genesis 1

▸ **OBJECTIVE: You will be able to summarize the creation narrative from Genesis 1.**

The biblical creation story begins with the words "In the beginning, God created the heavens and the earth" (Genesis 1:1). The Hebrew word **Elohim** (*'ĕlōhîm*) is *a name for the Creator God used in the Old Testament.* This is a general designation for a deity or powerful spiritual being.

The Bible thus begins with two fundamental claims. First, God exists. Second, God is the Creator of everything else that exists.

While all Christians agree with these two claims, discussions about Genesis 1 often get bogged down in the creation versus evolution debate or in whether the days of Genesis are literal 24-hour days or longer periods of time. As intriguing as these questions are, they go beyond the purpose of this chapter. Instead, we want to focus on how Genesis 1 highlights the purposefulness and orderliness of God's creation. It shows a God who speaks creation into existence *ex nihilo* (out of nothing).

Genesis 1:2 says that "the earth was without form and void." The rest of the chapter then sets out how God remedied this by forming the universe and filling it. This pattern can be observed in comparing days 1–3 with days 4–6.

FORMING	FILLING
Day 1: light and darkness	Day 4: sun, moon, and stars
Day 2: sky, atmosphere	Day 5: birds and water creatures
Day 3: land and vegetation	Day 6: animals and humans[6]

figure 6.a

God created in an orderly fashion through his spoken word. First, he gave shape to the world (sky, for example), and then he filled it with life (birds, etc.). The text also repeatedly emphasizes that all of God's creation is "good."

The high point of Genesis 1 comes in verse 26. Up until this point, God simply spoke and "it was so" (v. 15). In verse 26, however, God said, "Let us make man [human beings] in our image, after our likeness." What did God mean by "us?" Christians have traditionally interpreted this verse to mean that the "us" refers to the Trinity. This interpretation makes sense if we consider Colossians 1:15–16, which identifies Jesus as the Creator. Many scholars also see evidence of the Holy Spirit in the "Spirit of God" who was "hovering over the face of the waters" (v. 2).

The "us" language indicated that something unique was about to happen. Alone among all other created things, people were made in God's image. The Latin word **imago Dei** refers to *the idea that human beings were created in God's likeness.* We'll explore what this means in depth later, but for now, it is essential to notice two things. First, human beings, both male and female, are made in God's image (v. 27). Second, they are given a measure of authority and responsibility. They are to "be fruitful and multiply" and to have "dominion over . . . every living thing" (v. 28).

After creating humans, God said that all he made was very good (v. 31). It's a goodness full of great awe and wonder, so good that it makes one want to burst from sheer joy! The rest of the Bible concurs, celebrating God's awesome power, wisdom, and creativity in creating the world and everything in it, including human beings (see Psalms 8, 19, 104; Proverbs 8).

3. Genesis 2

▸ **OBJECTIVE: You will be able to discuss the account of the creation of humans found in Genesis 2.**

Genesis chapter 2 begins by showing that God "rested on the seventh day from all his work" (v. 2). In the Bible, the number seven represents perfection or completion.[7] The seventh day thus represents the completion of God's work. Why did God need to rest from his work? Did he get worn out? Did his work completely drain him of energy? A look at the rest of the Bible reveals that this is not so. For example, Isaiah 40:28 says that God, "the Creator," does not "faint or grow weary." God's rest isn't like collapsing on the couch after a long day; rather, it is a rest in the satisfaction of a job well done.

After the brief overview of creation described in Genesis 1:1–2:3, the text zeroes in on the special creation of humans. It also begins using the word *Yahweh*, from the Hebrew for "I AM" (*hāyâ*, shown in many English-language Bibles as "the LORD"). **Yahweh** is *the personal and covenantal name for God used in the Old Testament.*

Genesis 2:7 describes how the LORD God formed the man "from the ground and breathed into his nostrils the breath of life." Then God placed the man in the garden of Eden "to work it and keep it" (v. 15). This means that work is not the result of sin. On the contrary, humans were created to work. If this sounds crazy to you, think of a time when you put hard work into something you really cared about—maybe learning an instrument, building or designing something new, writing a poem, completing a school project, or even just bringing order to a messy room. Isn't there something fulfilling about accomplishing these tasks? That's because it's in our design to work.

In the garden where the man was placed, there were two special trees: the *Tree of Knowledge of Good and Evil* and the *Tree of Life* (v. 9). God specifically instructed the man not to eat from the Tree of Knowledge of Good and Evil "for in the day that you eat of it you shall surely die" (v. 17). Beyond this one command, the man had complete freedom to work in the garden and enjoy the fruits of his labor.

Yahweh: **the personal and covenantal name for God used in the Old Testament**

All was well in God's new creation except one thing: the man was alone. To remedy this "not good" situation, God created another human—a woman. God said, "It is not good that the man should be alone; I will make him a helper fit for him" (v. 18). Some people have the impression that God created the woman as an afterthought because the man was lonely. Others have seen the woman as a mere helper to the man, in a sort of secondary role. However, both of these interpretations are inaccurate.

For starters, the text does not say that the man was lonely. It says that he was alone and that this was not good. This is because humans were not intended to exist in isolation. They were created for relationship. Second, the Hebrew word for "helper," *ʿēzer*, (v. 18) in no way implies a second-class position. In fact, this same word is used to describe God in his relationship to Israel (see Psalm 33:20, 70:5; Hosea 13:9).[8]

When the man sees the woman, he calls her "Woman" (Hebrew *'ishah*) because she was taken out of "Man" (Hebrew *'ish*). The similarity of their names reflects their fundamental equality; both are image-bearers, cooperating together in the task God has given them.[9] Their relationship is one of harmony and deep intimacy; they were "both naked and were not ashamed" (v. 25).

4. God: The Creator

▸ OBJECTIVE: You will be able to articulate various attributes of God including his transcendence and immanence.

As the creation narrative unfolds in Genesis 1–2, we learn that humans are relational beings. Specifically, Genesis sees us in four primary relationships—with God, self, other people, and the natural world.[10] In this section, let's look more closely at the God we are meant to be in relationship with.

God is the main character in the first two chapters of Genesis (and, indeed, the whole Bible). He is also the most active character—he speaks, creates, rests, commands, and instructs. He is the one in charge, having absolute power and authority. However, God's authority is not domineering or abusive. God uses his authority to create a beautiful world. In Genesis 1–2, God is revealed as a creative, artistic Designer. As one philosopher said, "God created the world by imagination."[11]

Psalm 19:1 proclaims, "The heavens declare the glory of God, and the sky above proclaims his handiwork." The universe reflects the *glory* of God. Have you ever considered the fact that the universe did not have to be as amazing and beautiful as it is? God didn't have to make colors, sounds, beautiful landscapes, or tasty foods. The world could just as easily have been a barren wasteland or a concrete jungle. But that would not reflect who God is, because God loves beauty! The poet Gerard Manley Hopkins got it right when he declared, "The world is charged with the grandeur of God."[12]

But why did God create people and this amazing world? Did God create because he was bored, lonely, or needy? No! In the Trinity, the Father God already had a loving relationship with the Son (Jesus) and Holy Spirit (see Luke 3:22 and John 17:24). God did not *need* the world. God is an "outgoing, life-giving God."[13] He created a world where he could be known so that we might share in the love of the Father, Son, and Holy Spirit (Ephesians 1:4–5). This is why one theologian says, "the creation of all things is above all an expression of God's will to love."[14]

Scripture also reveals that God is both immanent and transcendent. **Transcendence** refers to *an attribute of God that describes him as being both above and outside of his creation.* He is separate and outside of it.

transcendence:
an attribute of God that describes him as being both above and outside of his creation

The **immanence** of God is *an attribute of God that describes him as being both within and among his creation.* This means that God is active in his creation. Paul preached, "In him we live and move and have our being" (Acts 17:28). Colossians 1:17 says that Jesus holds all of creation together. If he removed his hand, the universe would cease to exist!

In Chapter 13, we will discuss many more of God's attributes. For now, Genesis 1–2 reveals that God is transcendent, immanent, active, powerful, creative, generous, involved, personal, and overflowing with a desire to pour out love on all creation!

5. Humans Beings: Rulers and Sub-Creators

▸ **OBJECTIVE:** You will be able to analyze three ways in which human beings bear God's image.

Genesis 1:27 says that humans were made in the image of God. What does that mean? The most common Christian views of what it means to be made in God's image can be loosely categorized under three headings:

- **Rule:** This view connects the image of God with God's granting of authority to humans to subdue and have dominion over creation (Genesis 1:28–30). In this view, bearing God's image means that we are responsible for caring for, cultivating, and bringing God's creation to abundance.
- **Resemblance:** This view says we are "like God" with respect to certain attributes we share, such as intelligence, creativity, morality, and the ability to communicate.
- **Relationship:** This view says that we reflect God's image by existing in loving relationship with God, ourselves, other people, and nature.[15]

Let's consider the first aspect: rule. Image (Hebrew *tselem*, meaning *shape*, *resemblance*) was a very important concept in the ancient Near Eastern culture in which the Bible was written. Kings set up images of themselves in conquered cities to remind people who was in charge. Such images symbolized authority over a certain domain.[16] God's domain is the entire universe, but he didn't set up a statue of himself on Earth. Instead, he created living, moving images: human beings. That's one reason why, in the rest of the Bible, we are forbidden from making statues or images of God—because we ourselves are God's image (Exodus 20:4–6, Isaiah 44:9–20, Jeremiah 51:17, Habakkuk 2:18–19).

In Genesis, people are given great authority and responsibility in God's domain (Genesis 1:28–30). **Stewardship** is *the process of managing something that has been entrusted to one's care.* People are to bear God's image by ruling as wise stewards over his creation. Of course, God is the ultimate ruler and authority in the universe (Deuteronomy 10:14, Psalm 24:1, Romans 13:1). When God made us in his image, he invited us to participate with him in wisely ruling over creation, bringing it to its fullness and abundance.

The second aspect (resemblance) says that we bear God's image because we resemble him in certain attributes. One particular attribute that stands out is creativity. The novelist Dorothy Sayers observes, "the desire and the ability to make things" is one characteristic that is "common to God and man."[17] For Christian apologist G. K. Chesterton, humans are different from other creatures because we are creators as well as creatures.[18] Of course, we cannot create out of nothing, as God did. However, we can take the existing materials that God has made and make new things from them. As J. R. R. Tolkien would say, we are "sub-creators,"[19] taking what God has created and exercising our God-given creativity to make culture. As author Andy Crouch points out:

> Grain is good, but bread is very good. This is the essential pattern of all culture at its best. Eggs are good, omelets are very good. Trees are good, a beautiful wooden chair is very good. Sound is good, music is very good. When human beings do what they were created to do, the latent possibilities in creation come to fruition, a flourishing reality that would never exist without the application of human intelligence and intentionality. This is what image bearing is for.[20]

People, then, are not mere bystanders in God's world. We have a job to do! Genesis implies creation has a lot of potential that needs to be developed. Men and women are to use their ruling capacity and creativity to make the world beautiful and bring out its full potential.[21] Therefore, every time we use our authority and creativity in a God-honoring, constructive pursuit, we are bearing God's image well.

6. Humans: Relational and Sexed Beings

▸ **OBJECTIVE: You will be able to describe God's plan for people as relational and sexed beings.**

A third aspect of what it means to bear God's image focuses on our relational nature. As we have already seen, God was not alone before creation. He was in relationship as the Trinity—Father, Son, and Holy Spirit. God is fundamentally relational. Since humans are made in God's image, they too are relational beings. We are made for loving relationship, first with God, but also with ourselves and with others (Leviticus 19:18, Deuteronomy 6:5, Matthew 22:37–39).

The Bible describes our relationship with God in various ways. To name just a few, God is our Creator (Revelation 4:11), Parent (Psalm 103:13), Protector (Psalm 121:1–8), Provider (Matthew 6:25–33), Savior (Luke 1:47), Friend (John 15:13), and Lord (Isaiah 42:8). Each of us has a longing in our hearts that nothing but God can satisfy. True life does not exist outside of a relationship with God. If we are to be who God made us to be, then we must first find our identity in relationship with God.

God created us to be his children (Isaiah 64:8). God created each person with a unique personality and with gifts and abilities (Psalm 139:13–14, 1 Peter 4:10). Having a good relationship with ourselves means understanding who God made us to be and seeking to grow so that we can fulfill his purposes for us (Romans 11:29, 1 Timothy 4:7–8).

Genesis 2:18–20 makes it clear that a human being in isolation is not in a good situation. If you've ever felt alone, without friends or family, you know how true this is. We were not meant to be alone. God didn't just want to be in relationship with us himself; he wanted us to share in relationship with others. That's why God made another person in Genesis 2. The desires that people have for friendship, community, and marriage all have their source in how God created us.

stewardship: the process of managing something that has been entrusted to one's care

The Bible upholds the value of friendships like that of David and Jonathan (1 Samuel 18, 20) or Ruth and Naomi (Ruth 1–4). It speaks of how friends and community can provide support (Ecclesiastes 4:9, Proverbs 27:17) and encouragement (Hebrews 10:24–25). In Genesis, God gave the first human pair "*joint* dominion" over his creation;[22] they were to work together under God's authority. To live well in God's world, we need to be in relationship with others.

Genesis 1:27 says that God created humans male and female. Notice that this is the second thing that God says about humans—they are sexed beings. This means that our sexuality is a profound gift. It reveals a deep longing for intimacy—it is meant to point us back to God, who made us for intimacy with himself, so that we might join in the life of love already shared in the Trinity. Sexual expression in marriage is not the ultimate goal of life.[23] Those who remain single bear God's image just as much as those who are married. Jesus is our model. We are all "being transformed into the same image" to be like him (2 Corinthians 3:18).

The Bible celebrates the act of sex in its proper context of a loving marriage relationship. In order to fulfill God's creation mandate to "be fruitful and multiply" (Genesis 1:28), a man and a woman united in marriage must join together in physical intimacy. In Genesis 2:21–22 we see that the woman was taken out of the man. Upon seeing the woman (Genesis 2:23), the man proclaims:

Creation of Adam and Eve, ErlÖserkirche, Bahnhofstraße, Weener, Germany

> "This at last is bone of my bones
> and flesh of my flesh;
> she shall be called Woman,
> because she was taken out of Man."

Man and woman were different from each other, but they were to become again "one flesh" (Genesis 2:24) in a union of intimacy.[24] This was the first marriage. Adam and Eve were "both naked and were not ashamed" (Genesis 2:25). Already being in relationship with God, they could be at peace with themselves and with each other. Marriage is meant to be a loving union on emotional, spiritual, and physical levels—a relationship characterized by "a total self-giving, a total self-donation."[25]

7. Nature: God's Gift

▸ **OBJECTIVE: You will be able to correlate the biblical mandate for stewardship to our relationship with nature.**

In the last three sections, we have explored how people were created to be in relationship with God, themselves, and others. But there is one final relationship that often gets passed over—the relationship between us and nature.

The way that people interact with the natural world depends on how they view themselves in relation to nature.[26] If we think that we are the absolute masters of nature and that nature is merely an object for our use, then we will feel free to exploit and abuse it any way that serves our needs. Sadly, many people throughout history have viewed the human relationship with nature in this way. Human activity has resulted in rampant pollution of the environment, the destruction of soil in order to satisfy the ever-increasing demands of consumers, inhumane treatment of animals in food production, and many other problems. Such problems have often been blamed on the Christian worldview, which some say allows and even celebrates the exploitation of the natural world.[27] But does Genesis give us permission to exploit the world for our own ends? Nothing could be further from the truth!

Genesis 1–2 leaves no doubt that the physical world is a good place. It is a holy place, the place where God makes himself known.[28] It is a beautiful place, designed to showcase his glory. As one scholar puts it, "We find in Genesis a world-affirming perspective. . . . It is a sacred place, designed precisely as *the* place in which life, including human life, can flourish."[29]

The world exists for God (1 Corinthians 8:6, Colossians 1:16); it is also a gift. God put the man in the garden to work and keep it (Genesis 2:15). The Hebrew word for *work* (*'ābad*) also means *to serve*. The word for *keep* (*šāmar*) means *to watch* or *to preserve*. Both words imply bringing something to maturity. That God gives humans dominion over creation and tells them to subdue it (Genesis 1:28) in no way implies that they can simply do whatever they like with it.

We are *stewards* in God's world. We do not have the right to tarnish and destroy his property but are charged with protecting it, preserving it, and working for its flourishing. This is the biblical mandate for stewards all throughout Scripture. God expects his people to wisely care for land, plants, trees, domesticated and wild animals, birds, fish, and even creeping things (Genesis 1:26; Leviticus 25:1–12; Deuteronomy 22:6, 25:4; Isaiah 35:8–10).

Like animals and plants, people are a natural part of creation. But God also gave us an exalted place here (Genesis 1:26–30; Psalm 8:4–6); our stewardship involves caring about humans too. Sometimes, this means that we will need to alter landscapes or cut down trees in order to plant food or build housing. If we do this wisely and carefully, we will not tarnish God's world. Rather, we will be doing our job in bringing abundance out of the earth.

God's creation must be approached with love and respect. God created the world out of love and we are "to give the world back to God in works of love."[30] Our attitude should be one of faithfulness, gratefulness, and humility, remembering that creation is God's gift.[31] We can care for creation, while also upholding the dignity of people by creating cultures where we can flourish.

8. Genesis Confronts Ancient Creation Myths

▸ **OBJECTIVE: You will be able to distinguish between the false ideas in creation myths and the truth of the Genesis creation story.**

This brings us back to where we started at the beginning of this chapter. Did the writer of Genesis merely borrow from other creation myths in the ancient world? Is Genesis 1–2 in any way unique? Though there are similarities between the Genesis creation story and other ancient creation myths, the differences between them are far greater. In fact, Genesis 1–2 is actually a refutation of other creation myths popular in the ancient Near East. Consider these distinctive elements in the biblical story:

- **There is only one God, not many.** In ancient creation myths, the sun, moon, and stars were often seen as gods. In Genesis, they are God's creation.
- **The universe has a divine origin.** The gods of ancient creation stories are

presented as part of a universe that has always existed. They shape or elicit creation from preexisting matter. In Genesis, creation has a beginning. God creates the world out of nothing (*ex nihilo*).[32]

- **God is sovereign.** While many creation myths begin with a violent power struggle among the gods, in Genesis God has no challenger. He is the absolute Sovereign over the universe.
- **Creation is purposeful.** In some creation myths, the creation is a byproduct or accident of the gods' struggle. In Genesis, God deliberately and purposefully speaks creation into existence.
- **Creation is not the result of a sexual act.** The pagan gods of ancient myths are often embodied, gendered, and sexually active, and their activity results in creation. In Genesis, God has no spouse and is not sexually active.
- **God is good and loving.** Often, the gods of the ancient world are portrayed as perverse, immoral, petty, jealous of humans, and power hungry. The God of the Bible, by contrast, is good, loving, and just.
- **Humans are valued in God's creation.** In many ancient myths, humans are created as slaves because the gods are lazy and want other people to do their work. In Genesis, humans are specially made in God's image to participate in God's wise rule of creation.[33]

Genesis 1–2 is a direct challenge to ancient pagan ways of thinking about the world and humans' place within it. Before we move on, let's take the last example (Humans are valued in God's creation) and zero in on it to see how Genesis confronts and undermines the low view of humanity put forth by other ancient myths.

In ancient Egyptian culture, the pharaoh was unique among humans. He alone was considered to be the image of God. This was a common view in the ancient world—only special classes of people (such as kings) were considered to be God's image. Since the majority of humans in the ancient world were considered slaves of the gods, kings could take human life by their command. (Think of how Pharaoh commanded the Israelites to throw their male babies into the river in Exodus 1:16, 22.) As the sole image-bearer of God, Pharaoh dominated the Israelites, abusing and enslaving them.

Adam naming animals mural, Agios Nikolaos Anapafsas Monastery, Meteora, Greece

Now, imagine being an Israelite in that culture and hearing the Genesis story. This Israelite would understand that Pharaoh was not, in fact, the sole bearer of the divine image; rather, every human being—each man and each woman—bears God's image! This Genesis idea undermined Pharaoh's godlike authority. It implied that everyone had equal value because *all* were made in God's image. In this view, all humans have inherent dignity and should be treated with respect. Later in Genesis, God warns against murder on the grounds that people are made in God's image (Genesis 9:6). To abuse or assault another human being is an attack on God.

9. Genesis Confronts Alternative Worldviews

▸ **OBJECTIVE: You will be able to determine seven ways the biblical creation story is distinct from other worldviews.**

The Genesis account of creation confronts and undermines ancient pagan worldviews, but does it have anything to say to our modern society? Yes! In contrast to other worldviews, the Genesis creation story. . .

- **affirms the direct involvement of a personal God in creation.** Unlike *atheism*, which says that God does not exist, the biblical account affirms that God does exist and that he is a personal and loving Creator.
- **affirms the distinction between creation and the Creator.** This directly contradicts *pantheism*, which claims that the universe is god.
- **affirms that the universe is good and purposeful.** This confronts *gnosticism* (the idea that the material world is evil), and *nihilism* (the idea that there is no meaning or purpose in the universe).
- **affirms the special creation of humans.** This counters any evolutionary theory that proposes that life arose by random accident and that human beings are merely highly evolved animals.
- **affirms the goodness of the body and sexuality.** Genesis rejects any notion that our bodies are inherently evil or that our sex is something we can alter however we like. Rather, our bodies and our sex are God's good gifts.
- **affirms the distinction and equality between male and female.** This confronts the modern notion that men and women are interchangeable. At the same time, it rejects any notion that men are superior to women or women superior to men.
- **affirms the dignity and value of all human beings.** This undermines any view that devalues people based on age, gender, sex, race, class, national or ethnic origin, physical or intellectual abilities or characteristics, or circumstances of conception.

The above distinctives have major implications for how we live. Let's consider two of them in more detail to get an idea of how radical the biblical worldview is.

First, ask yourself some questions: What gives you value? Are you inherently valuable, or must you do something to become valuable? Are you valuable because of what you can accomplish? How much you possess? How fit your body is? The color of your skin? Your mental capacity? Without God to give us value, secular worldviews provide no foundation for human dignity. Without God, our value must inevitably be assigned by flawed human beings based on some arbitrary criteria. In contrast, the biblical teaching is that because you are made in God's image, you are inherently valuable and endowed with dignity from God. It does not matter how attractive you are, your age, mental capacity, size, body type, or skin color. Each and every human being matters to God because everyone bears his image. Each and every human being has dignity and value because God says so. Think about how seeing people this way could help with some problematic issues in our society like racism, sexism, abortion, and euthanasia.

Second, consider how much Genesis upholds the value of the body and sexuality. It has often been said that Christianity represses sexuality and sees it as evil. But the Christian worldview (beginning in Genesis) upholds the value of the body and the inherent goodness of sexuality. Jesus became a human, with a physical body. The Bible includes the Song of Solomon, celebrating sex and romantic love. Let it be said clearly: The Bible teaches that the body and sexuality are *profoundly* good. "God saw everything that he had made, and behold, it was very good" (Genesis 1:31). In contrast, modern secular views reduce people to sexual beings who may treat their bodies as raw material to use and be used by others in the pursuit of pleasure.

10. Conclusion

Genesis 1–2, the beginning of the biblical metanarrative, reveals a good and loving Creator, who made the world in an orderly fashion. He has unlimited power and authority, but he does not use them to manipulate or abuse others. Rather, God channels his power and creativity to make a beautiful world, and he chooses to share some of his authority with us. He is both separate from his creation and actively involved in it. Creation is primarily an act of God's overflowing love.

The first chapters of Genesis portray a creation that is good and beautiful—a sacred place where God is revealed and known. The world is not inherently evil. It is not to be discarded, abused, or treated irreverently. It is not God, but since God loves it, we should, too.

The creation story unveils humans as God's image bearers—stewards and caretakers of all their surroundings. They are endowed with dignity and worth right from the beginning. Both male and female bear God's image and have equal worth. They are relational beings. They are made to be in relationship with God (being under his authority and participating in his mission), with themselves (bearing God's image through creativity and action in the world), with others (in family, friendship, and community), and with nature (ruling wisely as stewards rather than exploiting the world for their own ends).

The Bible's creation story also confronts the negative and dehumanizing tendencies of many worldviews, both ancient and modern. It provides a way forward for living well in God's world. Creation is God's first act in the great drama that spans the Bible into our modern day and beyond. We must begin at the beginning of the biblical metanarrative—Genesis 1 and 2—with careful study and reflection on God's Word, so that we may learn how to live purpose-filled lives in the world.

This was the situation at the beginning of our story: God created human beings to be in loving relationship with him and to participate in his rule by stewarding the world for God's glory. All was well. But something went wrong in God's world, something that plunged our world into evil and destruction. That's what the next chapter is all about.

ENDNOTES

[1]John D. Currid, *Ancient Egypt and the Old Testament* (Grand Rapids, MI: Baker Books, 1997), 36–40.

[2]"Ta'aroa," Encyclopedia.com, https://www.encyclopedia.com/humanities/news-wires-white-papers-and-books/taaroa.

[3]John H. Walton, *Ancient Near Eastern Thought and the Old Testament: Introducing the Conceptual World of the Hebrew Bible* (Grand Rapids, MI: Baker Books, 2006), 46.

[4]John D. Currid, *Against the Gods: The Polemical Theology of the Old Testament* (Wheaton, IL: Crossway, 2013), 33–35.

[5]Currid, *Against the Gods*, 37–38.

[6]Currid, *Against the Gods*, 104–105.

[7]See Significant Numbers in "Number" entry of the *International Standard Bible Encyclopedia*, https://www.internationalstandardbible.com/N/number.html.

[8]Iain Provan, *Seriously Dangerous Religion: What the Old Testament Really Says and Why It Matters* (Waco, TX: Baylor University Press, 2014), 87.

[9]Provan, *Seriously Dangerous Religion*, 90–91.

[10]Craig G. Bartholomew and Michael W. Goheen, *The Drama of Scripture: Finding Our Place in the Biblical Story* (Grand Rapids, MI: Baker Academic, 2004), 39.

[11]The philosopher was Nikolai Berdyaev. As quoted in Dorothy Sayers, *The Mind of the Maker* (San Francisco: HarperCollins, 1987), 29.

[12]Gerard Manley Hopkins, "God's Grandeur," https://poets.org/poem/gods-grandeur.

[13]Michael Reeves, *Delighting in the Trinity: An Introduction to the Christian Faith* (Downers Grove, IL: IVP Academic, 2012), 24.

[14]Craig Gay, *Modern Technology and the Human Future: A Christian Appraisal* (Downers Grove, IL: IVP Academic, 2018), 137.

[15]Angus Ritchie and Nick Spencer, *The Case for Christian Humanism: Why Christians Should Believe in Humanism, and Humanists in Christianity* (London: Theos, 2014), 51–52, https://www.theosthinktank.co.uk/research/2014/12/05/the-case-for-christian-humanism.

[16]D. J. A. Clines, "The Image of God in Man," *Tyndale Bulletin* 19 (1968), 53–103, https://ia802704.us.archive.org/2/items/pdfy-SLVx2c60Fa59pgFJ/The%20Image%20Of%20God%20In%20Man.pdf.

[17]Sayers, *The Mind of the Maker*, 22.

[18]G. K. Chesterton, *The Everlasting Man* (London: Hodder & Stoughton, 1925), 24.

[19]J. R. R. Tolkien, "On Fairy Stories," in *Tales from the Perilous Realm* (London: HarperCollins Publishers, 2008), 315–400.

[20]Andy Crouch, *Playing God: Redeeming the Gift of Power* (Downers Grove, IL, IVP Books, 2013), 105–106.

[21]Gay, *Modern Technology*, 144.

[22]Provan, *Seriously Dangerous Religion*, 92.

[23]Julie Slattery, "What's the Purpose of Your Sexuality, Really?," https://www.authenticintimacy.com/resources/16353/whats-the-purpose-of-your-sexuality-really.

[24]Provan, *Seriously Dangerous Religion*, 89.

[25]Christopher West, *Theology of the Body Explained: A Commentary on John Paul II's Man and Woman He Created Them* (Boston: Pauline Books & Media, 2007), 29.

[26]Lynn White, "The Historical Roots of our Ecologic Crisis," in I. G. Barbour ed., *Western Man and Environmental Ethics* (Reading, MA: Addison-Wesley, 1973), 24.

[27]See, for example, Lynn White, "Ecologic Crisis," 25–27.

[28]Provan, *Seriously Dangerous Religion*, 32.

[29]Provan, *Seriously Dangerous Religion*, 46.

[30]Gay, *Modern Technology*, 146.

[31]Wendell Berry, "The Gift of Good Land," in *The Art of the Commonplace: The Agrarian Essays of Wendell Berry*, ed. Norman Wirzba (Berkley, CA: Counterpoint, 2002), 297.

[32]Many theologians argue that this is one of the distinguishing marks of the Christian narrative. For example, see Ian A. McFarland, *From Nothing: A Theology of Creation* (Louisville, KY: Westminster John Knox Press, 2014), xii–xiii.

[33]See Kenneth J. Turner, "Teaching Genesis 1 at a Christian College," in *Reading Genesis 1–2: An Evangelical Conversation*, ed. J. Daryl Charles (Peabody, MA: Hendrickson, 2013), chap 6.

7

Act 2: The Fall

1. All Was Well

▸ **OBJECTIVE: You will be able to compare the harmony of the original creation with the state of the world today.**

In the last chapter, we left the biblical story at the end of Genesis 2. The powerful, wise, and loving God made a rich and abundant universe, filled with his glory. Human beings were specially created in God's image and given the job of stewarding this world. At that time there was no sin or exploitation of the natural world, no abuse in human relationships, and no shame, evil, or suffering. All was well; this was God's original intention for the world.

The Hebrew word **shalom** (*šālôm*) means *peace, harmony, wholeness, prosperity, welfare, and tranquility.* A state of *shalom* is a state where everything is good and in order.

The original *shalom* of creation can be seen in each of the four relationships we discussed in the previous chapter. The world God made was a place where he could dwell in close relationship with his creation. Adam and Eve knew God personally; he had given them life and sustained them. Adam and Eve were also properly ordered within themselves and ready to fulfill their calling. The first human pair were in right relationship with each other. Deriving their value from God, the man and the woman could live in harmony, unity, and intimacy. Finally, humans were in right relationship with creation and acting as stewards to bring forth abundance and beauty from the earth.

shalom: means peace, harmony, wholeness, prosperity, welfare, and tranquility

If you take a look around at our world today, you'll quickly realize that we aren't in a *shalom* situation. Something has gone wrong with the original creation. All of us know that we aren't living in Eden anymore. The Bible's metanarrative continues in Genesis 3 and unfolds in a world corrupted by evil, broken by sin, and plagued by suffering.

Nearly every worldview recognizes there is some kind of problem in our world, but there is wide disagreement over what the problem is. Some worldviews accept evil and suffering as a natural part of life, while others teach that evil and suffering are illusions. Some suggest the problem is humanity itself, while others argue that individual human beings are good, but human systems and societies are corrupt.

The Christian worldview also has an answer for what is wrong with the world—a reasonable and compelling answer. To put it bluntly, the Bible teaches that the problem with our world is sin. Sin is the reason for evil and suffering in the world. But sin, evil, and suffering played no part in God's creation; they are intruders in God's world. This is not the way the world was supposed to be.

What is sin? Where did it come from? In this chapter, we'll explore what the Bible says about these questions. We'll also look at the consequences of sin and what God has been doing about sin since it first entered the world.

2. What Is Sin?

▸ **OBJECTIVE:** You will be able to explain the three words used in the Bible for sin.

Before we look at how sin entered the world, we need to be clear about what sin is. For many people, the word *sin* conjures up images of an angry God who likes to spoil all of our fun. But sin doesn't mean failing to follow a list of petty rules; it is far more serious. In this section, we'll take a look at three words used in the Bible for sin—*sin*, *transgression*, and *iniquity*—to get a better idea of what sin actually is.[1]

Sin. The most common word used in the Bible for sin is, well, *sin* (Hebrew *ḥaṭṭā'āṯ*, Greek *hamartia*). To **sin** is *to miss the goal, to fail to love God and others.* The first part of this definition is well-known, but it only makes sense if we know what the goal is. In the last chapter, we saw that God's goal was for us to be in right relationship with himself and others. Therefore, to sin is also *to fail to love God and others.*[2]

We see many instances of sin in the Old Testament. When Cain got angry, God warned him that sin was "crouching at the door" (Genesis 4:7), waiting to control him. It eventually did when Cain murdered his brother, Abel (Genesis 4:8). When the prophet Nathan confronted King David for his adultery and murder, David acknowledged that he had sinned (2 Samuel 12:7–14, Psalm 51:4). David sinned against Bathsheba, against her husband Uriah the Hittite, and against God.

In the New Testament, Paul speaks of how both Jews and Gentiles are guilty of sin (Romans 3:9) and how we must not let sin "reign" in our lives (Romans 6:12). John makes it clear that when we fail to love others, we also fail to love God (1 John 4:20). Through sin, all of humanity has fallen short of God's goal of love. (Romans 3:23)

Transgression. A less familiar Bible word for sin is *transgression* (Hebrew *pešaʿ*, Greek *paraptōma*). **Transgression** is *the act of rebelling or breaking trust with another person.* Imagine telling a friend a sensitive secret. If that friend maliciously shares that secret with other people, your friend has transgressed against you.

In Genesis 37, Joseph's brothers had a responsibility to protect him. Instead, they betrayed him and sold him into slavery. Later in Genesis 50, they asked Joseph to forgive them for their transgression. In the New Testament, Jesus admonished his disciples to forgive others who had transgressed against them so that they could be forgiven by God. (Matthew 6:15, 18:35; Mark 11:25–26). The book of James challenges us to confess our transgressions to each other so we may be healed (James 5:16).

Iniquity. The word **iniquity** (Hebrew *ʿāôn*, Greek *anomia*) refers to *crooked, wicked, and perverse behavior.*

In the book of 1 Samuel, God told Samuel he would punish the house of Eli for their iniquity. Eli's sons were supposed to serve God faithfully in the tabernacle. Instead, they abused the sacrificial system and had sex with the women who were helping with the sacrifices. Their behavior was totally wicked (1 Samuel 2:12–35). In the New Testament, Jesus appropriately condemned the Pharisees for appearing to be righteous on the outside while being full of hypocrisy and iniquity on the inside (Matthew 23:28).

So, sin in the Bible isn't just not living up to God's standard despite your best efforts. It involves a failure to love God and neighbor, the violation of trust through breaking of relationships, and wicked behavior. Sin, in all its forms, corrupts and pollutes our world. But where did sin come from in the first place?

3. The Beginning of Sin

▸ **OBJECTIVE: You will be able to describe what the fall is and how it happened.**

The story of how everything went wrong in God's world is what theologians call *the fall*. **The fall** is *the belief that sin entered the world when Adam and Eve chose to disobey God.* The fall is the second act in the Bible's metanarrative.

Genesis 3:1 introduces a new character, the serpent: "Now the serpent was more crafty than any other beast of the field that the Lord God had made." Genesis does not explain what the serpent was doing in the garden or who the serpent was, but other verses of Scripture seem to identify the serpent as Satan (see Romans 16:20; Revelation 12:9, 20:2). The serpent is clearly more than just a simple reptile. He is intelligent, speaks, asks clever questions, and is antagonistic toward both God and humans.

When the serpent encountered the woman in the garden, the first thing he did was challenge God's command. "Did God actually say, 'You shall not eat of any tree in the garden'?" (Genesis 3:1). Of course, we, the readers, know that God told Adam he could eat freely from any tree in the garden except one: the Tree of Knowledge of Good and Evil (Genesis 2:16–17).

The woman's response to the serpent is fascinating. She corrected the serpent saying, "We may eat of the fruit of the trees in the garden, but God said, 'You shall not eat of the fruit of the tree that is in the midst of the garden . . . '" Then she added, " 'neither shall you touch it, lest you die' " (Genesis 3:2–3). The Bible does not report that God had said anything about *touching* the tree; it only reports that he told the man not to *eat* of it (Genesis 2:16–17).

Upon hearing the woman's response, the serpent went from challenging God's word to outright rejection of it: "You will not surely die" (Genesis 3:4). The serpent suggested that God lied. Then he questioned God's goodness and motivation, saying, "For God knows that when you eat of it your eyes will be opened, and you will be like God, knowing good and evil" (v. 5). The serpent's promise is ironic, considering that human beings were already like God: we bear his image. In Genesis 1–2, God gave freedom and blessing, but the serpent suggested that God is actually stingy and restrictive.[3] The serpent wanted to convince Adam and Eve that God had been holding out on them. He wanted to break the trust between the Creator and humanity.[4]

What was it the serpent suggested God was holding back? It seems the wisdom offered by the Tree was a wisdom that makes one independent from God.[5] The woman saw the desirability of this independence and seized it, as did her husband (v. 6). They demonstrated that they were not content with the knowledge that God had given them. They were not content to bear God's image; instead, they wanted to be gods, ruling on their own terms.[6] They wanted to define good and evil for themselves. They wanted to make the rules in God's world.

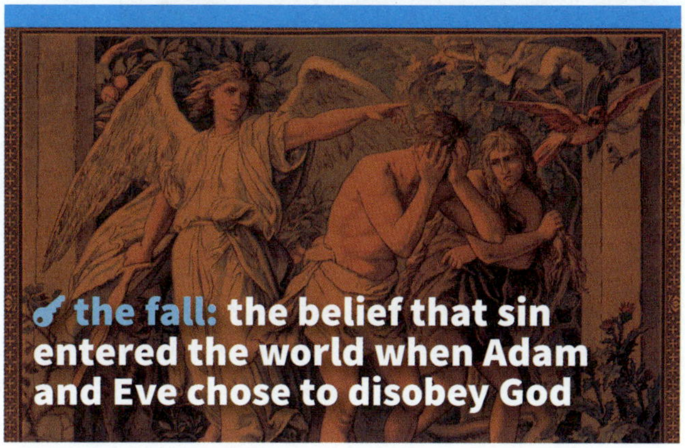
the fall: the belief that sin entered the world when Adam and Eve chose to disobey God

This was the first sin. The fall was not primarily about eating a piece of fruit. Adam and Eve sinned by failing to love God. They transgressed by rebelling against him. They chose iniquity by rejecting their role as stewards.

4. Consequences of Sin: Broken Relationships with God and Nature

OBJECTIVE: You will be able to identify the physical and spiritual consequences of the fall in people's relationship with God and nature.

The first consequence of Adam and Eve's sin was death. In a Christian view of the world, death is unnatural. According to Paul in 1 Corinthians, death is the great enemy (1 Corinthians 15:26), an invader in God's world. Christians have the hope of eternal life in God's kingdom, but this hope should never cause us to minimize death in the present. When Jesus went to raise Lazarus from the dead, Jesus wept with those who mourned for Lazarus (John 11:33–35). Jesus took the time to feel the weight and tragedy of death. Because of sin, it is only a matter of time until our bodies tragically decay and die. Job puts it strikingly, "Man wastes away like a rotten thing, like a garment that is moth-eaten" (Job 13:28).

Adam and Eve would die *physically* (because they could no longer eat from the Tree of Life), but also *spiritually* because to be away from God's presence leads to eternal death.

True life, they discovered, was not found in being "like God" in the serpent's sense, but in being "with God."[7] Their spiritual death was the fracturing and distortion of their relationship with God.[8] In rebelling against him, the man and woman mistrusted, ignored, and rejected God. Their shame caused them to hide from God (Genesis 3:8–10).

When God asked Adam if he had eaten from the Tree of Knowledge of Good and Evil, Adam blamed "the woman whom you gave to be with me" (v. 12). Adam blamed Eve; he also blamed God for making her in the first place. The trust between God and humans was broken.

Today, both the physical and spiritual consequences of the fall are felt by all humanity. We all experience pain, suffering, and eventual death. The spiritual consequences of humanity's broken relationship with God are evident in our attitudes. We no longer trust God. Instead, some ignore him. Others fear him as an angry judge or see him as uninterested and distant. Many atheists say that to enjoy life, we must abandon God. Others dislike the idea of God having authority and so reject him entirely.

The fall also had physical consequences for nature and for our relationship with creation. Plants decay, forests burn, rivers dry up, and animal predators tear their victims to pieces. As one famous hymn puts it, "Change and decay in all around I see."[9] The book of Romans says that "creation waits with eager longing;" it groans because it has been "subjected to futility," and it is under "bondage to corruption" (Romans 8:19–22).

In Genesis 3:17–19, God cursed the ground so it would not yield fruit easily. In Genesis 1–2, Adam and Eve's responsibility to cultivate the earth represents "all kinds of human labor and culture making," so when the ground was cursed, all work fell under the curse. Work would be frustrating.[10] We see dimensions of this today in work that is tedious, boring, painful, dehumanizing, and often characterized by the frantic struggle to get ahead or stay afloat. The pressures, demands, and problems with work over time cause us to stop seeing ourselves as stewards of creation, but as its masters and even foes—abusing, exploiting, and destroying creation for our own gain. Creation longs to be free from the curse and to be reconciled with the humans who were meant to care for it.

5. Consequences of Sin: Broken Relationships with Self and Others

▸ **OBJECTIVE: You will be able to infer the consequences of the fall in people's relationships with themselves and with other people.**

The fall also has consequences for our relationship with ourselves. When Adam and Eve ate from the Tree of Knowledge of Good and Evil, they became internally broken. Suddenly, they realized that they were naked and were ashamed (Genesis 3:7). While physically nothing had changed (they were naked in Genesis 1–2 as well), Adam and Eve were no longer comfortable in their own skin. They sewed fig leaves together to cover themselves up. Later, God made them clothes to cover their nakedness (v. 21).

Internal brokenness causes us to see ourselves in the wrong way, to justify our sinful actions, and to deceive ourselves into calling good evil and evil good. When we live contrary to the way God designed us, we become plagued by guilt, fear, shame, and anxiety. No longer content with our identity as beings in God's image, or with the gifts and tasks he has given us, we seek to define ourselves through who or how much we know, how much we can possess, or what we can accomplish. Such things can never fully satisfy us (Ecclesiastes 1:12–2:26).

The internal fracturing of humans leads to a more obvious fracturing of the relationships we have with other people. The first signal of this in the text is that Adam and Eve no longer felt safe with one another. What had previously been a relationship of intimacy was now marred by shame and confusion. The second signal is that when God questioned Adam, he refused to take responsibility for his own sin. Instead, Adam blamed Eve. Can you imagine the frustration, pain, and tension this caused in Adam and Eve's relationship?

Genesis 3:16 states that the woman would experience pain in childbearing and her "desire shall be contrary to [or shall be toward her] husband, and he shall rule over [her]." The meaning of this part of the verse is not easy to decipher. It could mean that the woman's desire will be to dominate her husband or that she will turn away from God's rule to her husband's rule.[11] For the man to "rule" over the woman might mean that he will treat her "as if she were *part of* the creation over which humans are given dominion, rather than being herself a coruler *over* creation."[12] However this verse is interpreted, it is clear that what it describes is not a good thing. What had previously been a relationship of complete oneness and trust would be characterized by division and distrust.

The fallout from this broken relationship is tragic, but the fall affects all relationships, not just those between men and women—it affects friendships, parent/child relationships, sibling relationships, and boss/coworker relationships. Throughout the Bible, we see betrayal, sibling rivalry, selfishness, dishonesty, abuse, and injustice all perpetuated by people seeking to get the upper hand over others.

Today, the consequences of broken relationships are no less severe. Consider, for example, physical and emotional abuse, child labor, exploitation, sex slavery, gossip, lying, stealing, murder, hatred, harassment, discrimination, abortion, and euthanasia. All of these examples illustrate instances in which people (who all bear God's image) are mistreated in some way. Sin has caused a enormous mess in human relationships.

6. Who Is to Blame?

▸ **OBJECTIVE: You will be able to discuss the doctrine of original sin and whether God is to blame for people's sin.**

As we look at the sin that has caused such a mess in our world, it is our natural tendency to look for someone to blame. Many people believe that we don't really have any natural bent toward evil;[13] therefore it is our society, culture, or upbringing that is to blame for our problems. Going one step further, some secularists argue that our guilt and shame over sin are unnecessary; they are psychological trauma foisted on us by the tyrannical God of Christian faith. As the late atheist Christopher Hitchens argued, "Once you assume a creator and a plan, it makes us objects in a cruel experiment whereby we are created sick and commanded to be well."[14] Hitchens said religion itself is largely to blame for evil. Many others, like Hitchens, see the God of the Bible as a selfish, cruel deity who curses people forever because of eating a simple piece of fruit.

Christians would say that these views do not accurately describe the Bible's teaching on sin and evil. The first sin was not merely about snatching a piece of fruit. The Scriptures also affirm that God is not the author, creator, or instigator of evil (see Genesis 1:31, 1 Corinthians 14:33, James 1:13, 1 John 1:5). Rather, Genesis 3 shows evil is the result of rebellion against God.

Though Scripture teaches that people were not created evil, sin entered the world, and as a result, sin has infected all of us. "Just as sin came into the world through one man, and death through sin, so death spread to all . . . because all sinned" (Romans 5:12). In this verse, Paul is referring to the fall of Adam and Eve in Genesis 3. Though both sinned, Paul uses Adam (the one man) as the representative of their sin. Because of the first sin in the garden of Eden, now all of us inherit a sin nature. This is what theologians call *the doctrine of original sin*. The **doctrine of original sin** is *the belief that Adam and Eve's first sin corrupted the nature of their descendants.*

This doctrine teaches that we are so *thoroughly* fallen that nothing remains unaffected by our fallenness. It also says that we are so *absolutely* fallen that there's nothing we can do to fix ourselves. The fall affects us so deeply—both physically and psychologically—that our attempts at self-repair only highlight how broken our condition really is. The doctrine of original sin isn't just about imperfect human beings who make mistakes; it is about rebels going against their Creator, incapable of doing what is good on their own.

The Bible is clear that no one is exempt. We are all sinners (Romans 3:9–26), our hearts are deceitful (Jeremiah 17:9), and we have all "turned aside" and "become corrupt"

(Psalm 14:1–3). Christian writer and apologist G. K. Chesterton understood this truth well. Responding to the question "What's wrong with the world?" he supposedly replied simply: "I am."[15]

The Scriptures are clear that sin is an outsider in our world that invades and corrupts everything. It is like a parasite that latches on to a living host and sucks away life and nutrients. But sin cannot be blamed solely on society, religion, or false guilt. The problem lies deep within each of us, and on our own there is nothing we can do to fix it.

7. God's Grace in the Midst of Judgment

▸ **OBJECTIVE: You will be able to summarize how God responded to Adam and Eve's sin and showed grace to them by promising redemption.**

Admittedly, this chapter hasn't been very encouraging so far. We've talked about sin, how it entered the world, it's terrible consequences, and how each one of us is part of the problem. Is there any hope? How does God's great story continue? The good news is that God didn't exit the world after the fall. He stayed involved and worked to redeem his people.

Redemption begins in Genesis 3. Wait, isn't that the chapter where everything went wrong? The one where God dealt out judgment? Yes, but if you look closely, you will see that even in the midst of judgment, God was gracious. The first thing we see is that God did not give up on Adam and Eve. After they had eaten the fruit from the Tree of Knowledge of Good and Evil, God called out to them, "Where are you?" (Genesis 3:9). Now why would God need to ask this question? Didn't he know where they were? Of course he did! When he called out to them, he was offering them the chance to confess and be honest about what they had done. God could just as easily have struck them down—hadn't he warned them that when they ate from the Tree they would die? Instead, God graciously reached out to them. He refused to abandon them.

The most important act of grace is stated in Genesis 3:14–15. In these verses, God condemned the serpent for the evil he had done. The serpent was cursed "above all beasts of the field" and would eat dust all its life. But there's more. God said there would be a conflict between the serpent and the offspring of the woman, who would "bruise [the serpent's] head," though the serpent would "bruise his heel." This cryptic promise is what theologians call *the protoevangelium*. It is the first (*proto*-) announcement of the gospel (the evangel, or good news). God's promise in Genesis 3:15 is the first appearance of his plan to restore and redeem humanity through Jesus' death and resurrection. The serpent would bite the heel of the woman's offspring, but the serpent would be crushed. This looks ahead to Jesus, who in his death on the cross is mortally wounded by Satan, but ultimately crushes Satan by rising from the dead. Jesus' victory on the cross is the blow that defeats death and sin once and for all.

The final act of grace in this chapter may seem like one more curse, but God did not curse humans. He cursed the ground and the serpent. Yet God sent Adam and Eve out of the garden so they would not "take also of the tree of life and eat, and live forever" (Genesis 3:22). How is this grace? Apparently, if humans had continued to eat from the Tree of Life, they would have lived forever—but this would not be a pleasant existence. Death limits the suffering that humans will experience in a fallen world.

8. The Way of Cain and the Flood

▸ OBJECTIVE: You will be able to give examples of sin in the lives of Adam and Eve's descendants.

After these events, Eve gave birth to a son and named him *Cain*. Would this be the promised Offspring who would crush the head of the serpent? One can imagine that Adam and Eve's hopes were high. In Genesis 4:1, Eve says that she has "gotten a man with the help of the LORD." The Hebrew of this verse is tricky, and scholars are divided on how it should be interpreted. Some scholars take this statement to mean that Eve gave birth to Cain with God's help.[16] Others see Eve's statement as an arrogant assertion of her own godlikeness, suggesting that, like God, she too can create life.[17]

Cain and Abel offer sacrifices, by George Wesley Evans, Preceptive Illustrations of the Bible, *1750*

The trouble began when Cain and his brother Abel brought sacrifices to the Lord. Abel brought a lamb from his flock and Cain brought "fruit of the ground" (v. 3). God accepted Abel's sacrifice but rejected Cain's. Hebrews 11:4 says that Abel's offering was given through faith, implying that Cain's was not. According to Hebrews 11:6, "And without faith it is impossible to please him, for whoever would draw near to God must believe that he exists and that he rewards those who seek him." Rather than having faith, it seems that Cain's attitude was arrogant and rebellious.[18] In Genesis 4:6–7, God made it clear to Cain that if he did what was right, he would be accepted. But, if he did not, he should watch out, because sin was waiting to overcome him. God portrays sin as a wild animal waiting to pounce on Cain and devour him.

Cain allowed sin to get the better of him and ended up murdering his brother Abel. God gave Cain a chance to confess his crime, but Cain refused to own up to it. So, God punished Cain by banishing him. Yet God also offered grace. He placed a mark on Cain so that no one could take revenge on him. Cain's descendants went on to form cultures and civilizations—building cities, playing music, and forging tools (all examples of people using their God-given talents potentially for good). However, human wickedness continued. In Genesis 4:23–24, Lamech boasted about how he had just killed a young man merely for hurting him. This wicked man is also the first man in the Bible to have more than one wife.

Meanwhile, Eve was granted another son, Seth, who also had descendants. "At that time," Genesis 4:26 says, "people began to call on the name of the LORD." To call on the name of the Lord is to recognize him as God and to worship him.[19] From this moment on, human beings followed one of two paths. Some humbly acknowledged God as Creator and worshipped him. Others followed the "way of Cain" (Jude 1:11), rebelling against God by perpetuating evil. One notable example of a person who called on the name of the Lord was Enoch. The Bible has only a few verses to describe him, but we know "he walked with God" (Genesis 5:21–24), had faith, and pleased God (Hebrews 11:5). For this, he was taken up into heaven without dying.

By Genesis 6, it becomes clear that most humans chose the way of Cain. In fact, people became so corrupt that their "every intention . . . was only evil" (Genesis 6:5), and God decided the world needed a fresh start. Human beings had completely failed as God's stewards, instead filling the world with sin. So, God instructed a righteous man named *Noah* to build an ark to escape the flood with which God would destroy the earth. This was a radical act of faith on Noah's part (Hebrews 4:7). Noah and his family, along with animals and birds of every kind were saved from the flood inside the ark. The flood covered the earth for 150 days and destroyed almost every living thing.

9. God's Covenant with Noah and the Tower of Babel

▸ OBJECTIVE: You will be able to articulate what a covenant is, how God made a covenant with Noah, and what happened to humans after the tower of Babel.

After the flood, God made a covenant with Noah, his family, and "every living creature" (Genesis 9:9–10). Because there are several key moments in the Bible where God makes a covenant with someone, we need to stop and consider this concept. A **covenant** is *an agreement between two parties that involves both rights and responsibilities.*

A covenant is different from a contract. In a contract, each party is *self-centered*: "What's in it for me?" "What are my rights?" "What can I expect?" If a contract is broken, the parties usually go to court. A covenant, on the other hand, is *other-centered*: "What do I promise to do for others?" "How will I serve them?" "How can I exceed their expectations?" Marriage is an example of a covenant. When two people marry, each person makes a vow that clarifies what he or she will do, not what the other person will do.

In the Bible, we read that God explicitly initiated at least four covenants. In each case, God chose his covenant partner and set out the expectations without human input. In this sense, a covenant is similar to a vow or promise. God's covenants both *declare promises* of God's commitment and *express expectations* of human faithfulness.

The first covenant God made was with Noah. God decided that he would never again "curse the ground" (Genesis 8:21) or destroy all living things on the earth by means of a flood. He placed a rainbow in the sky as a reminder of his covenant with all creation.

God also expressed hopes for Noah and his descendants. They were to "be fruitful and multiply and fill the earth" (Genesis 9:1). This is the same command God gave to Adam and Eve in the garden of Eden. In some ways, the earth after the flood was a new creation, and Noah was to partner with God in bringing life and abundance from it. Unlike the original creation, however, animals and people would now fear one another. God specified that human beings were free to eat animals (Genesis 9:2–3). In addition, God instructed Noah and his sons that anyone who killed a person should be punished (Genesis 9:6).

Tower of Babel, artwork based on 16th century painting by Pieter Brueghel the Elder

What is important about this covenant is that God knew Noah and his descendants would break it (Genesis 9:7–13). Nonetheless, God promised not to destroy the earth with a flood again. Even if (and when) human beings failed, God would not. This is good news, because before Noah's story ends, we see that the flood did not stop people from sinning. After the flood, Noah planted a vineyard and got drunk. While he was drunk, Noah lay naked in his tent and his son Ham shamed him.[20] This resulted in Noah cursing Ham's son Canaan (Genesis 9:20–28).

We see further evidence that the rebellious heart of people had not changed. Some people decided to build a tower that would reach to heaven—the tower of Babel. They wanted to make a name for themselves. God knew that if the people were all united against God, their wickedness would soar to incredible heights. So, God confused their language, graciously allowing people to still speak to at least some others. People groups were able to form around common languages and spread out on the earth.[21]

10. Conclusion

In this chapter, we saw how *shalom* was shattered when Adam and Eve believed the lies of the serpent and rebelled against the God who made and loved them. We saw that sin is not a made-up concept to spoil our fun. Rather, sin is a failure to love God and others as we should, an act of betrayal or rebellion, and a willingness to choose what is wicked over what is good. Sin is a failure to be who God created us to be. When we sin, we don't just break a law, we act against our design.

When sin happens, relationships break down. The greatest fallout is the breaking of our relationship with God. The Bible is clear that we are estranged from God because of our sin. God wishes to reach out to us in love and forgiveness, but often we are too mistrustful of God to see this. Our sin causes us to doubt his goodness and believe lies about him. Our sin also causes breakdowns in our relationships with nature, ourselves, and others. Sin results in hurt, frustration, pain, suffering, violence, destruction, abuse, and inner turmoil. Try as we might, we cannot remove sin from the world. We are all part of the problem, broken by sin. We cannot fix ourselves, and we cannot blame anyone else.

The good news is that there is hope. God loves us more than we could ever know. He has not, and will not, abandon his world or the people in it. The stories in Genesis 1–11 (Adam and Eve, Cain and Abel, Noah and the flood, and the tower of Babel) reveal important truths about God's response to sin. We learn that God is grieved by our sin and will not forever tolerate our destroying his world and the people in it. He will not allow rebellion and wickedness to continue unabated. Yet even in the midst of judgment, God is incredibly gracious, continually reaching out to people, offering them forgiveness, mercy, and love.

All throughout the rest of the Old Testament—from Genesis 3 on—God is relentless in working to save, protect, and preserve his people and his creation. He seeks to forgive, heal, and restore. God's commitment knows no bounds. In the next chapter, we'll see how God chose one person and one nation to bring blessing to the whole world. We'll see the continuing effects of the fall, but we'll also see how God worked through his people, despite their sin, to bring blessing to all the earth.

ENDNOTES

[1] See Bible Project, "Bad Words Series: Khata/Sin," BibleProject.com, video, 5:43, https://bibleproject.com/explore/video/khata-sin

[2] Michael Reeves, *Delighting in the Trinity: An Introduction to the Christian Faith* (Downers Grove, IL: IVP Academic, 2012), 65–68.

[3] Iain Provan, *Seriously Dangerous Religion: What the Old Testament Really Says and Why It Matters* (Waco, TX: Baylor University Press, 2014), 111.

[4] John Sailhamer, *The Pentateuch as Narrative: A Biblical-Theological Commentary* (Grand Rapids, MI: Zondervan, 1992), 103.

[5] Provan, *Seriously Dangerous Religion*, 113–114.

[6] Provan, *Seriously Dangerous Religion*, 114.

[7] Sailhamer, *Pentateuch as Narrative*, 110.

[8] Craig G. Bartholomew and Michael W. Goheen, *The Drama of Scripture: Finding Our Place in the Biblical Story* (Grand Rapids, MI: Baker Academic, 2004), 43–44.

[9] Henry Francis Lyte, "Abide with Me," Hymnary.org, https://hymnary.org/text/abide_with_me_fast_falls_the_eventide.

[10] Timothy Keller, *Every Good Endeavor: Connecting Your Work to God's Work* (New York: Dutton, 2012), 89–90.

[11] Chesna Hinkley, "What to Say When Someone Says That Patriarchy Is God's Plan," CBE International, April 9, 2019, https://www.cbeinternational.org/resource/article/mutuality-blog-magazine/what-say-when-someone-says-patriarchy-gods-plan.

[12] Provan, *Seriously Dangerous Religion*, 118.

[13]See for example, David G. Allan, "Breaking News Alert: People Are Inherently Good, Nonviolent," CNN, December 11, 2018, https://www.cnn.com/2018/12/11/health/nonviolence-good-wisdom-project: Abraham Maslow, *Humanistic Psychology I*, ed. David Welch, George A. Tate and Fred Richards, (Buffalo, NY: Prometheus Books, 1978), 11.

[14]"Munk Debate on Religion—Christopher Hitchens Opening Remarks," YouTube, January 31, 2011, https://www.youtube.com/watch?v=rYMyxa5fysI.

[15]"What's Wrong with the World?", The Society of G. K. Chesterton, April 29, 2012, https://www.chesterton.org/wrong-with-world/.

[16]See John Walton, *Genesis: The NIV Application Commentary* (Grand Rapids, MI: Zondervan, 2001), 260–63.

[17]See Provan, *Seriously Dangerous Religion*, 192; Sailhamer, *Pentateuch as Narrative*, 112.

[18]Tremper Longman III, *How to Read Genesis* (Downers Grove, IL: InterVarsity Press, 2005), 115.

[19]Walton, *Genesis*, 278–79.

[20]Many commentators acknowledge a certain amount of ambiguity as to what actually happened in this story. See Bartholomew and Goheen, *Drama of Scripture*, 51; Iain Provan, *Discovering Genesis: Content, Interpretation, Reception* (Grand Rapids, MI: Eerdmans, 2015), 125; Sailhamer, *Pentateuch as Narrative*, 129; and Walton, *Genesis*, 345–49.

[21]Longman, *How to Read Genesis*, 121.

8

Act 3: Redemption Initiated—Israel

1. The Family of Abraham

▸ **OBJECTIVE: You will be able to explain God's covenant with Abraham and list the two descendants who received the covenant blessing.**

In the previous chapter, we saw how Adam and Eve rebelled against God, bringing sin and destruction into the world. We also saw that God continued to be gracious and committed to his creation. But we were left wondering how God would crush the head of the serpent and how God would deal with the mess sin caused.

In Genesis 12:1–3, God chose a man named *Abram* (later renamed *Abraham*) and called him to move to a new country. God promised that Abraham and his wife, Sarah, would have a son (Genesis 17:19, 18:10). Eventually, Abraham's descendants would be as numerous "as the stars of heaven and as the sand that is on the seashore" (Genesis 22:17). God also promised to give Abraham the land of Canaan, where he and his family would become a nation and prosper (Genesis 13:14–17, 15:18–21, 17:8).

Central to all this was God's promise to bless Abraham's family so they, in turn, could bless all the families of the earth (Genesis 12:2–3, 18:18; Galatians 3:8). Abraham and his family were to "keep the way of the LORD" by doing what was just and right (Genesis 18:19). The ultimate blessing was that the Offspring who would crush the head of the serpent would come from Abraham's family (Genesis 22:18, Acts 3:25–26, Galatians 3:16). This was God's covenant with Abraham.

However, on numerous occasions, both Abraham and Sarah doubted God's promises or took matters into their own hands.[1] They mistreated a slave woman, Hagar, who gave birth to Abraham's son Ishmael. He was not the heir God had promised to Abraham and Sarah. Sarah later gave birth to the child God had promised—a son, Isaac (Galatians 4:22–23). In Genesis 22, God commanded Abraham to sacrifice Isaac. By this time, Abraham had learned that God was absolutely trustworthy. He obeyed God without question, believing that God could raise Isaac from the dead (Hebrews 11:17–19). When Abraham lifted the knife to sacrifice Isaac, an angel stopped him, praised Abraham for his faith, and reaffirmed God's covenant promises (Genesis 22:9–18).

The angel stops Abraham, 19th c. mosaic, All Saints Church, London, UK

The covenant blessing was then passed to Isaac, who had his own troubled history.[2] He had two sons, Esau and Jacob. After stealing his father's blessing from Esau, Jacob fled to a foreign land where he married two sisters, Leah and Rebecca, and had 12 children. Through many failures,[3] Jacob learned to trust in God's promises. Later, Jacob was renamed *Israel*, meaning "God strives," or "he strives against God" (Genesis 32:28).[4]

The final story in the book of Genesis is about Jacob's favorite son, Joseph (Genesis 37–50). Joseph's jealous brothers sold him as a slave in Egypt. Joseph was very successful there until he was falsely accused and thrown in prison. However, through a wild series of events, Joseph was taken out of prison and elevated to second in the kingdom, where he shrewdly stewarded Egypt's food resources during a famine. Genesis ends with Joseph forgiving and blessing his brothers, then bringing his whole family to stay with him in Egypt. Speaking to his brothers, Joseph concluded: "As for you, you meant evil against me, but God meant it for good, to bring it about that many people should be kept alive, as they are today" (Genesis 50:20).

The stories of Genesis 12–50 reveal how God was faithful to his covenant with Abraham's family. Even when they failed to be faithful, God continued to redeem.

2. The Exodus

▸ **OBJECTIVE:** You will be able to relate the Passover to the exodus from Egypt.

At the beginning of the book of Exodus, Abraham's descendants, called *Hebrews,* (now known as *Israelites*) had become so numerous that Pharaoh (the king of Egypt) worried they could overpower the Egyptians. Therefore, the Egyptians enslaved and mistreated the Israelites (see Exodus 1:6–14). But God had compassion on Israel and raised up Moses to deliver them (Exodus 3:7–10).

Moses' story began when Pharaoh commanded that all newborn Israelite males be thrown into the Nile River. In defiance, Moses' mother kept him for three months, and then hid him in a basket among the reeds in the river, where he was rescued by Pharaoh's daughter. Moses grew up in the royal house but identified with his fellow Israelites (Hebrews 11:24–26). After murdering an Egyptian for beating an Israelite, Moses fled and became a shepherd in Midian. There God revealed himself to Moses through a burning bush. He instructed Moses to go back to Egypt and lead Israel out of slavery, promising to be with him. It was at this time that God revealed himself as the great *I AM* (Exodus 3:14). This title identifies God as eternal and timeless. It can mean that "God is always there, was always there, and will always be there."[5] God also told Moses that his name was *the LORD*, or *Yahweh* (Exodus 3:15, 6:2–3).[6] After much arguing with God, Moses went back to Egypt with his brother Aaron.

Moses and Aaron confronted Pharaoh, but he refused to release Israel, saying, "Who is the LORD, that I should obey his voice and let Israel go?" (Exodus 5:2).[7] With fearsome plagues, God showed himself to be the supreme Ruler of the universe. Pharaoh still would not acknowledge God. In a final plague, God struck the firstborn son of each family in Egypt, but made provision for the Israelites, commanding them to sacrifice a lamb and paint its blood on the doorposts of their homes. When God saw the blood, he would "pass over" the house and spare it (Exodus 12:1–28, 43–51). **Passover** is the name of *an annual Jewish celebration to commemorate God rescuing Israel from slavery in Egypt.*

The firstborn of all families in Egypt whose doors did not have the blood were killed, including Pharaoh's firstborn. Following this, Pharaoh allowed the Israelites to leave Egypt and Moses led them to the Red Sea. But Pharaoh changed his mind and went after the Israelites. Once again, God displayed his power—this time by parting the sea so the Israelites could cross over in safety. Once they were through, the sea engulfed and drowned their pursuers (Exodus 14).

The Israelites camped at Mount Sinai, where God made a new covenant with them. Revealing himself as a God of great love and faithfulness, God called them to be a kingdom of priests. Through Moses, gave them a mission to bless the world (Exodus 6:1–8, 19:1–6).

He promised to be with them and bless them. In this covenant, God also gave his people the Ten Commandments and many other instructions to follow (Exodus 20–23). Keeping the laws and commandments was not a way for the Israelites to earn God's favor. Rather, obedience to the law was to be a response to God's grace to Israel (Exodus 19:4, 20:2). For their part, the Israelites promised, "All that the LORD has spoken we will do" (Exodus 19:8).

3. The Tabernacle in the Wilderness

▸ **OBJECTIVE:** You will be able to explain the purpose of the tabernacle.

▸ **OBJECTIVE:** You will be able to differentiate between the two categories of Old Testament laws, the two types of sacrifices, and the three major festivals.

Despite God's miraculous deliverance, however, the people continually complained, doubted, and even contemplated going back to Egypt (Exodus 14:10–12, 15:22–24, 16:1–3, 17:1–3). Almost immediately they fell into idol worship (Exodus 32). God wanted to be among his people, but how were sinful people going to be able to live in the presence of a holy God?[8]

The answer—the tent of meeting. In Exodus 25–31, God graciously provided a detailed set of instructions for building a tent, known as the **tabernacle**, as *a sacred place of meeting where God's presence dwelt among the Israelites.*

The tabernacle was a kind of miniature Eden where God could be personally known.[9] Inside the most sacred space in the tabernacle was the ark of the covenant, the place where God descended to speak to his people (Numbers 7:89).

But there was still the problem of sin. The book of Leviticus is taken up with explaining how sinful people can dwell in God's presence. Central to this were the priests, who were to represent the people before God and perform the rituals in the tabernacle.

Leviticus is also filled with laws, sacrifices, and festivals, many of which seem odd to us today. Through these, God wanted to shape a kingdom of priests, a holy nation—that is, people who relied on him, who would practice justice and mercy, and so demonstrate to the world that Yahweh is the true God.

- **Laws:** The laws God gave the Israelites fall generally into two categories—ceremonial and moral.[10]
    - Ceremonial laws: dietary restrictions, sacrifices, washing before entering the tabernacle, and other laws were about keeping the people of Israel ceremonially pure so they could live in God's presence.
    - Moral laws: the Ten Commandments, instructions about sexual integrity, justice, restitution, and other laws were designed to help Israel reflect God's character to the nations.

- **Sacrifices:** The book of Leviticus details five different kinds of sacrifices, which can be put into two categories.[11]
    - Thanksgiving sacrifices: grain offerings and peace offerings celebrated God's goodness and gratefully acknowledged his blessings.
    - Sacrifices for sin: burnt offerings, sin offerings, guilt offerings were a way of confessing and acknowledging sin to God and receiving his gracious forgiveness.
- **Festivals:** The people of Israel were instructed to celebrate seven feasts or days of remembrance. One was the Passover. Two others are listed here:[12]
    - Feast of Tabernacles: a remembrance of God's provision for the Israelites while they lived in tents after leaving Egypt.
    - Day of Atonement: *an annual holy day when all the sins of Israel were confessed and atoned for.* The Israelites offered a goat as a sacrifice for all of Israel; another goat symbolically carrying their sins was banished to the wilderness. *Atonement* means *restitution for wrongdoing.*

Day of Atonement: an annual holy day when all the sins of Israel were confessed and atoned for

In the wilderness, God provided for his people—guiding them with a cloud by day and a pillar of fire by night, giving them water in dry places, sending manna from heaven, and defending them against their enemies. Yet the Israelites continued to rebel—doubting God's promises, complaining, and rebelling against Moses' leadership (Numbers 11:1, 16:1–3, 20:1–5, 21:4–5). Due to their failure to trust God, he let them wander in the wilderness for 40 years.

4. The Promised Land and the Judges

▶ **OBJECTIVE:** You will be able to describe the pattern Israel fell into during the period of the judges.

Faithful to his covenant promises, God finally allowed the Israelites to enter the Promised Land. On the eve of this event, Moses encouraged the Israelites to be faithful to the covenant and reminded them of all that God had done for them (as recorded in the book of Deuteronomy). With Moses' words ringing in their ears, the people of Israel, now led by Joshua, crossed over into Canaan.

God instructed the Israelites to drive out the nations that were already living in the land. This is often known as the conquest of Canaan (as recorded in the book of Joshua), and it has raised many questions about how a loving God could command such a thing. We cannot explore the details of these questions here,[13] but we should note that God's judgment on the Canaanites was not arbitrary. The Canaanite nations were extremely wicked. In their cities, women were abused, children were sacrificed, and sex slavery and idolatry were rampant.[14]

God commanded the destruction of these nations as a punishment for their wickedness (Deuteronomy 9:3–5). God knew that if they weren't driven out, Israel would fall into the same evil practices (Deuteronomy 7:1–6). But Israel was not God's favorite team, which he always supported regardless of their actions.[15] In fact, God promised that if Israel practiced the same sins as the Canaanites, they would suffer the same way (Deuteronomy 28:15–68).

The book of Judges details the bloody history of Israel following the conquest and settling of Canaan. The stories follow a pattern: First Israel falls into idolatry and sin, so God allows them to be oppressed by another nation; then Israel cries out to the Lord, so he raises up a judge to deliver them. Following this, Israel turns back to God for a time; eventually, they fall back into idolatry and the cycle repeats.[16]

Old biblical engraving depicting Ruth in Boaz's Field (1873)

The judges who ruled in Israel were a mixed bag. Some, like the prophet and judge Deborah, were noted for their faithfulness and courage (Judges 4–5). Others, like Gideon (Judges 6–8) and Samson (Judges 13–16), accomplished great things but were deeply flawed individuals who lived immoral lives or led Israel back into sin.

One redemptive story from this time concerns a woman named *Ruth*. Interestingly, Ruth was a Moabite from one of the nations that was usually seen as Israel's enemy. Having married into an Israelite family, she came to trust in and worship Yahweh (Ruth 1:16–17). When her husband died, she remained with her mother-in-law and went with her to Bethlehem. There, Ruth eventually married a righteous man named *Boaz*. Together, they had a son, Obed, whose own son Jesse would be the father of Israel's greatest king, David (Ruth 4:22).

At the end of the period covered in the book of Judges, Israel was in turmoil. Something needed to change. God raised up Samuel as a righteous judge, prophet and priest to guide his people. Samuel faithfully followed God and urged the people to turn back to God, but they had other ideas. They demanded a king so that they could be like all the other nations (1 Samuel 8). For better or worse, a king is exactly what they would get.

5. The First Kings of Israel

▸ **OBJECTIVE:** You will be able to summarize details about the first three kings of Israel.

▸ **OBJECTIVE:** You will be able to explain the purpose of the temple.

The first king of Israel was Saul. At first, Saul was humble and reluctant to lead, but power eventually went to his head. He usurped Samuel's duties (1 Samuel 13:8–15), made foolish vows (1 Samuel 14:24–46), and failed to carry out God's commands in full (1 Samuel 15). Because of this, God rejected him and his descendants from ruling in Israel.

In Saul's place, God raised up a shepherd boy named *David* to lead Israel. At a young age, David earned fame by defeating the giant Goliath and leading Saul's army to victory (1 Samuel 17–18). But Saul grew jealous and David fled into the wilderness to escape Saul's wrath. David was a fugitive for ten years. During that time, God prepared him for leadership. David had to practice patience and humility. On two separate occasions, David had an opportunity to kill Saul but instead chose mercy and awaited God's timing.

After Saul's death, David assumed the kingship. He ruled Israel with righteousness. He was "a man after [God's] heart" (Acts 13:22). In 2 Samuel 7, God made a covenant with David. This covenant included a great name for David, a place of rest for Israel, and an eternal dynasty for David's family (see 1 Chronicles 17:11–14, 2 Chronicles 6:16). For their part, David's descendants were to lead Israel in being faithful to God so that Israel could be what God had promised Abraham they would be—a blessing to all nations.[17] God promised to fulfill his covenant even if David and his family failed. Indeed, David did fail in many ways. He had multiple wives and concubines, treated his children poorly, committed adultery and murder, and showed direct disregard for God's commands. Yet David repeatedly repented and turned back to the Lord.

After David's death, his son Solomon became king. Regarded by many as the wisest man who ever lived, Solomon started out well. When God visited him in a dream and told him he could have whatever he wanted, Solomon asked for wisdom (1 Kings 3:1–15). As a result, God richly blessed him. People came from all over the world to hear Solomon's wisdom, and Israel became a wealthy nation. Solomon replaced the tabernacle with a magnificent **temple**, *a permanent sacred building where God was worshipped and made his presence known to Israel*.

At the dedication of the temple, Solomon called on God to be faithful to his promises to David, to hear the prayers of Israel, and to show mercy and forgiveness. He also called on the people of Israel to worship God and to be fully committed to him (1 Kings 8). As grand as the temple was, Solomon knew that it was an act of incredible humility on God's part to come dwell there. He said, "But will God indeed dwell on the earth? Behold, heaven and the highest heaven cannot contain you; how much less this house that I have built!" (1 Kings 8:27).

temple: a permanent sacred building where God was worshipped and made his presence known to Israel

Despite his great wisdom, however, Solomon drifted away from God. He took hundreds of wives and concubines and began to worship foreign gods (1 Kings 11:3–5). He also imposed harsh policies on the people of Israel and abused his power. Despite all that he had worked to build, his kingdom would soon be divided.

6. The Northern Kingdom: Israel

▸ **OBJECTIVE: You will be able to describe the consequences of sin in the northern kingdom and how that sin interfered with Israel's mission.**

Following Solomon's death, his son Rehoboam ascended to the throne. In arrogance and foolishness, he increased the workload that his father had put on the Israelites. In response, Israel rebelled, and ten tribes split off to follow another king, Jeroboam (1 Kings 12). They became known as *the northern kingdom*, *Samaria*, or simply, *Israel*.

Jeroboam led the people away from God and into idol worship, turning his back on God and doing more evil than all who came before him (1 Kings 14:9). All subsequent kings would be measured by this standard: Did they do what was right in God's eyes, like David, or did they do what was evil and lead Israel astray, like Jeroboam?[18]

Elijah at the Brook Kerith, chromolithograph, published ca. 1880

Without exception, the remaining kings of the northern kingdom are described as wicked. One notorious example is King Ahab. Described in the Bible as weak and faithless, Ahab and his wife, Queen Jezebel, led Israel into idolatry by promoting worship of Baal and Asherah. For Ahab, the sins of Jeroboam were trivial, and he far exceeded them (1 Kings 16:30–33).

Because of Israel's great sin, God raised up the prophet Elijah to call its people back to repentance. Elijah had to go into hiding because Jezebel was hunting down and killing the Lord's prophets (1 Kings 18:4). Upon his return, he called for a showdown between Yahweh and Baal (1 Kings 18:16–46). On Mount Carmel, he devised a test. He would construct an altar and make a sacrifice to Yahweh, while the prophets of Baal would do the same for Baal. Then, Elijah and the prophets of Baal would each call on their god to send fire to consume the sacrifice. Whichever god answered would be the true God. Despite numerous tries, the false prophets couldn't get Baal to answer them, but it only took one prayer for Yahweh to send fire from heaven to consume Elijah's sacrifice.

Despite this, Ahab and Jezebel refused to turn to God. They chased Elijah off into the wilderness where he had a remarkable encounter with God. In the wilderness, God spoke to him in "a gentle voice" (1 Kings 19:12, NIV). God had shown his great power on Mount Carmel, but later he revealed himself to Elijah in a whisper.

Eventually, God raised up Jehu as King of Israel to punish Ahab's house and cleanse the land of idolatry. However, after doing this job, Jehu fell into the same sins (2 Kings 10). Meanwhile, Elijah's servant Elisha continued to call Israel to repentance. In a significant story, a military commander from Aram named *Naaman* came to Elisha for healing from leprosy. After being healed he declared, "Behold I know that there is no God in all the earth but in Israel" (2 Kings 5:15). This was the kind of thing that Israel had always been meant to do: to show God's goodness to the world so that others would believe in Yahweh.[19]

The Israelites' persistence in sin kept them from achieving their mission, and God could not let this go on forever. Just as he had promised he would in Deuteronomy 28:15–68, God brought punishment on the Israelites for their unfaithfulness to the covenant and for practicing the very same evils that the nations they had driven out had done. In 722 BC, the northern kingdom was overrun by the Assyrians and Israel was taken into exile.

7. The Southern Kingdom: Judah

▸ **OBJECTIVE: You will be able to distinguish Jehoshaphat, Hezekiah, and Josiah from the other kings of Judah and Israel by indicating how they served the Lord.**

When the kingdom was divided at the beginning of Rehoboam's reign, only the tribes of Judah and Benjamin stayed loyal to the house of David. They became known as *the southern Kingdom of Israel*, or simply, *Judah*. Though there were numerous villains who ruled in Judah throughout its history, there were several kings who followed in God's ways. Three of most important were Jehoshaphat, Hezekiah, and Josiah.

Jehoshaphat was the fourth king of Judah and his assessment in Scripture is generally positive. 2 Chronicles 17:3 says, "The LORD was with Jehoshaphat, because he followed the earlier ways of his father David." Because he was devoted to God's ways, he removed shrines for worshipping false gods, ended male temple prostitution (1 Kings 22:46), called on God's aid in the face of trouble, and led the people in the worship of God. He sent officials into the towns to teach people God's law (2 Chronicles 17:7–9) and instructed judges to be faithful to God in administering justice (2 Chronicles 19).

Hezekiah was the thirteenth king of Judah. At the start of his reign, Hezekiah determined to serve God faithfully. He began by appointing priests to cleanse the temple of all idolatry. Then, he rededicated the people of Israel to the Lord with a great animal sacrifice. He reestablished proper worship in the temple as well as the celebration of Passover (2 Chronicles 29–30). Hezekiah urged the people to repent of their sins and turn to God so that they would not experience the fate of the northern kingdom, which had already gone into exile.

Hezekiah shows the Babylonian messengers his treasures. Wood engraving.

The defining moment of Hezekiah's reign occurred when King Sennacherib of Assyria came mocking the God of Israel and threatening to destroy Judah. Hezekiah wisely fortified the walls and cried out to God for help. God sent an angel to crush the Assyrians, leaving Sennacherib to withdraw in disgrace (2 Kings 18–19, 2 Chronicles 32). But in his later years, Hezekiah grew proud, though he did repent (2 Chronicles 32:24–26). He foolishly flaunted all his wealth before some Babylonian officials. The prophet Isaiah warned that all this wealth, along with many of Hezekiah's descendants, would be carried off in exile to Babylon (2 Kings 20:12–21).

The remaining kings of Judah were all wicked with the exception of Josiah, who began his reign at age eight. The key event of his reign was when the high priest Hilkiah rediscovered the Book of the Law during renovations to the temple. When Josiah heard the words of the book, he realized that Judah was deep in sin and in danger of incurring God's wrath (2 Kings 22). So, he called all the people together to renew the covenant. He then began a vigorous campaign of removing idol worship from Judah (2 Kings 23). For all this, the Bible says that there was never a king before or after him that "turned to the Lord . . . with all his heart and with all his soul and with all his might" (2 Kings 23:25).

Sadly, the same sins that plagued the northern kingdom of Israel eventually came to dominate life in the southern kingdom. Despite numerous warnings, its people persisted in sin. Around 586 or 587 BC, Judah was conquered by the Babylonians and taken into exile.

8. The People of God in Exile

▸ **OBJECTIVE: You will be able to give examples of how Daniel, Shadrach, Meshach, and Abednego modeled faithfulness to God.**

A key biblical book about the exile is Daniel. For Daniel and his friends, the challenge of exile was how to remain faithful to God under intense pressure to conform to Babylonian culture. Daniel, Hananiah (Shadrach), Mishael (Meshach), and Azariah (Abednego) were appointed to serve in King Nebuchadnezzar's government. Part of their training regimen included a daily provision of food and wine, some of which Israelites were forbidden to eat. Determined not to defile himself, Daniel proposed a ten-day test, where they would be fed nothing but vegetables and water. At the end of those ten days, they looked healthier than everyone else. For their faithfulness, God blessed them with great knowledge and understanding (Daniel 1).

In Daniel 2, Nebuchadnezzar ordered his wise men to tell him about a dream he had and to explain what it meant. When they could not, he ordered that they all be killed. Hearing about this, Daniel intervened, praying to God for understanding. After telling and interpreting the dream, Daniel and his friends were appointed to high office. In Daniel 3, Nebuchadnezzar made a huge gold image and ordered everyone to worship it. When Shadrach, Meshach, and Abednego refused, they were thrown into a fiery furnace. But God delivered them, and Nebuchadnezzar acknowledged Israel's God. Later, under the Persian king Darius, Daniel was thrown into a den of lions for worshipping the God of Israel. God rescued him and the king recognized Israel's God (Daniel 6).

These stories provide a model of faithfulness to God in the midst of exile. It is a faithfulness that is tactful, diplomatic, nonviolent, and patient.[20] Daniel and his friends did not use their positions to try and overthrow their rulers. Instead, they trusted God and refused to compromise. They followed the prophet Jeremiah's instructions: "But seek the welfare of the city where I have sent you into exile, and pray to the LORD on its behalf, for in its welfare you will find your welfare" (Jeremiah 29:7).

Chapters 7–12 detail Daniel's visions of the future.[21] In Daniel 7, Daniel had a remarkable vision in which he saw four grotesque beasts coming out of the sea and the Ancient of Days (a name for God) seated on his throne, surrounded by thousands. The beasts represented kings, with the fourth beast being a king whose rule would be extremely oppressive to God's people. It was slain and the other three beasts were stripped of their power. Next, Daniel saw "one like a son of man"[22] coming on the clouds of heaven, approaching the Ancient of Days (Daniel 7:13). To him was given an everlasting kingdom and the authority to rule over all nations.

Daniel's second vision (Daniel 8) had similar themes. These dreams caused Daniel great distress, so he prayed to God, repenting for all the people of Israel (Daniel 9). God assured Daniel that he need not fear because his prayers had been heard and God would save his people.

We will return to the details of these unusual visions in the next chapter, but for now, it is enough to note that the visions reveal a future time of tribulation for Israel, but one in which, ultimately, God will have the final say.

Beasts and the Ancient of Days, from the 10th century Spanish manuscript Silos Apocalypse

9. The Prophets

▸ **OBJECTIVE: You will be able to define the word *prophet* and discuss the types of messages prophets were entrusted to deliver.**

When the Israelites first entered Canaan, God had them drive out nations that were steeped in idolatry and wickedness. When Israel began practicing those same things, God eventually expelled them from the land. In the Bible, this happens very slowly and much to God's sadness.[23] In Isaiah 5:1–7, Israel is portrayed as a vineyard that God lovingly planted and cared for, and yet it bore no good fruit. Where God hoped for justice, he "saw bloodshed;" instead of righteousness, he "heard cries of distress" (v. 7, NIV). God had set apart the nation of Israel to bless the world. As it turned out, God's chosen people were often just as wicked as the nations they were supposed to witness to.

At all times throughout the history of Israel, God commissioned prophets to speak his word to his people. We have already seen a few—Deborah, Elijah, Elisha, and Isaiah. A **prophet** is *a person authorized to speak on God's behalf,* usually to give a specific message at a specific time. In Scripture, some prophets spoke messages that included predictions for the future, but mostly they highlighted God's covenant promises. Whenever God's people became entangled in sin, the prophets challenged them to turn from their wicked ways and worship God, who was always ready to forgive (2 Chronicles 7:14, 24:18–19; Joel 2:13; Zechariah 1:3).[24]

prophet: a person authorized to speak on God's behalf

UNITED KINGDOM OF ISRAEL	
Kings [26]	**Prophets** [27]
Saul (1030–1010) David (1003–970) Solomon (970–930)	Samuel Nathan, Gad

SOUTHERN KINGDOM		NORTHERN KINGDOM	
Kings	**Prophets**	**Kings**	**Prophets**
Rehoboam (930–913)	Shemaiah	Jeroboam (930–909)	Ahijah
Abijah (913–911)			
Asa (911–870)	Azariah	Nadab (909–908)	
	Hanani	Baasha (908–855)	Jehu
		Elah (855–844)	
		Zimri (844)	
		Omri (844–873)	
		Ahab (873–852)	Elijah, Micaiah
Jehoshaphat (870–846)		Ahaziah (852–851)	
Jehoram (851–843)		Jehoram (851–842)	
Ahaziah (843–842)		Jehu (842–814)	
Queen Athaliah (842–836)			
	Zechariah (son of Jehoida)		Elisha
Joash (836–798)		Jehoahaz (817–800)	
Amaziah (798–769)		Jehoash (800–784)	
			Amos, Jonah, Hosea
Azariah (785–733)[28]	Amos	Jeroboam II (789–784)	
Jotham (758–743)		Zechariah (784–747)	
		Shallum (747)	
Ahaz (743–714)		Menahem (747–737)	
	Isaiah, Micah	Pekahiah (737–735)	
		Pekah (735–732)	Obed
Hezekiah (722–698)		Hoshea (731–722)	
Manasseh (698–642)	Jeremiah, Nahum		
Amon (641–640)	Zephaniah		
Josiah (639–609)	Huldah		
Jehoahaz (609)			
	Habakkuk		
Jehoiakim (608–598)	Uriah		
Jehoiachin (597)			
Zedekiah (596–586)	Obadiah		

EXILE AND BEYOND	
Event	**Prophets**
Exiles in Babylon	Daniel, Ezekiel
Exiles Return to Jerusalem	Haggai, Zechariah, Malachi, Joel

figure 10.a

The prophets highlighted the folly of worshipping statues and carved images (Isaiah 44:6–23, Jeremiah 10:1–16) and condemned Israel for turning away from the living God to worship idols (Ezekiel 14:6, Hosea 11:2). The prophets also condemned Israel's injustice—oppression of the poor (Isaiah 10:1–2, Amos 5:11–12), sexual immorality (Jeremiah 5:7–8, Hosea 4:13–14), slaughter of innocent children (2 Kings 17:17, Jeremiah 7:30–34), and violence (Isaiah 59:7, Ezekiel 9:9). They warned that continued unfaithfulness to God's covenant would eventually lead to judgment (2 Chronicles 34:24–28, Isaiah 9:8–20) and exile (Isaiah 5:13, Hosea 9:1–3).

19th century fresco by Leopold Bruckner, St. Nicholas Basilica, Trnava, Slovakia

As we have seen, the northern Kingdom of Israel went into exile in 722 BC because of persistent idolatry and injustice. Between 605 and 586 BC, the southern kingdom of Judah was sent into exile, having failed to heed the warning of Jeremiah 11:1–17. Yet God would not abandon his people, even in exile.

Through the prophets, God promised that he would eventually restore Israel, rule the world with justice, and accomplish his purposes (Isaiah 40–66, Jeremiah 29:10–14).[25] After exile would come restoration (Deuteronomy 4:29–31, 30:1–10). The prophets promised:

- The coming king (Zechariah 9:9–13, 12:10–14)
- The day of the Lord (Zechariah 9:14–17, 12:1–9, 14:1–21; Malachi 4:1–3)
- The restoration of Judah and Israel (Zechariah 10)
- The coming of the Lord's messenger (Malachi 3:1–4, 4:5–6)

In Jeremiah 31:31–34, God spoke through Jeremiah of a new covenant that he would establish with his people. It would include a new heart and forgiveness of sins. Isaiah spoke of a suffering Servant who would carry the sins of the world and take on evil at its root (Isaiah 53). The Offspring who would crush the head of the serpent would give his life and bring hope to the world (Genesis 3:15). Even though the kings of Israel and Judah had mostly failed to follow God's ways, a righteous King would come to rule the world with justice (Isaiah 9:6, Jeremiah 23:5).

10. Conclusion

In this chapter, we've looked briefly at the storyline of the Old Testament. Of course, there is much more to explore. Books like Psalms, Proverbs, and Ecclesiastes provide essential insight and encouragement for the people of God on how to live wisely and faithfully. Books like Job, Ecclesiastes, and Jonah explore the problem of suffering, the mysterious nature of life, and God's love for the outsider. Reading the Old Testament for yourself is the best way to immerse yourself in this great story that not only sets the stage for Jesus, but also speaks to each of us in the many challenges we face. In the next chapter, we'll see the final events of the Old Testament unfold as a few Israelites are allowed to return to Jerusalem and rebuild the temple. But for now, let's recap where the story has gotten us so far.

God created a perfect world and made humans in his image to rule and reign with him over all creation. However, humans rebelled against God. This brought sin into the world and sent people on a downward spiral of chaos and ruin. Determined not to give up on his creation, God chose one family to bring blessing to all the families of the earth. The descendants of Abraham, Isaac, and Jacob formed a great nation called *Israel*. Through Israel, God desired to set up a kingdom of priests that would show God's lovingkindness to all nations. He rescued Israel from slavery, made a covenant with them, and made it possible for them to live in his presence. But over and over, Israel failed to live up to the covenant. They quickly fell into idolatry and wickedness.

God raised up judges and kings to lead his people, but most fell prey to the destructive power of sin. The prophets warned of God's judgment and urged the leaders and the people to return to God, but they refused. Eventually, the people of God were captured by their enemies and taken into exile. Even then, God did not abandon them. He was with those who were faithful, and he revealed himself as sovereign over all nations. As Daniel's time was drawing to a close, a new king came to power who would allow the Israelites to return to their homeland.

Adam, Abraham, Moses, and David, St. Mary Abbot's Church, London, UK

The metanarrative of the Bible reveals that God is absolutely committed to the world and the people he created. He is patient, kind, generous, forgiving, and merciful, but also just, and unwilling to let sin run on forever without judgment. The characters in this grand story—Abraham, Moses, David, and many more—reveal God's persistence in working through broken and corrupt people to bring redemption and blessing to all. And just as God did not abandon Israel when they failed, so God does not abandon us even in our worst moments. The Bible reveals a God who is trustworthy and faithful, even when we are not (2 Timothy 2:13).

You might expect that the next chapter will tell the story of Jesus. But between the end of the Old Testament and the beginning of the New, some 400 years passed when the faith of God's people was put to the ultimate test. In the next chapter, we'll look at what happened in the time between Malachi and Matthew.

ENDNOTES

[1]See Genesis 12:10–20, 16:1–6, 18:12–15, 20:1–18, and 21:9–12.

[2]See Genesis 25:27–28 and 26:1–10.

[3]See Genesis 25:29–34; 27:36; 29:25–28, 30; 30:2–5, 9, 29–43; 37:3–4; 42:1, 36–38; 43:6; 49:5–7.

[4]Chad Brand et al., "Israel," in *Holman Illustrated Bible Dictionary* (Nashville: Holman Bible Publishers, 2003), 844.

[5]Paul Spilsbury, *The Throne, the Lamb, & the Dragon: A Reader's Guide to the Book of Revelation* (Downers Grove, IL: InterVarsity Press, 2002), 61.

[6]In Hebrew, God's name is spelled with four Hebrew letters: yud, hey, vav, hey—YHVH. Because Hebrew manuscripts did not include vowels, to make it pronounceable in English it is rendered as *Yahweh* or *Jehovah*. Where God's name is found in Hebrew, most English Bibles today show it as LORD to distinguish it from other Hebrew words that can also be translated Lord.

[7]See John D. Currid, *Ancient Egypt and the Old Testament* (Grand Rapids, MI: Baker Books, 1997), 104–120.

[8]See the video "Leviticus," Bible Project, video, 7:22, https://bibleproject.com/explore/video/torah-leviticus/.

[9]Iain Provan, *Seriously Dangerous Religion: What the Old Testament Really Says and Why It Matters* (Waco, TX: Baylor University Press, 2014), 36–40.

[10]There is not always clear distinction between moral and ceremonial laws in the Old Testament, so one must be careful, for example, of assuming that something is in the ceremonial category simply because it sounds odd to us today. Christians are not wholly agreed on the use or purpose of the law in the Old Testament. Nearly all Christians argue that the ceremonial laws have been fulfilled by Christ and Christians are no longer bound by them, whereas the moral laws do still hold some force over us today (though exactly how is not agreed). Furthermore, some Christians add a third category of civil laws to distinguish between Israelite systems of justice and the Ten Commandments. See "What Is the Difference between the Ceremonial Law, the Moral Law, and the Judicial Law in the Old Testament?" Got Questions, https://www.gotquestions.org/ceremonial-law.html.

[11]Brand et al., "Sacrifice and Offering," in *Holman Dictionary*, 1428–31.

[12]The other four were "Unleavened Bread," "First Fruits," "Feast of Weeks," and "Feast of Trumpets." See Jessie Blackman and Susha Roberts, "7 Feasts That Point to Christ," Wycliffe, https://www.wycliffe.org/feast/7-feasts-that-point-to-christ.

[13]This question will be addressed in greater detail in the forthcoming second volume in this series.

[14]Paul Copan, *Is God a Moral Monster?: Making Sense of the Old Testament God* (Grand Rapids, MI: Baker Books, 2011), 159–61; Clay Jones, "We Don't Hate Sin So We Don't Understand What Happened to the Canaanites: An Addendum to 'Divine Genocide' Arguments," *Philosophia Christi* 11, no. 1 (2009): 53–72.

[15]This analogy from apologist Brent Kunkle, https://maventruth.com/team/brett-kunkle/.

[16]"Introduction to Judges," The Gospel Coalition, https://www.thegospelcoalition.org/course/judges/#overview.

[17]Craig G. Bartholomew and Michael W. Goheen, *The Drama of Scripture: Finding Our Place in the Biblical Story* (Grand Rapids, MI: Baker Academic, 2004), 91.

[18]Brand et al., "Jeroboam," in *Holman Dictionary*, 889.

[19]See Walter L. McConnell, III, "Mission in the Old Testament: Israel as a Light to the Nations," *Themelios* 39, no. 2, https://www.thegospelcoalition.org/themelios/review/mission-in-the-old-testament-israel-as-a-light-to-the-nations/.

[20]Tim Mackie, "Faithfulness in Exile: A Five-Part Sermon Series on the Book of Daniel," Exploring My Strange Bible Podcast, https://bibleproject.com/podcast/series/faithfulness-in-exile/.

[21]Eugene H. Merrill, Mark F. Rooker, and Michael A. Grisanti, *The World and the Word: An Introduction to the Old Testament* (Nashville: B&H Academic, 2011), 409–13.

[22]"Son of Man" is a title that Jesus repeatedly applied to himself in the Gospels; for example, see John 8:28 or Luke 9:26.

[23]Bartholomew and Goheen, *Drama of Scripture*, 107.

[24]Merrill, Rooker, and Grisanti, *The World and the Word*, 361–66.

[25]Bartholomew and Goheen, *Drama of Scripture*, 111.

[26]List of kings and approximate dates taken from Iain Provan, V. Philips Long, and Tremper Longman III, A Biblical History of Israel, 2nd ed. (Louisville, KY: Westminster John Knox Press, 2015), 269, 328. Other sources were also consulted.

[27]The prophets in this chart are listed in and around the approximate time of their known work. Some prophets, such as Isaiah, had careers that spanned across the reigns of multiple kings, so positioning is not exact. This chart includes the four major prophets and twelve minor prophets who each have a biblical book ascribed to them; their names are italicized. Other prophets from this period are also listed. There are many more prophets in the Bible.

[28]King Azariah is also known as *King Uzziah*.

9 Interlude—The Second Temple Period

1. Daniel's Vision and the Return from Exile

▸ **OBJECTIVE:** You will be able to name the empires represented in Daniel's vision.

▸ **OBJECTIVE:** You will be able to give examples of the challenges Jews returning from exile faced.

At the close of our last chapter, the people of Israel had been sent into exile. While in Babylon, the prophet Daniel had a strange vision in which he saw four beasts that represented four kings (or kingdoms) that would rule on Earth. The beasts can be associated with the following empires:[1]

- **First Beast:** Babylonian Empire (Daniel 7:4)
- **Second Beast:** Medo-Persian Empire (Daniel 7:5)
- **Third Beast:** Greek Empire (Daniel 7:6)
- **Fourth Beast:** Roman Empire (Daniel 7:7—Rome is not explicitly identified in the text.)

Daniel's vision, from the 11th century French manuscript Apocalypse of Saint-Sever

In this and the next three sections, we will see how the beasts appeared in Israel's history. During Daniel's life, the Babylonian Empire (the first beast) was conquered by the Medes and Persians (the second beast). In 539 BC, King Cyrus of Persia took control of the empire. The prophet Isaiah had spoken of Cyrus as one who would be God's instrument in returning the Jewish exiles to their homeland (Isaiah 44:23–45:8). In 538 BC, Cyrus issued a decree allowing the Jewish exiles in Babylon to return to Jerusalem and rebuild the temple (Ezra 1:1–4). Under the leadership of Zerubbabel, a descendant of King David and Joshua the priest, many Jews returned to Jerusalem to complete this task (Ezra 1–3).

All this was very encouraging, and the returned exiles were filled with hope. However, things didn't turn out the way they had expected. The rebuilding of the temple caused some to rejoice, but those who had seen the previous temple wept (Ezra 3:10–13). While work on the temple was going on, some people living around Jerusalem, identified as "adversaries of Judah and Benjamin" (Ezra 4:1), came to help but were told to get lost. After this, they began to cause trouble for the returned exiles (Ezra 4–5).

Sixty years later, Ezra, a priest and expert on the Torah, came to Jerusalem and began instituting reforms and encouraging the Jewish people to observe God's laws (Ezra 7–10).[2] He renewed festivals, instructed the people to follow God, and took particular issue with Jews marrying foreign wives (Ezra 9–10).[3]

Not all Jews had returned to Jerusalem to rebuild the temple. The biblical book of Esther tells the story of Jews who still remained in Persia during the reign of King Xerxes (486–465 BC), which may have occurred around the same time that Ezra was in Jerusalem.

The story focuses on Esther, a young Jewish woman, who was elevated to the position of queen alongside Xerxes. Her surrogate father, Mordecai, was faithful to God; he refused to bow down before Xerxes' political advisor Haman. Upset over this slight, Haman hatched a plot to have all the Jews in Persia executed. In a bold gesture, Esther came before Xerxes, eventually exposed Haman's plot, and became the rescuer of her people. The story ends with the Jews being saved, Esther praised, and Mordecai elevated to high office.

Back in Jerusalem, some twenty years after Ezra's arrival, Nehemiah came to help the Jewish people rebuild the walls of

Jerusalem. Though he had the support of King Artaxerxes, Nehemiah was opposed by some of the same people who tried to previously hinder the rebuilding of the temple. Nehemiah's leadership was also somewhat ambiguous. When his program of reform and rebuilding didn't meet with success, he lost his temper and beat people, pulled out their hair, and forced them to take oaths (Nehemiah 13). Given the many years that God's people had spent in exile for their sin, Nehemiah's frustration over their indifference is understandable, but his own actions left much to be desired.

2. Alexander the Great and Hellenization

▸ **OBJECTIVE: You will be able to recount the rise of Greek culture during the intertestamental period.**

The biblical prophets had spoken of a day when God would once again dwell among his people, the nations would worship Yahweh, and God's people would be given new hearts to truly love God and others. But the return from exile hadn't resulted in the glorious kingdom the Jews had hoped would be restored. Instead, the people of Israel and their leaders fell into some of the same sins that had sent them into exile in the first place. As the last Old Testament prophet, Malachi, called out Israel for profaning God's name, practicing injustice, and continuing in unfaithfulness, a curtain of silence descended on Israel. There would be no direct prophetic word from God for the next 400 years.

The interval between the final events of the Old Testament and the coming of Jesus in the New Testament is often referred to as *the intertestamental period*, which lasted from roughly 400 BC to the early first century AD when John the Baptist began his ministry. It is also sometimes called *the second temple period*, spanning from the rebuilding of the Jerusalem temple in 515 BC to the destruction of that temple in AD 70.[4]

The Medo-Persian Empire endured for 200 years before it was conquered by Alexander the Great around 333 BC. In just a few short years, Alexander conquered most of the Mediterranean world, which amounted to a huge empire. Alexander initiated *the spread of Greek culture throughout the conquered lands of ancient Europe, North Africa, and the Middle East* in a process called **hellenization**. People across his empire began patterning their lives on Greek values and embracing Greek culture (including language, arts, ideas, religion, and government).

However, the young Alexander's glory did not last. At 32 years of age, Alexander abruptly died, and his kingdom was divided among four of his military commanders (many believe this was a fulfillment of Daniel's prophecy in Daniel 8:5–8, 21–22). Two of these were Ptolemy and Seleucus. The Ptolemies ruled Judea (the territory that included the city of Jerusalem) until 198 BC, when the Seleucid general Antiochus III defeated Ptolemy V in a decisive victory. Throughout much of the Greek era, the Jewish people living in Judea had experienced relative independence.[5] On the whole, they were free to live their lives in peace and to worship Yahweh in obedience to the Torah. There were no major uprisings against the ruling powers.[6]

Though Alexander's empire did not survive his death, the influence of the Greek culture he had introduced lasted almost 1,000 years.[7] Hellenization established Greek as the common language throughout the Mediterranean world. During this period, the Old Testament was translated from Hebrew into Greek (this is the translation known as *the Septuagint*).[8] This common culture and language would aid the spread of the gospel after Jesus' death. But hellenization also had a dark side. The push for hellenization could run right over a local culture, and this became a particular problem for Jews. The Jewish people divided over how to respond to this pressure. Some, seeking to fit in, accepted Greek ideas without debate. Others saw hellenization as a threat to the Jewish way of life and regarded those who accepted hellenization as traitors.[9]

3. Antiochus IV and the Maccabees

▸ **OBJECTIVE: You will be able to explain the factors that led to the Maccabean Revolt.**

The pressure to hellenize came to a high point when the Seleucid monarch Antiochus IV came to power in 168 BC.[10] Antiochus took the name *Epiphanes* (which means *God manifest*) and arrogantly asserted his authority over the Jews.[11] In a violent campaign, he attacked Jerusalem and raided the temple (1 Maccabees 1:20–24, Apocrypha). Later, Antiochus outlawed many Jewish customs such as Sabbath observance, circumcision, and temple sacrifice. He demanded the Jews build altars to worship idols, threatening death for those who disobeyed (1 Maccabees 1:41–50). He outraged the Jews by offering a pig on the altar, profaning the temple[12] and renaming it "the temple of Olympian Zeus" (2 Maccabees 6:2). Soon, prostitution was practiced there, and Jews were forced to take part in celebrations for Greek gods (2 Maccabees 6:2–7).[13] The Jews nicknamed Antiochus *Epimanes* (a play on Epiphanes meaning *the madman*).[14] Some saw Antiochus' actions as a parallel to Daniel 9:24–27 and 11:21–45.[15] Clearly, the Jews suffered greatly under Antiochus, and eventually, this led the Jews to revolt.

Mattathias blesses his sons, 1877 woodcut by Julius Schnorr von Carolsfeld

An old priest named *Mattathias* stirred a revolt when he defied the king's order by refusing to offer a sacrifice to pagan gods. When another Jew went ahead with the sacrifice, Mattathias killed him and the king's official who was enforcing the law. Mattathias and his five sons then fled to the wilderness with many other Jews (1 Maccabees 2), eventually forming a rebellion under the leadership of Mattathias's third son Judah, who earned the nickname *Maccabee*, which means *the hammer*.

Their campaign against Antiochus met with great success. The Maccabees proved to be able military leaders, zealous for the God of Israel. On December 25, 164 BC, Judah Maccabee rode into Jerusalem with his army (amidst shouts of 'hosanna' and the waving of palm branches) and cleansed the temple. This event started **Hanukkah**, *a yearly Jewish festival that celebrates the cleansing and rededication of the temple.*[16] John 10:22 tells us that Jesus was at a Hanukkah celebration.

The Maccabees continued to do battle with their enemies. By 142 BC, they won Jewish independence. For all practical purposes, the Maccabean leaders were seen as Moses—or messiah-like figures. They had conquered Israel's enemies and restored true worship in the temple. People dreamed that Judea would once again become the great kingdom that it was under David. But it quickly became apparent that neither Judah Maccabee nor any of his brothers was the one that Israel had been hoping for.[17]

After Judah's death, the Maccabee family and their descendants, the Hasmoneans, became tyrants. They took over the high priesthood and acted like kings. Some, like Alexander Janneus, were almost as bad as Antiochus IV. Under his rule, hellenization went ahead full steam and he brutally punished his enemies (crucifying over 800 men while murdering their wives and children in front of them).[18] The Maccabean campaign for freedom had begun as an attempt to free Israel from foreign domination so that the Jews could live in obedience to the Torah and worship Yahweh, but it quickly descended into chaos and wickedness. The hard-won independence would not last. In 63 BC, the Roman general Pompey conquered Jerusalem, ushering in almost 500 years of Roman rule.[19]

4. Herod, Pilate, and Roman Rule

▸ OBJECTIVE: You will be able to paraphrase how the rise of the Roman Empire set the stage for the birth, life, and death of Christ.

Rome may have been the fourth beast Daniel spoke of. At first, the Romans chose to rule the Jews through the "client king," Herod the Great.[20] Though he claimed to be a Jew, Herod was really the son of an Edomite and had been made governor of Galilee with the help of Rome. Later, the Roman Senate appointed him "king of the Jews."[21] He assumed total leadership of Judea in 37 BC. Herod is mentioned in the Bible in connection with Jesus' birth (which occurred sometime between 7–4 BC).[22] In Matthew 2, Herod acts very much like Pharaoh in the Exodus account. Having heard prophecies about a coming ruler, Herod, fearful of any who would challenge his leadership, ordered the slaughter of all boys under two in Bethlehem (where the Messiah was supposed to be born).

This action is characteristic of what we know about Herod from history. He was power-hungry and paranoid about losing his power. For this reason, he had many of his own family killed, and he drowned and burned those who opposed him. Even on his deathbed, he ordered the slaughter of many of his enemies. Herod was ruthless, but he was also a competent leader. Keen to gain the support of the Jewish people, Herod made significant improvements to the Jewish temple. By the time of his death in 4 BC, the temple was a magnificent structure.

Even so, Judea became a hotbed for rebellion. Various figures claimed to be the messiah who would lead the Jews to victory against their Roman oppressors. Frequent uprisings made keeping the peace in Judea a difficult task. Shortly after Herod's death, Rome had Roman governors, called *prefects*, rule Judea. Pontius Pilate, who handed Jesus over to be crucified, was one of these. According to historians, Pilate was brutal, unfair, and a poor administrator. A few years after Jesus' crucifixion, Pilate was sent back to Rome to answer for his poor leadership. Eventually, he committed suicide.[23]

Overlapping with Herod's reign and continuing afterward was a period of relative peace and stability in the Roman Empire outside Judea. In 31 BC, Octavian defeated Mark Antony and Cleopatra to become the first emperor of Rome. Octavian's reign ushered in the *Pax Romana* ("Roman Peace"), a period that would last for 200 years. During this time, the Romans built numerous roads and highways, which made travel across the empire much easier and safer than it had been before. It was the golden age of Rome.

Yet, Rome could be a cruel master. Octavian took the name Caesar Augustus (*Augustus* means "majestic one"), and the cult of emperor worship began. Caesar Augustus (as well as those who came after him) claimed to be "king of kings" and demanded absolute obedience and loyalty.[24] It was dangerous to defy Rome or question Caesar's lordship. The empire notoriously used crucifixion as a way to put down rebels. It was one of the most humiliating and brutal forms of torture ever invented. Crucifixion was so horrible that Roman citizens did not even speak of it in polite society. The Romans used crucifixion to crush opposition, to "show subject peoples who was in charge and . . . break the spirit of any resistance." During Roman rule, thousands of Jews were executed in this way.[25]

Statue CAESAR Augustus PATRIAE PATER, Rome, Italy

5. Key Jewish Symbols

▸ **OBJECTIVE: You will be able to describe the four key Jewish symbols during the second temple period.**

This brief timeline of events from Babylon to Rome brings us to the time of Jesus. But before we talk about him, we need to look at some core symbols, groups, and beliefs that arose or became prominent during the second temple period. Let's begin with symbols. New Testament historian N. T. Wright has identified four symbols that shaped the everyday life of the Jewish people:[26]

Temple. For Jews, the temple in Jerusalem was the center of all religious and political life. The temple (and the tabernacle before it) was supposed to be the place where God came to dwell among his people. Throughout the second temple period, Jewish identity was under threat from foreign influence, particularly hellenization. One of the ways that Jews maintained their identity was by keeping up the sacrifices, worship, and prayer at the temple. By Herod's day, there were three courts around the temple. The outer court was open to foreigners, but only Jewish men and their wives could enter the middle court. The inner court was reserved for Jewish men in a state of purity; within that space was the sanctuary, where only the priests were allowed to perform sacrifices and rituals.[27]

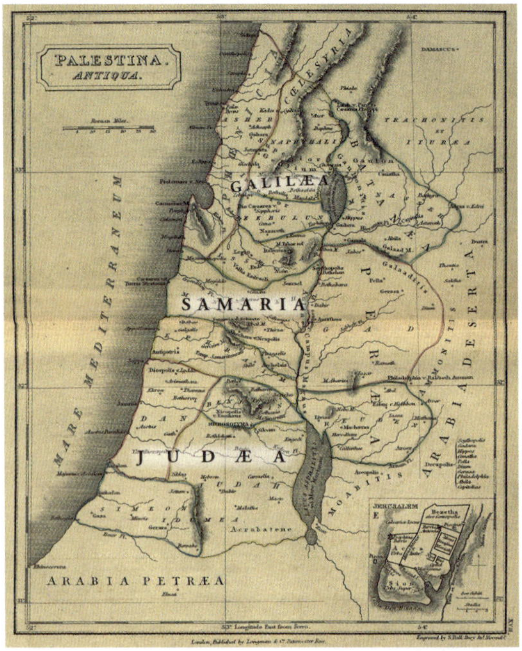

Land. When God promised Abraham that he would make of him a great nation in Genesis 12, he also promised to give Abraham land on which his people could settle and prosper. As we have seen, the Israelites conquered the land, settled it, and then were kicked off it because of their sin. But with the return from exile, Jews in this period believed that the land of Judea belonged only to God's people. It was supposed to be like a new Eden where God's people could live in a state of *shalom*. The land was a great point of tension during the second temple period because many people occupied the land—not only descendants of the tribes that Israel had conquered, but also foreign invaders. Pagan temples, Greek gymnasiums, and Roman symbols were seen as blights on the land. Jews eagerly awaited the day when God would cleanse the land of foreign influence.

Torah. Throughout a long and troubled history, Israel had learned the dangers of idolatry. In order to stay on the land, the Jewish people believed that they had to be faithful to the commands given in the Torah. The five books of the Torah provided instructions for how to worship in the temple and for the behavior that was to characterize God's people. Instruction in the Torah was offered in the temple. Torah study and observance became especially important for those Jews living outside of Judea. It set Jews apart from their pagan neighbors, marking them out as God's people.

Racial Identity. According to Jewish thinking of the time, the true people of God consisted of descendants of Abraham. They saw themselves as the only inheritors of God's promises. The Jews had been commanded not to intermarry (to prevent idolatry, Deuteronomy 7:1–5), so Ezra stressed lineage (Ezra 2:1–62) and decried intermarriage (Ezra 9–10). It is thought that Jewish-Samaritan tensions after the exile escalated into ethnic prejudice,[28] though politics and theology played a major role in their mutual contempt.[29] Moreover, the mark of a true Jewish male was circumcision, so Antiochus IV's outlawing of the practice was seen as a threat to Jewish identity. For most Jews, practicing circumcision and avoiding intermarriage were the primary ways to be set apart for God.

6. The Diaspora, the Synagogue, and the Samaritans

▸ **OBJECTIVE: You will be able to discuss the role of synagogues post-exile and how Jews and Samaritans related to one another.**

Not all Jews lived in Judea. Many chose not to return from the Babylonian exile; others were dispersed among the nations. In fact, by the first century AD there were approximately five million Jews living outside Judea, greatly outnumbering the Jews in Judea. The largest population of Jews resided in Alexandria, in Egypt, but there were many Jewish communities in other lands. These groups became known collectively as *the Diaspora*. Though they had their own distinctive practices, these groups looked to Jerusalem as their homeland and to the temple as the true house of worship.[30]

For those Jews living outside of Judea, who had no access to the temple, the study of the Torah became critically important. Sometime during the exile or soon after, Jews began gathering together in the local **synagogue**, *a Jewish meeting place for Torah study, prayer, and discussion* of issues relevant to the Jewish community.

Not all synagogues served the same function,[31] and they were not seen as a replacement for the temple, but rather as a supplement to it. Synagogues appear frequently in the New Testament. Jesus is found teaching there on more than one occasion (Luke 4:15–37, John 6:22–59), and the apostle Paul often began his missionary activity in the synagogue of whatever city he happened to be in (Acts 17:2-3).

In addition to the Diaspora Jews, there were the **Samaritans**, a people group who were likely descendants of the *Israelites from the northern kingdom who lived in Samaria and had intermarried with the Assyrians* after the conquest of the northern kingdom in 722 BC,[32] though their specific identity is hard to pin down. The New Testament is clear that Jews and Samaritans had a strong dislike for one another (Luke 9:52–54, 10:25–37; John 4:1–42).

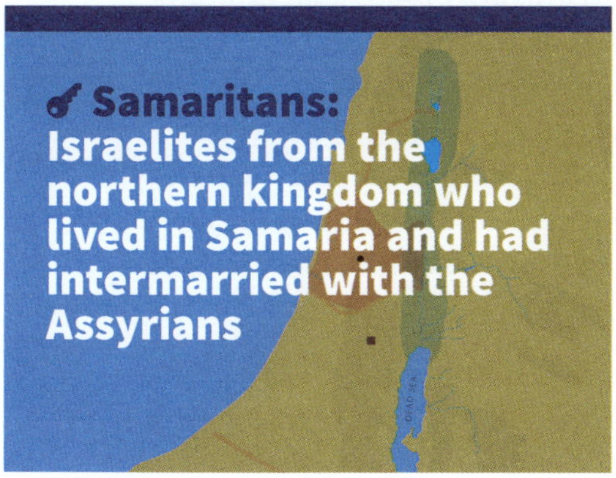

When the Jews returning from exile refused to let the Samaritans help rebuild the temple, the Samaritans built their own temple on Mount Gerizim[33] as a rival to the temple in Jerusalem. Because of this, Jews regarded them as outside of God's true people and looked at them with disdain. On the whole, the Jews in Judea held a superior and deeply prejudiced attitude toward Samaritans.

The Samaritans also hated the Jews. Some may have been among those who attempted to hinder the rebuilding of the temple and wrote letters to foreign rulers accusing the Jews of treachery against the government (Ezra 4–5). The ancient historian Josephus records that during the terrible reign of Antiochus IV, the Samaritans wrote a letter to Antiochus in which they disowned the Jews, claimed they weren't related to them, and asked Antiochus to let them dedicate their temple to Jupiter Hellenius (that is, Zeus).[34] It is no wonder that Jewish "hatred" for Samaritans was so strong "that to be called a Samaritan was a grievous insult."[35] In light of this, Jesus' actions in regard to Samaritans were countercultural. He spoke willingly and kindly to a Samaritan woman (John 4:1–42), and he told a story to Jews in which a Samaritan turned out to be the good guy (Luke 10:25–37).

7. Jewish Factions

▸ **OBJECTIVE: You will be able to list and describe the four Jewish factions that emerged during the second temple period.**

In response to the continuing pressure of hellenization and the oppression of Roman rule, the Jews splintered into at least four different groups during the second temple period—the Pharisees, Sadducees, Essenes, and Zealots.

Pharisees: The **Pharisees** were *Jewish leaders who taught strict observance of the Torah and oral tradition.* They were the largest group of leaders and were popular and respected by the common people. They resisted hellenization, stood for the old ways or traditions of Israel, and obeyed oral laws passed down from their ancestors. The Pharisees were concerned with ensuring all Jews were obeying the laws of God and live purely as God's chosen people.[36] Only then, they believed, would God come to rescue his people. In the New Testament, the Pharisees are identified numerous times as the primary adversaries of Jesus. In Matthew 23:1–36, Jesus called them out for their showy observance of traditions while being inwardly prideful, corrupt, and wicked. He called them *hypocrites* who laid heavy burdens on others but refused to carry those burdens themselves. Instead of faithfully leading Israel in obedience to God, Jesus said that the Pharisees were like the blind leading the blind.

Sadducees: In contrast to the Pharisees, the **Sadducees** were *Jewish priests and teachers from the upper classes who cooperated with the ruling powers.* They gladly worked with the Hasmoneans and Romans to maintain the peace and their own power.[37] They also held the majority on the Sanhedrin (a ruling council of priests, elders, and teachers in Jerusalem that put Jesus on trial in Mark 14:53–65).[38] We know that, unlike the Pharisees, they held only to the Torah and did not observe the oral laws and traditions.[39] They are often found in opposition to Jesus in the New Testament, and from him we learn that they did not believe in the resurrection (Matthew 22:23–46).

Essenes: The Essenes were an extreme group. In their eyes, the temple in Jerusalem had become so corrupt that they could no longer worship there, the priests were illegitimate, and the people were failing to live in obedience to God and observe the Sabbath.[40] In opposition, the Essenes left for the desert and formed communities centered around self-control, avoidance of luxury, and intense ritual. They believed themselves to be the "true Israel," the sole inheritors of God's promises to Abraham.[41] Though not mentioned in the New Testament, many scholars believe that a group of Essenes living in Qumran were responsible for producing the Dead Sea Scrolls.

Sadducees: Jewish priests and teachers from the upper classes who cooperated with the ruling powers

Zealots: The Zealots were political revolutionaries who tolerated "no king but God!" They advocated for the violent overthrow of the Romans[42] and were willing to die for their convictions. The Zealots may have arisen around the time of Jesus' birth. Up until the time of the destruction of the temple in AD 70, they were involved in numerous uprisings and skirmishes with the Romans.[43] Among them was a group who went even further—the *Sicarii*, known for carrying daggers and stabbing compromising Jews. It is possible that one of Jesus' disciples may have originally been a Zealot (Luke 6:15).

8. Literature and Theology in the Second Temple Period

▸ OBJECTIVE: **You will be able to give examples of literature from the second temple period.**

At the beginning of this chapter, we noted that there were no new revelations from God during the second temple period. However, there were numerous books being written by Jews—including 1–2 Maccabees, Judith, Tobit, Bel and the Dragon, Wisdom of Solomon, and many more. These books record the history of the Jews, tell stories about God's people in exile, or offer wisdom for living in a pagan culture. Today, these books make up the Apocrypha, which we briefly discussed in Chapter 2. We have already talked about 1–2 Maccabees. Let's consider a few other books.

The book of Tobit tells the story of two Jewish exiles from the northern Kingdom who both experience persecution—Tobit loses his job because of his faithfulness to God, while Sarah, another faithful Jew, experiences persecution from a demon that killed off her husband every time she got married (seven times). Both are righteous characters who eventually are vindicated by God through the help of an angel.[44]

The book of Susanna tells the story of a faithful Jewish woman who is falsely accused of adultery by two wicked Jewish elders trying to blackmail her. She refuses to compromise and is almost stoned, but the young prophet Daniel intervenes. The two wicked Jewish elders are exposed and Susanna is proclaimed innocent. Susanna's story is considered "one of the world's first detective stories."[45] It is included in Catholic and Orthodox Bibles as two chapters at the end of the book of Daniel.

The Trial of Susanna before the Elders, painting, c. 1500

Bel and the Dragon is another story about the prophet Daniel, in which he demonstrates the foolishness of idol worship to the Babylonian king.

In a time when God seemed silent, these stories would have encouraged the Jews to remain faithful to God in whatever setting they found themselves. These and many other books of the Apocrypha also provide an interesting look into Jewish thought during the second temple period. For example, though the Bible speaks often of angels and demons, during the second temple period, ideas about these spiritual beings and the role they play in human affairs were extensively developed.[46] Jews also held tightly to monotheism (belief in only one God) during this time. The Jews believed that the exile had been the result of their idolatry; therefore, they needed to repent and abstain from idolatry at all costs. Belief in the resurrection from the dead also became popular. Daniel 12:2 prophesies about some people being raised to life and others to destruction. It is hard to say exactly what most Jews believed during this time about resurrection, but at least some believed that all God's people would be raised together when God redeemed Israel. However, no one was expecting any one person to rise from the dead before that time.

In addition to the Apocrypha, several other important writings from the second temple period have survived. Philo, a Jewish philosopher living in Egypt, attempted to integrate Greek and Jewish ideas in his writings. The Jewish historian Flavius Josephus wrote much of the history of the second temple period. Strangely, he argued that the emperor Vespasian was actually the world ruler that the prophet Daniel predicted in Daniel 2:44, the messiah figure that Israel had been waiting for.[47] It was also during this time that the Dead Sea Scrolls were produced. Together, these sources provide invaluable information for our understanding of Jewish thought and life during the second temple period.

9. The Hopes of Israel

▸ **OBJECTIVE: You will be able to restate the five hopes of the Jewish people during the second temple period.**

Much of the Jewish writing from the second temple period is full of expectation and hope. But what exactly were the Jews hoping for? They hoped for at least five things:[48]

Salvation from their enemies. Jews who were familiar with the Scriptures knew that God had rescued his people from slavery to the Egyptians. They hoped that God would rescue them again—this time from their Roman oppressors. Though Rome seemed unbeatable, the Jews knew that the prophet Daniel had spoken of four kingdoms, all of which would be crushed. Ultimately, "one like a son of man" would be given all power and authority to rule over all nations (Daniel 7:13–14). The prophet Zechariah had also spoken of the coming of the Lord when Jerusalem would be raised up and Israel's enemies would be judged (Zechariah 14).

The establishment of a state of shalom. Long ago, God promised Abraham that the land of Canaan would be home to his descendants. Yet, for most of the second temple period, it was a battleground. Judea changed hands numerous times—first Babylon, then Persia, then Greece, and now Rome. What the average Jew would have most wanted was shalom, including freedom to go about one's business and to worship God without fear of oppression or brutality. One day, they hoped, God would grant them that peace.

The arrival of God's kingdom and rule over Israel and the world. The Old Testament kings of Israel and Judah had failed to lead the nation well. Now, the Jews hoped for a true king from the line of David who would rule with justice and faithfulness. Additionally, they believed that when God finally arrived and established his rule, his kingdom would extend far beyond Israel. God would rule over *all* nations. And with a true king ruling in Jerusalem, Israel would be placed at the head of all the nations.

The forgiveness of sins. People like Ezra, Nehemiah, and Mattathias, and groups like the Pharisees and the Essenes were all concerned about Israel's disobedience to God. They knew that Israel had been exiled due to unfaithfulness to God's covenant. God's people were failing to be the people they were created to be—people who truly loved God and others. Israel had a sin problem. Jews believed that when God arrived, he would deal with their sin, cleansing them from their wickedness and giving them new hearts so that they could live freely and faithfully in his presence.

A messiah who would lead Israel. The word *messiah* refers to *the Lord's anointed*. It should be noted that not all Jews expected a messiah, and those who did had different ideas about what the messiah would actually be like. It seems that for many Jews of the time, the particular kind of messiah they wanted was one who would be a military figure, one who would ride into Jerusalem and crush the Romans in battle.[49]

These hopes sustained the faith of many Jews through the unpredictable and chaotic period of the second temple. Meanwhile, God never abandoned his people, but continued to work in hidden ways.

10. Conclusion

The history we have surveyed in this chapter provides important background for understanding the next great act in the biblical drama. Israel's story was still waiting for a satisfying ending. The period of 400 years from Malachi to John the Baptist was a very discouraging time for God's people. When the Jews returned from Babylon to rebuild the temple in Jerusalem, many hoped that the moment when all would be set right had finally arrived, yet the return from exile didn't work out like they had expected. As nation after nation ruled over Judea, Jews faced mounting pressure to conform to the dominant culture. Antiochus IV's rule sent the nation into crisis. Some would have thought that Judah Maccabee's cleansing of the temple was the beginning of God's promises finally being fulfilled. However, the Maccabees soon proved themselves to be poor, corrupt leaders. When Rome took over, the situation seemed all the more hopeless.

God had promised to be faithful to his covenant with Abraham, Isaac, and Jacob, but where was he? When would he fulfill his promises? When would Israel be rescued from oppression? When would they be free to live and worship in peace? Jews living all over the world hoped that soon they would get some answers. In the meantime, they tried to remain faithful to God, but how to do so and prepare for God's coming were divisive issues. The Pharisees thought it best to meticulously obey the Torah and the traditions while resisting the foreign powers. The Sadducees tried to get on with the dominant culture as best as they could to maintain peace and comfort. The Essenes decided to withdraw from society altogether, while the Zealots used violence to try to overthrow their oppressors.

In the midst of all this, Jewish authors sought to encourage the people to remember God's past faithfulness and to demonstrate how God would vindicate his people. Moreover, many doctrines arose to help explain what was going on and to affirm that God was still sovereign. Living in this time certainly required great endurance and hope.

Many people today can relate. The world seems to be trapped in a hopeless cycle of violence and chaos. When we look at what is going on in the world, it is hard not to get discouraged. Where is God? Why doesn't he do something? And so, people today look for a messiah-like figure who will arise and put everything right. They turn to political leaders or join causes they think have the answer, but none ultimately succeed. Is there any hope?

In the next chapter, we'll see that God's apparent silence during the second temple period was not a sign that he had abandoned his people. Indeed, God would be faithful to his covenant promises, save Israel, and defeat the true enemy. But his work wouldn't look anything like what God's people had expected. And it wouldn't come on their timeline. Instead, at just the right time, "God sent forth his Son . . . to redeem" (Galatians 4:4–5).

The promised one who would crush the head of the serpent was about to arrive. And his coming would be good news not just for the Jews in the first century, but also for everyone who's ever lived, including you and me.

ENDNOTES

[1]Not all scholars agree on the interpretation of the beasts given here. Though the first three beasts seem to be identified in the text, the fourth beast is not. The book of Daniel is not written in chronological order. Chapters 2 and 7 both occur during the Babylonian period, and scholars see some similarity between the four kingdoms of the statue in chapter 2:31–35 and the four beasts in chapter 7:1–8. In addition, the ram and the goat in chapter 8:1–14 are seen as comparable to the second and third beasts from chapter 7. The assumption of Rome as the fourth beast comes from the fact that in chapter 2:39–40, the kingdoms come one right after another. As Rome was the next great world empire after Greece, it is highly probable that it is the fourth beast. Some, however, separate the Medo-Persian empire so that the four beasts are identified as Babylon, Media, Persia, and Greece. See Joyce G. Baldwin, *Daniel: An Introduction and Commentary* (Downers Grove, IL: InterVarsity Press, 1978), 136–62.

[2]Craig G. Bartholomew and Michael W. Goheen, *The Drama of Scripture: Finding Our Place in the Biblical Story* (Grand Rapids, MI: Baker Academic, 2004), 110–11.

[3]The Scriptures do not usually advocate the dissolution of marriages. Jesus' teaching in the New Testament suggests that marriage was intended as a lifelong, faithful union (Matthew 5:31–32, 19:3–9; Mark 10:2–12). Paul says believing spouses should *not* divorce unbelieving spouses who consent to live with them (1 Corinthians 7:10–16), contrary to what happened in the book of Ezra.

[4]Andreas J. Köstenberger, L. Scott Kellum, and Charles L. Quarles, *The Cradle, the Cross, and the Crown: An Introduction to the New Testament* (Nashville: B&H Publishing Group, 2009), 59.

[5]F. F. Bruce, *New Testament History* (New York: Doubleday, 1969), 2–3.

[6]Shaye J. D. Cohen, *From the Maccabees to the Mishnah*, 3rd ed. (Louisville: KY, Westminster John Knox Press, 2014), 2.

[7]Cohen, 2.

[8]James C. VanderKam, *An Introduction to Early Judaism* (Grand Rapids, MI: Eerdmans, 2001), 14.

[9]John R. Bartlett, "1 Maccabees," in Michael D. Coogan, ed., *The New Oxford Annotated Apocrypha: New Revised Standard Version*, 5th ed. (New York: Oxford University Press, 2018), 205–207.

[10]What follows is described in two books from the Apocrypha—1 and 2 Maccabees.

[11]Bartlett, "1 Maccabees," 207.

[12]VanderKam, 20.

[13]VanderKam, 20.

[14]Köstenberger, Kellum, and Quarles, 68.

[15]Baldwin, *Daniel*, 172–73, 191–92.

[16]Bartholomew and Goheen, 120–21.

[17]Bartholomew and Goheen, 121.

[18]Köstenberger, Kellum, and Quarles, 70–73.

[19]Bartholomew and Goheen, 121.

[20] Köstenberger, Kellum, and Quarles, 74.

[21]Rodney Stark, *The Triumph of Christianity: How the Jesus Movement Became the World's Largest Religion* (New York: HarperCollins, 2011), 34–35.

[22]Köstenberger, Kellum, and Quarles, 138.

[23]Köstenberger, Kellum, and Quarles, 77.

[24]R. Alan Street, *Caesar and the Sacrament: Baptism: A Rite of Resistance* (Eugene, OR: Cascade Books, 2018), 1, 19–21.

[25]N. T. Wright, *The Day the Revolution Began: Reconsidering the Meaning of Jesus's Crucifixion* (New York: HarperCollins, 2016), 19, 53–55, 58.

[26]N. T. Wright, *The New Testament and the People of God* (Minneapolis, MN: Fortress Press, 1992), 224–32.

[27]VanderKam, *Early Judaism*, 202.

[28]Wright, *The New Testament and the People of God*, 230–32.

[29] Isidore Singer and Cyrus Adler, *The Jewish Encyclopedia*, Vol. 10, (Funk & Wagnalls Company, New York, 1906), 669–681.

[30]"Diaspora: Judaism," Encyclopedia Britannica, https://www.britannica.com/topic/Diaspora-Judaism.

[31]Cohen, 110–14.

[32]"Samaritan: Judaism," Encyclopedia Britannica, https://www.britannica.com/topic/Samaritan.

[33]Stark, 36.

[34]Flavius Josephus, *The Antiquities of the Jews in Josephus: The Complete Works*, trans. by William Whiston, A.M. (Nashville: Thomas Nelson, 1998), 389.

[35]Craig A. Evans, "Introduction: Finding a Context for Jesus," in *The Missing Jesus: Rabbinic Judaism and the New Testament*, eds. Bruce Chilton, Craig A. Evans, and Jacob Neusner (Leiden: Brill, 2002), 2. As quoted in Stark, *The Triumph of Christianity*, 36.

[36]Wright, *The New Testament and the People of God*, 181–90.

[37]Bartholomew and Goheen, 126.

[38]Köstenberger, Kellum, and Quarles, 95.

[39]"Sadducee: Jewish Sect," Encyclopedia Britannica, https://www.britannica.com/topic/Sadducee.

[40]Cohen, 160.

[41]Bartholomew and Goheen, 125–26.

[42]Cohen, 163–65.

[43]Stark, 42–43.

[44]VanderKam, 69–71.

[45]Amy C. Merril Willis, "Susanna: Contents and Genre," in Michael D. Coogan, ed., *The New Oxford Annotated Apocrypha*, 197.

[46]Cohen, 81.

[47]N. T. Wright, *Jesus and the Victory of God* (Minneapolis, MN: Fortress Press, 1996), 65, 199, 500–01.

[48]Wright, *The New Testament and the People of God*, 280–338.

[49]Stark, 44–45.

10

Act 4: Redemption Accomplished—Jesus

1. The Incarnation of Jesus

▶ **OBJECTIVE:** You will be able to conclude three ways the Incarnation is significant.

The history we surveyed in the last chapter sets the stage for Act 4 of the Bible's metanarrative: redemption, accomplished through Jesus. After roughly 400 years of apparent silence from God, an angel named *Gabriel* appeared to announce two pregnancies. The first announcement was to a priest named *Zechariah* about his wife, Elizabeth. The other announcement was to a woman named *Mary* and her fiancé, Joseph. Gabriel said to Mary:

> "Do not be afraid, Mary, for you have found favor with God. And behold, you will conceive in your womb and bear a son, and you shall call his name Jesus. He will be great and will be called the Son of the Most High. And the Lord God will give to him the throne of his father David, and he will reign over the house of Jacob forever, and of his kingdom there will be no end." —Luke 1:30–33

This promise echoed the great hopes of Israel for a righteous leader who would establish God's kingdom. Gabriel explained that Mary would become pregnant, despite being a virgin, through the power of the Holy Spirit. She humbly accepted God's will for her. "Behold, I am the servant of the Lord; let it be to me according to your word" (Luke 1:38). Soon after, with Joseph at her side, Mary gave birth to Jesus in a stable in Bethlehem, fulfilling the prophecy of Micah 5:2. (Elizabeth had given birth to Jesus' cousin John a few months earlier; he would fulfill prophecies given in Isaiah 40:3 and Malachi 3:1.)

Jesus' birth was the **Incarnation**, *the action of the eternally divine Son of God becoming a human being.* Consider three ways the Incarnation is significant:

The Incarnation is essential for salvation. Early church teachers and councils emphasized that Jesus had to become human so we could be saved. According to Athanasius of Alexandria, the Incarnation is the "heart of Christianity."[1] Though Jesus was the Creator and Lord of all the earth, he "emptied himself, by taking on the form of a servant, being born in the likeness of men" (Philippians 2:5–11). Jesus is both fully God and fully human. Gregory of Nazianzus famously said of Jesus, "That which he has not taken up he has not saved." In other words, Jesus had to take on humanity in order to save human beings.[2] He suffered "in the flesh" (1 Peter 4:1) so "that he might bring us to God" the Father (1 Peter 3:18).

The Incarnation affirms that creation is good. When Jesus became human, this confirmed that our problem is not that we are human, but that we are not human enough (because our humanity is corrupted and broken by sin). Jesus was tempted, as we are, yet he never sinned (Hebrews 4:15). The Incarnation means that matter—our bodies and all of creation—is good. Jesus didn't come to save us *from* the physical world but to redeem us so that we might truly bear his image in this world.

The Incarnation means that Jesus suffers with us. John 1:14 says that "the Word [Jesus] became flesh and dwelt among us." *The Message* paraphrase puts it this way, "The Word became flesh and blood, and moved into the neighborhood." Jesus, though he is God, did not remain aloof but came among us to experience what we experience. He got tired

(John 4:6), he needed sleep (Matthew 8:24), he needed to eat (Matthew 4:2, 21:18). He experienced joy and sorrow (John 15:11, Matthew 26:37).[3] Jesus came to be with us, to share in our pain and to be the personal presence of God among us.

2. Jesus' Announcement of the Kingdom of God

▸ **OBJECTIVE: You will be able to relate Jesus' ministry to the gospel and the kingdom of God.**

Jesus began his public ministry around age 30. His first act was to get baptized in the Jordan River by his cousin, the prophet John the Baptist. Why was John baptizing people? John's baptism would remind Jews of the Exodus story where God saved his people from slavery by bringing them through the waters of the Red Sea and across the Jordan River into the Promised Land. John was hinting that a new exodus was at hand.[4] God's salvation for Israel was about to appear.

kingdom of God: the just and peaceful rule of God over all creation

All four Gospels (Matthew, Mark, Luke, and John) tell how Jesus came to be baptized by John. When Jesus came up from the water after being baptized, the heavens opened up and "the Holy Spirit descended on him in bodily form, like a dove. Then a voice from heaven called out, 'You are my beloved Son; with you I am well pleased'" (Luke 3:22). The people watching this event might have been reminded of the Roman ritual of using the flight of birds to choose their kings.[5] This action and the Father's words to Jesus proclaimed that Jesus was the King who would bring salvation through the Holy Spirit's power.[6] Following his baptism, Jesus spent 40 days in the wilderness, where he was tempted by the devil (this story should remind us of the 40 years that the nation of Israel spent wandering in the wilderness). Satan tempted Jesus to turn stones into bread, to jump off the temple and let the angels save him, and to worship him in exchange for all the kingdoms of the world. Jesus rejected the temptations by using the Scriptures (Matthew 4:1–11). He left the desert empowered to fulfill his mission.

Jesus began his ministry by announcing the kingdom of God. "The time is fulfilled, and the kingdom of God is at hand; repent and believe in the gospel" (Mark 1:15). To understand the purpose of Jesus' life, death, and resurrection, we need to know what Jesus meant by *the kingdom of God* and *the gospel*. Let's first be clear about what these words do not mean. The kingdom of God (sometimes called *the kingdom of heaven*) does not refer to a place in the clouds where people play harps and sing in an eternal choir, nor is the gospel simply a message about how we get to heaven when we die.

The **kingdom of God** refers to *the just and peaceful rule of God over all creation*.[7] The kingdom of God is where God is worshipped, there is justice, and people live in peace (see Isaiah 40–66).

When God's kingdom comes, it will mean for Israel "the end of exile"; but it also means the "defeat of evil," the forgiveness of sins, and the rescue of all creation from its bondage to sin and corruption.[8] The **gospel** (Greek, *euangelion*) means *good news,* specifically *the good news that Jesus is Lord and that through him, salvation and forgiveness are available to all.* The kingdom of God has arrived in Jesus (Matthew 4:23), God reigns (Isaiah 52:7), and all who trust in Jesus will be saved from the penalty for sin (Acts 10:34–43).

To spread the good news, Jesus called 12 disciples (which reminds us of the 12 tribes of Israel). He enlisted them to spread the message of God's kingdom.

3. Jesus' Identity

OBJECTIVE: **You will be able to contrast popular views of Jesus' identity with Jesus' own claim to be the Messiah.**

There are many views about who Jesus was. Some scholars view Jesus as a traveling philosopher who said wise things and gave advice for living a good life. Others view Jesus as a charismatic faith healer who had a mystical experience and sought to bring God's healing to others. Some see Jesus as just one more in a long string of Jewish prophets who announced the end of the world. Still others see Jesus as a social reformer whose main goal was to bring equality between rich and poor, the powerful and the oppressed, and men and women.[9]

Jesus certainly offered much wisdom, healed many people, called people to repentance, and taught in a way that valued the needy. However, none of these views can adequately account for the unusual things that Jesus said and did. Jesus saw himself as more than all of these things. He saw himself as the Messiah, the "Son of Man" who would rescue Israel and the world from the bondage of sin and corruption. Jesus' claim to be the Messiah entailed at least three roles:

1. **Prophet:** As a prophet, Jesus announced that God remained faithful to his covenant promises and that the people of Israel needed to repent. They needed to stop trusting in their own righteousness and turn to God (Matthew 4:17, 21:11; Luke 4:18–24; John 5:19–20, 30).

2. **Priest:** As a priest, Jesus offered himself as the sacrifice for our sins and he advocates for us before God the Father (John 1:29, Ephesians 5:2, Hebrews 7).

3. **King:** As a king, Jesus brought the kingdom of God to earth and will one day return to bring it to completion (1 John 3:2). He is the King of kings and Lord of lords, to whom all authority has been given (Matthew 28:18, Hebrews 2:8–9, Revelation 19:16).

On multiple occasions Jesus claimed to be this Messiah, the very God of Israel himself. Whenever he did this, he raised the anger of the Jewish leaders. When Jesus forgave the sins of a paralyzed man, the teachers of the law reacted with anger, "Who can forgive sins but God alone?" (Mark 2:7). They rightly understood that forgiving sins was God's job. In a dispute with the Jews, Jesus called himself "I AM" (this is the name by which God revealed himself to Moses), after which some people tried to stone him (John 8:58–59).

On another occasion, Jesus asked his disciples who they thought he was. Peter boldly answered, "You are the Christ, the Son of the living God" (Matthew 16:16). (The word *Christ* in Greek means *anointed* and was another way to refer to the Messiah.) When Jesus was on trial for blasphemy, he called himself the "Son of Man," claiming the power and authority of the Messiah (Daniel 7, Luke 22:66–71). All four Gospels are unanimous in stating that Jesus was more than just a prophet or healer. They affirm he was the God of Israel and Lord of all.

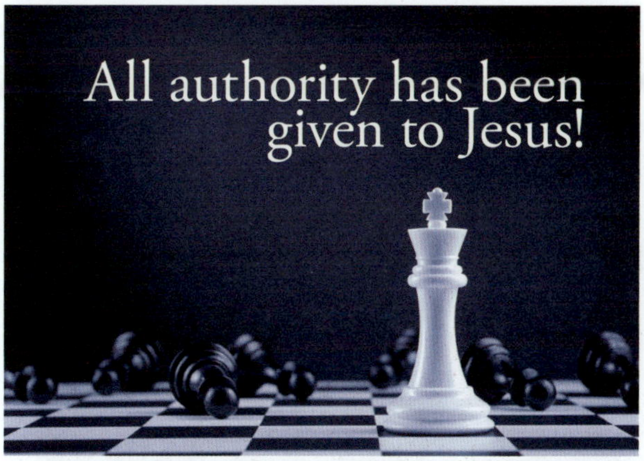

The violent reactions that Jesus got whenever he claimed to be God help explain why he often told his disciples not to tell anyone that he was the Messiah (Matthew 16:20, Mark 8:30). The people of Israel were expecting a messiah, but they didn't expect one like Jesus. They were hoping for someone who would overthrow the Romans and reestablish Israel's sovereignty. Instead, Jesus confronted the people of Israelites for trusting in their own attempts in righteous deeds.

4. Jesus' Parables

▸ **OBJECTIVE: You will be able to explain four lessons Jesus taught about the kingdom of God through parables and to interpret the parable of the tenants.**

The announcement of the kingdom was accompanied by parables. Jesus told parables to help people understand what the kingdom was about. For those who refused to believe that Jesus was the Messiah, the parables would hide the truth (Matthew 13:10–17). Biblical scholars Craig Bartholomew and Michael Goheen identify four lessons Jesus taught about the kingdom of God through the parables in Mark 4 and Matthew 13:

1. **The kingdom does not come all at once.** The Jews wanted the kingdom to come right away. Jesus taught that the kingdom was arriving through him, but that it was not yet fully realized.
2. **In the present, the kingdom does not come with irresistible power.** The Jews wanted to crown Jesus as a king, hoping that he would lead them in victory over their Roman oppressors. But Jesus taught that the kingdom would be characterized by humility, service, and loving and forgiving our enemies.

3. **The final judgment of the kingdom is reserved for the future.** The Jews wished for judgment to fall quickly on their enemies, but Jesus taught that such judgment would come at the very end. In the meantime, the faithful needed to imitate Jesus and faithfully work for God's kingdom.

4. **The full revelation of the kingdom is postponed to allow many to enter it during the present age.** The Jews hoped for a savior for Israel, but Jesus' kingdom was for the whole world, including non-Jews, slaves, and the unlikeliest of sinners.[10]

The parables also provided a significant warning to the leaders of Israel, calling them to repentance and faithfulness to God. For example, in Mark 12:1–12, Jesus told a story about a master who planted a vineyard and hired some farmers to take care of it. When harvest time came, the master sent a servant back to the vineyard to collect some of the harvest. But the farmers beat up the servant and sent him away empty-handed. The master sent other servants, but the farmers beat and killed them. Finally, the master sent his own son. The farmers, envious of the son, decided to kill him too, thinking that this would secure their possession of the vineyard. What would the owner do? Jesus said the master would come to bring judgment on the farmers.

Jesus' listeners understood his warning. The owner of the vineyard was God, the farmers were the leaders of Israel, the servants represented the prophets of the Old Testament, and the son was Jesus himself. God chose Israel as his special people, caring for them (Isaiah 5:1–7). He made a covenant with them and entrusted them with a mission, but they went their own way. He sent many prophets to Israel, but they were ignored, persecuted, and killed (Matthew 23:37). The Father even sent his Son, Jesus, but the leaders of Israel were going to kill him too (Mark 9:30–32). The message was clear: if Israel refused to listen to Jesus, they would face judgment. After Jesus told this parable, Mark says that the leaders of Israel started looking for a way to kill Jesus because they knew the parable was about them.[11]

Teaching in parables was just one way that Jesus proclaimed his message—the kingdom of God was near, and it was time for Israel to repent and believe the good news about Jesus.

5. Jesus' Miracles

▸ **OBJECTIVE: You will be able to discuss two miracles Jesus accomplished and what they were a sign of.**

As a sign of the kingdom and confirmation that he was the Messiah, Jesus performed many miracles. In the Old Testament, God saved the people of Israel from slavery in Egypt by performing great signs and wonders—a series of plagues, parting the Red Sea so the Israelites could cross safely, and providing food from heaven. Through the times of judges, kings, and prophets, God continued to show his power, defeating false gods and working miracles. In the New Testament, Jesus showed God's power and freed many people from demon possession, blindness, and crippling diseases. While he was in his hometown in Nazareth in the synagogue, Jesus unrolled a scroll and read the words:

> The Spirit of the Lord is upon me, because he has anointed me
> to proclaim good news to the poor.
> He has sent me to proclaim liberty to the captives and recovering
> of sight to the blind, to set at liberty those who are oppressed,
> to proclaim the year of the Lord's favor. –Luke 4:18–19

Then he announced, "Today this Scripture has been fulfilled in your hearing" (Luke 4:21). He proclaimed that the kingdom of God had come. Jesus would bring this kingdom with great signs and wonders. When John the Baptist began to doubt that Jesus was really the Christ, the Messiah, Jesus pointed to his miracles: "The blind receive their sight and the lame walk, lepers are cleansed and the deaf hear, and the dead are raised up, and the poor have good news preached to them" (Matthew 11:2–5).

Let's consider two of Jesus' miracles in more detail. In Luke 9:10–17, Jesus took his disciples out into the wilderness to get some rest, but the crowds followed him. Jesus had compassion on them and healed many people. As the day drew on, the disciples urged Jesus to send the crowds away so they could get something to eat. Jesus, however, took five loaves of bread and two fish and gave thanks for them. Miraculously, this small meal multiplied to feed well over 5,000 people. Jesus' miracle here prefigured his own offering of himself, giving his body and blood to satisfy our spiritual hunger and granting us access to eternal life (John 6:48–59).

One of Jesus' most famous miracles was the raising of Lazarus. The story is told in John 11. Jesus' good friend Lazarus had died and been in the tomb for three days. Like many Jews during this time, Lazarus' sister Martha believed that Lazarus would be raised together with other Jews at the end of time.[12] Jesus, however, offered something more immediate. Jesus told Martha, "I am the resurrection and the life" (John 11:23–26). He called her to have faith in him. Yet Jesus was not unmoved by her suffering or that of others who were grieving for Lazarus. He was deeply moved; he was shown Lazarus' tomb and he wept (John 11:33–35). Then, calling out to his Father, Jesus raised Lazarus from the dead. This miracle caused many to believe, but Israel's leaders were jealous of Jesus' popularity and plotted to put him to death.

These miracles were offered as a sign that the kingdom of God had come at last through Jesus the Messiah. Through his miracles, Jesus demonstrated God's love for the world and his power over sickness and death.

6. Jesus' Teaching

▸ **OBJECTIVE: You will be able to name Jesus' most famous ethical teaching.**

▸ **OBJECTIVE: You will be able to list and describe the eight categories of people that Jesus referred to as blessed in the beatitudes.**

In addition to his parables and miracles, Jesus' ethical teaching became famous. An *ethical teaching* refers to *an instruction about what is right and wrong.* It involves our thoughts, words, and actions. Jesus' teachings are not just about how to be a better person or how to have a happy life. They are about following God with our whole heart.

View of the Sea of Galilee from the Mount of Beatitudes, Israel

Jesus' most famous teaching is the Sermon on the Mount recorded in Matthew 5–7. He began with eight beatitudes, or blessings. According to Jesus, the following people are blessed:

1. **"The poor in spirit"** may refer to the poor and to those who are humble before God and look to him for protection.
2. **"Those who mourn"** refers to those who grieve, often in the midst of a difficult situation.
3. **"The meek"** refers to those who have a gentle spirit and are not arrogant or oppressive; they keep their strength under control.
4. **"Those who hunger and thirst for righteousness"** are people who long for God to set things right.
5. **"The merciful"** describes those who have a generous attitude and do not "gloat over others' shortcomings"; they do not take revenge.
6. **"The pure in heart"** are those who are pure inwardly, not just outwardly.
7. **"The peacemakers"** refers to those who reconcile and bring others together.
8. **"Those who are persecuted for righteousness' sake"** describes disciples who suffer because of their willingness to follow God's ways.[13]

Jesus went on to say that he had come not to abolish Old Testament law, but to fulfill it. Jesus' teachings—about anger, lust, divorce, and revenge—all intensify the Old Testament commands. They warn us not to think that we are fine if we are just sticking to the letter of the law. For example, Jesus said that hating someone is a way of murdering them in your heart (Matthew 5:21–22). Jesus was, and is, concerned with more than just our outward actions.

Jesus taught people to love their enemies, give generously to those in need, pray, and fast. He also warned against doing these things for the sake of getting attention. Rather than accumulating the praise of others on earth, we should store up treasures in heaven. Because God is a good Father, Jesus taught that we need not worry but can trust God for our material needs.

Famously, Jesus warned "Judge not, that you be not judged" (Matthew 7:1). People sometimes take this to mean no one can judge them for what they do or say. But Jesus doesn't say that we can never say that something is wrong; he warns that "with the judgment you pronounce you will be judged, and with the measure you use it will be measured to you" (Matthew 7:2). Jesus warns us against pointing out the speck in others people's eyes while ignoring the log that may be in our own eye (Matthew 7:3).

Jesus encouraged people to live by the Golden Rule, treating others the way we want to be treated (Matthew 7:12). Above all, Jesus wanted his listeners to understand that love for God and others is most important (Matthew 22:34–40).

Jesus' ethical teachings may seem overwhelming, but he himself told his disciples that they could not keep his commands or bear fruit unless they stayed close to him (John 15:4–17). Scripture is clear that following Jesus' teaching and bearing fruit is accomplished through the work of the Holy Spirit, who transforms us (Philippians 2:13, Galatians 5:22–23; more on this in Chapter 14).

7. The Crucifixion of Jesus

▸ **OBJECTIVE: You will be able to explain two aspects of Jesus' redemptive work on the cross.**

Jesus' parables, miracles, teachings, and claims to be God did not sit well with the Jewish leaders. They plotted his death. After three years of ministry, Jesus was betrayed by one of his own disciples, brought before the Jewish leaders on the false charge of blasphemy, and put to death by the authority of the Roman ruler Pontius Pilate. The death of Jesus is the central event in the gospel narratives. Jesus died willingly, recognizing his role in God's plan of redemption (see Matthew 20:20–28; Mark 8:31, 10:45, 14:21; Luke 20:9–19; John 10:18).

Jesus was put to death by crucifixion (related to the word *excruciating*). According to the Roman statesman Cicero, crucifixion was "a most cruel and disgusting punishment," a death reserved only for the lowest of criminals.[14] The convicted person would be severely beaten and then nailed or tied to a cross. Crucifixion was designed to prolong suffering and pain. Victims would sometimes hang on the cross for days. It was a death by which the Romans hoped to utterly degrade their victims and crush any spirit of resistance.[15]

Above Jesus' cross, the Romans placed a sign that read, "This is Jesus, the King of the Jews" (Matthew 27:37). It was intended as a cruel mockery, but ironically it communicated the truth about who Jesus was. A Roman centurion standing by recognized the truth, "Truly this man was the Son of God!" (Mark 15:39). Jesus was Israel's king, Lord of the universe, and yet he willingly died. In response to those who mocked and tortured him, Jesus cried out, "Father, forgive them, for they know not what they do" (Luke 23:34). He also felt the full weight of separation from the Father when he cried out, "My God, my God, why have you forsaken me?" (Matthew 27:46). After an unusually short time on the cross, Jesus cried out, "It is finished," and then he died (John 19:30). His work was done. He had accomplished what he had come to do.

What exactly did Jesus accomplish on the cross? According to Scripture, the cross is the place where Jesus accomplished our redemption (Ephesians 1:7, Colossians 1:14, Titus 2:14, Hebrews 9:11–15). **Redemption** means *to be rescued from the consequences of sin through the sacrificial death of Jesus.* In Jesus, we have been rescued from sin and delivered to a new life in Christ.

Let's talk about two important aspects of Jesus' redemptive work on the cross. First, on the cross, Jesus died as our substitute, the sacrifice for our sins, receiving the punishment that we rightly deserve (Romans 3:23–28, 8:3). According to Scripture, our sins have put us in debt, and the consequence of sin that must be paid is death (Romans 6:23). However, through his death on the cross, Jesus canceled "the record of debt that stood against us" (Colossians 2:14). He "bore our sins in his body on the tree, that we might die to sin and live to righteousness. By his wounds you have been healed" (1 Peter 2:24). When Jesus died on the cross, God himself suffered the just penalty for sin on our behalf.

Second, on the cross, Jesus defeated the enemies that held us in bondage. According to Romans 6, we were slaves under the power of sin and death. These powers held us back from being the people we were intended to be—people who truly love God and others. On the cross, Jesus did battle with the powers that held us captive. Jesus died on the cross as our substitute by taking the full guilt of human evil on himself and atoning for it so we could be forgiven and freed to live new lives in relationship with God (Colossians 2:13–15).

8. The Resurrection of Jesus

▸ **OBJECTIVE: You will be able to respond to skeptical objections to the resurrection.**

▸ **OBJECTIVE: You will be able to give the most plausible explanation for the disciples' transformation.**

The disciples expected Jesus to be the one who would redeem Israel (Luke 24:21) and overthrow the Romans. When Jesus died, their hopes were dashed. After Jesus' crucifixion, we find his disciples hiding in an upper room dejected, and confused. And yet, within a few years, Christianity spread all over the Roman empire. What caused the change?

The only reasonable explanation is the one the Gospels themselves provide. Jesus arose from the dead! The gospel writers record that after three days, Jesus miraculously came out of the grave (Matthew 28:1–10, Mark 16:1–8, Luke 24:1–12, John 20:1–10). Several women who had come to the tomb found the stone rolled away and the tomb empty. An angel told them Jesus had risen, and then commissioned them to go and share the good news with the other disciples. Jesus appeared first to Mary Magdalene and then to the eleven disciples (John 20:11–29). He calmed their fears, reassured them of his reality, and conquered their doubts. In his resurrection, Jesus showed that the powers of evil had no power over him. Jesus was stronger than death.

Yet many people in Jesus' day were skeptical. Some Jewish people believed they would be resurrected at the end of the world, but the idea of a single person rising from the dead in the middle of history was nonsense. Today, many people doubt that miracles are possible, so the resurrection is seen as absurd. Throughout history, skeptics have offered several alternatives to explain the resurrection.

One early theory was that the disciples had stolen the body (see Matthew 28:12–13). But is it really plausible to believe the disciples, who all fled when Jesus was captured, suddenly became fearless warriors who overpowered a band of Roman soldiers and stole Jesus' body? It does not seem likely. Others have argued that Jesus did not really die on the cross; rather, he only swooned and was later revived by the cool air of the tomb. But medical evidence is strongly against this. And, is it likely that a weak and mutilated Jesus would have convinced anyone that he was worthy of worship? Besides, his death was verified by Roman soldiers, who pierced his side with a spear just to make sure. Still others have suggested the disciples only hallucinated—they thought they were seeing Jesus alive from the dead, but it was only a dream. However, it is rare for more than one person to have the same hallucination. Yet after his resurrection, Jesus was seen by groups of people on several occasions. Once, he was even seen by over 500 people at the same time (1 Corinthians 15:6), making it extremely unlikely it was a hallucination.

The most plausible explanation for the disciples' transformation is that Jesus actually rose from the dead, as the Bible records. Jesus showed that sin and death had no power over him. The resurrection was a life-changing, world-altering event. The cross is only good news if Jesus didn't stay dead. In fact, Paul argues in 1 Corinthians 15:17 that if Jesus didn't rise from the dead, then our faith is worthless and we are still in sin. Pastor Tim Keller summed up what the resurrection means for us:

> If Jesus rose from the dead, then you have to accept all he said; if he didn't rise from the dead, then why worry about any of what he said? . . . That is how the first hearers felt who heard reports of the resurrection. They knew that if it was true it meant we can't live our lives any way we want. It also meant we don't have to be afraid of anything, not Roman swords, not cancer, nothing. If Jesus rose from the dead, it changes everything.[16]

9. The Ascension of Jesus

▸ OBJECTIVE: **You will be able to analyze two major implications of Jesus' ascension.**

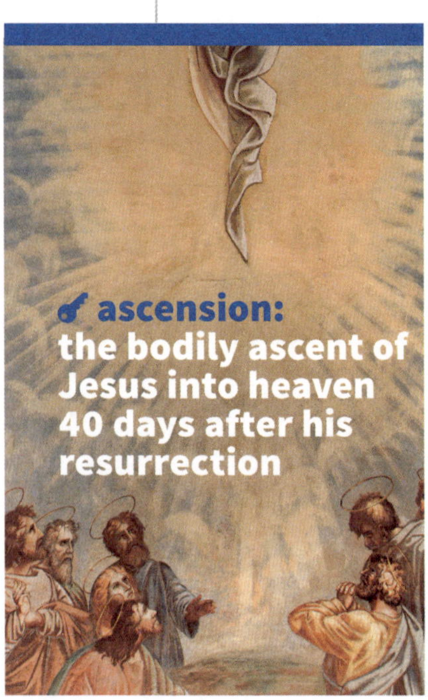

For many people, the resurrection is the last great event in the life of Jesus. But we must not overlook the **ascension**, which was *the bodily ascent of Jesus into heaven 40 days after his resurrection.*

Forty days after his resurrection, Jesus was with his disciples on the Mount of Olives. After blessing them and promising to return one day, he instructed them to wait for the coming of the Holy Spirit, after which they were to preach the good news "'in Jerusalem and in all Judea and Samaria, and to the end of the earth.' And when he had said these things, as they were looking on, he was lifted up, and a cloud took him out of their sight" (Acts 1:8–11) or as recorded in Luke, "he parted from them and was carried up into heaven" (Luke 24:50–51).

This is not just a footnote to the story of Jesus. The ascension has two major implications.[17] First, before ascending to heaven, Jesus announced, "All authority in heaven and earth has been given to me" (Matthew 28:18). Jesus is now sitting at the right hand of the Father where he rules and reigns over the whole earth (Ephesians 1:20–23). Of course, not everyone recognizes that Jesus is the King. That is why Jesus commissioned his disciples to spread the message of the gospel throughout all the earth. He commissioned them to "make disciples of all nations, baptizing them in the name of the Father and of the Son and of the Holy Spirit, teaching them to observe all that I have commanded you" (Matthew 28:19–20).

As Christians, we have the task of acknowledging Jesus as Lord and submitting to him. We are called to pick up our cross and follow him (Matthew 16:24–26). Yet Jesus said, "My yoke is easy, and my burden is light" (Matthew 11:30). Obedience to Christ is for our good. It enables us to be all that we were intended to be. We have the job of announcing this message to the world—that through Jesus, forgiveness of sins, reconciliation with God, and new life are available to all who will give him their allegiance.

The second major implication of the ascension is that "Jesus is available, accessible, without people having to travel to a particular spot on the earth to find him."[18] We no longer need to go to the tabernacle or temple to experience the presence of God. As God, Jesus is always present with us, just as he promised his disciples (Matthew 28:20). Furthermore, Jesus is our great High Priest. Having been made human himself, Jesus understands our weaknesses and struggles. He stands before the Father, allowing us to approach God with confidence, knowing that our sins have been forgiven (Hebrews 4:14–16). Jesus constantly makes intercession for us. Even as we wrestle with sin in our own lives, we can have confidence that nothing will ever separate us from his love (Romans 8:31–39).

10. Conclusion

The good news of the gospel is set out clearly in 1 Corinthians 15:3–4:

> For I delivered to you as of first importance what I also received: that Christ died for our sins in accordance with the Scriptures, that he was buried, that he was raised on the third day in accordance with the Scriptures . . .

Paul continues his letter assuming that Jesus Christ ascended to heaven, adding that the resurrected Jesus will return and reign in glory "that God may be all in all" (1 Corinthians 15:22–28).

The death, burial, resurrection, and ascension of Jesus were all part of God's rescue operation for the world. This is the meaning of redemption—through Jesus, the sin and death that enslaved us have been defeated once and for all, our sins have been paid for, and new life is available to all who will put their trust in him. Through Jesus, we are made new and commissioned to be part of God's rescuing work in the world.

In the next chapter, we'll explore what it looks like to live for Jesus as we await his return. In the meantime, what does all of this mean for you now? How can you receive forgiveness for sin? How can you become part of God's work in the world? How can you claim the redemption that Jesus offers?

The answer is both simple and challenging. You must put your faith in Jesus. This is not a blind sort of faith that means believing things without any proof. On the contrary, there is good evidence to believe in Jesus and that what the Bible teaches about Jesus is true.

Faith in Jesus is more like trust or allegiance. It means trusting that through Jesus, through his righteousness, you can be forgiven. It means to stop trusting in yourself—your good intentions, appearance, popularity, talents, or work—and trust in Christ instead. It means to repent, to turn away from sin and give your allegiance and obedience to the One who loves you, created you, and died to redeem you.

ENDNOTES

[1]Justo L. Gonzalez, *The Story of Christianity—Volume 1: The Early Church to the Dawn of the Reformation* (New York: HarperCollins, 2010), 200.

[2]Gonzalez, 297.

[3]"Incarnation," Chad Brand, Charles Draper, and Archie England, eds., *Holman Illustrated Bible Dictionary*, (Nashville: Holman Bible Publishers, 2003), 813.

[4]R. Alan Street, *Caesar and the Sacrament—Baptism: A Rite of Resistance* (Eugene, OR: Cascade, 2018), 46.

[5]Street, 56–57.

[6]Craig C. Bartholomew and Micael W. Goheen, *Drama of Scripture: Finding Our Place in the Biblical Story* (Grand Rapids, MI: Bakers Academic, 2004), 133.

[7] N. T. Wright, *Surprised by Hope: Rethinking Heaven, the Resurrection, and the Mission of the Church* (New York: HarperCollins, 2008), 201.

[8] Wright, 201–202.

[9] For these and other views of Jesus, see Andreas J. Köstenberger, L. Scott Kellum, and Charles L. Quarles, *The Cradle, the Cross, and the Crown: An Introduction to the New Testament* (Nashville: B & H Academic, 2009), 117–25.

[10] Bartholomew and Goheen, 146–49.

[11] See David E. Garland, *Mark: NIV Application Commentary* (Grand Rapids, MI: Zondervan, 1996), 450–54.

[12] D. A. Carson, *The Gospel According to John: The Pillar New Testament Commentary* (Grand Rapids, MI: William B. Eerdmans, 1991), 412.

[13] See R. T. France, *The Gospel of Matthew: The New International Commentary on the New Testament* (Grand Rapids, MI: Wm. B. Eerdmans Publishing Co., 2007), 160–70.

[14] John R. W. Stott, *The Cross of Christ* (Downers Grove, IL: Intervarsity Press, 2006), 29–30.

[15] N. T. Wright, *The Day the Revolution Began: Reconsidering the Meaning of Jesus's Crucifixion* (New York: HarperCollins, 2016), 52–63.

[16] Timothy Keller, *The Reason for God: Belief in an Age of Skepticism* (New York: Riverhead Books, 2008), 210.

[17] Wright, *Surprised by Hope*, 109–117.

[18] Wright, 111.

11

Act 5: Restoration Initiated—The Church

1. Already and Not Yet

▸ **OBJECTIVE: You will be able to express that the kingdom of God is already here but is not yet fully realized.**

As we learned in the last chapter, Jesus is God's good news to humankind. He initiated the new covenant with his blood (Luke 22:20) and fulfilled the covenants in the Old Testament. In the new covenant, Jesus mediates between God and humanity; forgiveness of sins is offered once and for all. Salvation and blessings are extended to everyone; the way is opened for people to truly love God and neighbor (Jeremiah 31:31–34; Hebrews 9:8–15).[1]

While he was on Earth, Jesus accomplished our redemption, the central event of the biblical metanarrative. He began his public ministry by proclaiming, "The time is fulfilled, and the kingdom of God is at hand" (Mark 1:15). Then he died on the cross, with the charge against him written above his head, "This is Jesus, the King of the Jews" (Matthew 27:37). But the story did not end there. Jesus arose. His followers proclaimed that he was "the first to rise from the dead" (Acts 26:23), previewing the resurrection of all believers. He ascended into heaven, and now we wait for his return.

church: the followers of Christ in all places and times

The return of Christ will lead to the full consummation of the kingdom of God. The word *consummation* refers to the idea of something being finalized or completed. The kingdom of God that Jesus had announced is *already* here, but it has *not yet* fully arrived. Jesus is King of the world and its rightful Ruler right now, but not everyone recognizes or acknowledges this. Our world is still plagued by evil, death, and broken relationships. When Jesus returns, he will banish sin and death once and for all (1 Corinthians 15:24–28); he will make all things new (Revelation 21:5); everyone will acknowledge that Jesus is Lord (Romans 14:11); and the kingdom will finally be realized.[2]

For the last 2,000 years, Christians have been living in an in-between time, awaiting Jesus' return. The early Christians faced great questions and challenges about how to follow Jesus, many of which we still wrestle with today. How were they to live in light of Jesus' resurrection? How was God going to work through them to accomplish his work in the world? These questions and many more are addressed in the remainder of the New Testament, beginning with the book of Acts.

In this chapter we will look at what happened immediately after Jesus' ascension. We'll discover the creation of the church and its God-given mission to be an agent of restoration in the world. We'll explore how the reality of Jesus-as-King over all creation truly changes everything. Finally, we will learn about the part that we have to play in God's great story as we live in this already-but-not-yet time. Let's start with how God begins his restoration through the mission of the church.

2. A New Community: The Church

▸ **OBJECTIVE: You will be able to describe the relationship between the church, the Great Commission, and Pentecost.**

In Matthew 16:18, Jesus promised, "I will build my church." **Church** includes *the followers of Christ in all places and times*. The word *church* is translated from the Greek *ekklesia*, a compound word from *ek*, meaning *out from*, and *kaleo*, meaning *to call*. The church is a group of people called out for a special purpose. Though in Matthew 16:18 the words *my church* refer to all Christians everywhere, the word *church* is also used to refer to smaller groups of Christians (such as congregations, denominations, and traditions) as well as to the buildings where such people meet.

The church is not called to isolation from the world. Instead, the church is tasked with the mission that Jesus gave the apostles before he left Earth. This mission is known as the **Great Commission**, which is *Jesus' command to make disciples, baptize, and instruct people about all he taught.* Jesus told the apostles to spread the good news of the gospel by making disciples in every nation, baptizing them in the name of the Father, the Son, and the Holy Spirit, and teaching people to obey his commands (Matthew 28:18–20).

Jesus promised the apostles that he would send the Holy Spirit to indwell and empower them for this mission (John 15:26–27, Acts 1:4–5). *The day the promised Holy Spirit filled the disciples* took place on the Jewish Feast of Weeks, or **Pentecost**, which was celebrated seven weeks, or fifty days, after Passover. Pentecost is from the Greek word for fifty, *pentekostos*.

When the apostles, Jesus' mother, and many more men and women who followed Christ were gathered on the day of Pentecost, the Holy Spirit arrived with the sound of wind and appeared as flames of fire on each person. All were filled with the Spirit and spoke in tongues (Joel 2:28–29; Acts 1:14–15, 2:1–4). Peter got up and preached about Jesus, urging people to repent and receive God's forgiveness, and 3,000 people accepted the gospel message that day (Acts 2:14–41).

Acts 2:42–47 and 4:32–37 describe the character of these early Christians. They were dedicated to the teaching of the apostles. They regularly got together in one another's homes to share meals and pray. Many still went to the temple. They also shared their possessions, some even selling their goods and distributing the proceeds to anyone who was in need. They also had a good reputation among their neighbors. These small communities of Christians (the church) were a testimony to the transformative power of the gospel.

The New Testament uses many metaphors and similes to describe the church, such as bride, army, nation, family, team, temple, flock, and hospital. Many of these metaphors come from Old Testament descriptions of Israel. Peter described the church's mission, in light of Israel's history, this way:

> But you are a chosen race, a royal priesthood, a holy nation, a people for his own possession, that you may proclaim the excellencies of him who called you out of darkness into his marvelous light. –1 Peter 2:9

The church consists of those who have been called together by the Holy Spirit from every tribe, language, people, and nation (Revelation 5:9) and it is tasked with proclaiming the good news about God's kingdom. Living faithfully in obedience to Jesus and loving one another, the church is God's witness in the world that redemption and restoration are possible.

3. Challenges and Growth

▸ **OBJECTIVE:** You will be able to relate how the early church grew despite the challenges it faced.

Despite the early success of the apostles in Judea, it was not long before they and other followers of Jesus began to experience persecution at the hands of Jewish leaders. Acts 4:1–2 describes how the priests and Sadducees were "greatly annoyed" that the apostles were preaching about Jesus. These leaders thought that Jesus' death would silence his followers, but here they were proclaiming that Jesus had risen from the dead. Hoping to stop the spread of the Jesus movement, they arrested Peter and John and put them on trial. Peter boldly criticized them for crucifying Jesus and proclaimed that Jesus is the only way to be saved (Acts 4:8–12). Eventually, they were released with a warning not to preach about Jesus. But Peter declared that they couldn't help speaking about all they had seen and heard (Acts 4:18–20).

Stoning of Stephen, by Juan Ribero de Rada, St. Stephen Convent, Spain

Later, an early church leader named *Stephen* was stoned to death for his witness (Acts 6–7). A Pharisee named *Saul* witnessed this event. Shortly after, he unleashed a great persecution on the believers in Jerusalem. Many were arrested and dragged off to prison (Acts 8:1–3). However, Saul's reign of terror did not last long. On the way to arrest some believers in Damascus, Saul was struck blind by a vision of the risen Christ. Within a few days he, too, became a follower of Jesus (Acts 9). His sight was restored. He quickly became one of the most influential leaders in the Christian movement. Eventually, he would be known as the apostle *Paul*.

Jesus had said his followers would be witnesses for him "to the end of the earth" (Acts 1:8). Thanks in part to the highly developed Roman roads and the shared language of Greek in the empire, the gospel was able to travel quickly and widely through the apostles and the work of ordinary believers.[3]

As the good news about Jesus spread, new church communities sprang up all over the Roman empire. Peter preached in and around Jerusalem (Acts 1–5), Phillip shared the good news in Samaria (Acts 8:5), and Paul took at least three missionary journeys[4] around Asia Minor between the years AD 47 and 54 to support local churches.[5] Various traditions say the apostles traveled all over the world preaching about Jesus. They include stories of Thomas taking the gospel to India, Matthew evangelizing in North Africa, and

Andrew sharing the good news in Russia. Whether these stories are historically accurate is uncertain. What we do know is that, wherever they went, believers proclaiming that "Jesus is Lord."

Though the good news spread like wildfire, it quickly became apparent that following Jesus in the Roman world would not be easy. The early Christian communities were fraught with various questions and problems about how they should relate to their Jewish neighbors and how they should live in a pagan culture. Did Gentile believers need to be circumcised? Should Christians eat meat that had been sacrificed to idols? Could Christians follow the sexual practices of their Roman neighbors? How should a believer's faith impact his or her relationships? These challenges prompted several apostles and church leaders to write to their brothers and sisters in Christ.

4. Letters to the Churches

▸ **OBJECTIVE: You will be able to discuss how the New Testament epistles addressed concerns of the early church.**

Letters of the apostles and other Christian leaders make up a large part of the New Testament. As explained in Chapter 2, an epistle is a short letter to a community or an individual. Of 21 epistles in the New Testament, 13 are attributed to Paul, 3 to John, 2 to Peter, 1 to James, 1 to Jude, and 1 (Hebrews) to an unknown author. These letters instructed believers and challenged them to remain faithful to Jesus.

As we read these letters, it is important to keep in mind that they were not written directly to us. Reading the epistles is like reading someone else's mail. Of course, as Scripture, these letters are for us, but we must carefully consider how they apply to us today because they were written to specific communities facing specific issues.[6] For example:

Paul Writes to the Ephesians 1886 wood engraving

Jews and Gentiles. Early on in the Christian movement, most new Christians were Jewish, since Jesus is the fulfillment of God's promises to Israel. But the message the apostles proclaimed was for everyone. In Ephesians 3:1–12, Paul says the church is the embodiment of a mystery hidden before Christ's coming: everyone may share in God's promises. This is what God has always intended—that all people might be blessed through the family of Abraham (Genesis 12:1–3). Through Jesus, non-Jews could be welcomed into God's family. Jews and Gentiles, slave and free, male and female—all can be united in the body of Christ.[7]

However, in the early church, there was some tension between Jewish Christians and Gentile Christians. Some Jewish Christians thought that Gentile believers needed to follow Jewish laws and customs, especially circumcision. Both Peter and Paul rejected this view when they saw how God had poured out the Holy Spirit on Gentiles who had received Christ (Acts 11:17–18, 15:8–9).[8] Paul warned Gentiles against thinking that God had abandoned Israel and chosen them instead: he emphasized that Gentiles were grafted into Israel, not the other way around (Romans 11). In Galatians 5:6, Paul made it clear to everyone that circumcision doesn't count for anything, only "faith working through love." This is not to say that Jewish laws and customs from the Old Testament do not matter. The author of Hebrews explains that the law and priestly rituals were good but have now been fulfilled in Christ.

Other Social Relationships. The epistles address how believers are to behave toward one another in family relationships (Ephesians 5:21–6:4, Colossians 3:18–21, 1 Peter 3:1–7), master/slave relationships (Ephesians 6:5–9, Colossians 3:22–4:1, Philemon, 1 Peter 2:18–25), and believers' relationship with governing authorities (Romans 13:1–7, 1 Timothy 2:1–2, 1 Peter 2:13–17). These are some of the most debated passages in the New Testament and require careful interpretation and theological reflection. Less controversial but enormously challenging are Paul and Peter's instructions to Christians about being united and at peace.[9]

Christian Ethics. The writers of the epistles taught that Jesus' followers should demonstrate their commitment through action (James 1:22). Christians were to love others (1 John 4:7–12), forgive (Ephesians 4:32), show mercy and compassion (Colossians 3:12–14), care for the fatherless and widows (James 1:27), practice sexual integrity (1 Corinthians 6:12–20), not take vengeance on anyone (Romans 12:19), bless their enemies (Romans 12:14), and remain faithful while waiting for Christ's return (Jude 1:22). The Holy Spirit helps believers to live this way (Galatians 5:22–25).

The New Testament epistles include encouragement, rebuke, warnings about false teachings, instructions about worship, and more. Together, they have shaped the nature and practice of the church for nearly 2,000 years.

5. The Church throughout History and Today

▸ **OBJECTIVE: You will be able to summarize major events in the history of the church from the first century to the present era.**

Revelation, the last New Testament book, was most likely written between AD 80 and 100. By that time, Christians were experiencing scattered persecution in the Roman Empire; many were martyred. Yet the church continued to grow at a rapid rate. The love that Christians showed for one another and their neighbors was very attractive to outsiders.[10] Christian apologists also sought to counter the critiques of pagan philosophers.

In 313, the Roman emperor Constantine ended the persecution and granted Christianity legal status in the empire. Over the next 500 years, church leaders gathered to discuss the faith, producing creeds that defined and preserved Christian doctrine. The Scriptures were translated into many languages. When the Roman empire eventually came to an end, Christian monks and nuns preserved important writings. The gospel spread throughout Europe. The church in North Africa also thrived and produced notable theologians, including Augustine of Hippo, until the Islamic conquest in the mid-600s. Later, war between Christian and Islamic forces led to the Crusades and eventually contributed to division between Roman Catholic and Eastern Orthodox churches. In 1054, doctrinal differences led to a major split in the Christian faith.

Back in Europe, throughout the Middle Ages, Christians led the way in education, art, and care of the poor. But the church gradually became increasingly corrupt and entangled with the state. Important doctrines were ignored and obscured by the pursuit of wealth and power.

In 1517, Martin Luther unintentionally kicked off the Protestant Reformation, which led to the recovery of the doctrine of justification and a renewed emphasis on Scripture. As a result, many new denominations were formed: Lutherans, Reformed, Anglican, Anabaptists, and Puritans, among others. The Bible was translated into even more languages, allowing for greater access to Scripture than ever before.

After the exploration of the Americas began, many Europeans migrated there, including Protestants seeking greater freedom of worship. The freedom of religion in the United States allowed many denominations to flourish. Two great awakenings contributed to religious revival, renewed missionary activity, the abolition of slavery, and the founding of many parachurch organizations for the common good.

In the 18th and 19th centuries, Protestant missionaries, many from the US and the UK, traveled around the world with the gospel and established churches in many countries. In the 20th century, Pentecostal and evangelical movements led to additional revival, missions, and fervor amidst religious skepticism, persecution, and two world wars. Today, Christianity is the largest religion on Earth,[11] and most Christians now live outside the West, mainly in Africa, Central and South America, and Asia. The gospel has led to transformation, greater concern for human life, and new communities dedicated to showing Jesus' love.

Church history is a valuable study on its own, and this extremely brief treatment of the last 2,000 years can hardly do justice to the rich tradition that has come down to us. If you are a Christian, you are a part of this story that began in Genesis and is still going on today. Christians have done amazing things in the world; they have also made terrible mistakes. Our challenge is how we can faithfully follow Jesus in our own time.

The message the church is to proclaim today is the same one the apostles preached—the gospel of Jesus Christ, which has implications for all of life, especially our relationships. Back in Chapter 7, we saw how the four relationships of creation were distorted and broken by sin. In the next four sections, we'll explore what the church's message of restoration means for our relationships with God, ourselves, other human beings, and the creation.

6. Restored Relationship with God

▸ **OBJECTIVE: You will be able to articulate how sin affects humans' relationship with God and how that relationship can be restored through Christ.**

God made us in his image to have a relationship with him, but sin broke that relationship (Romans 6:23). Sin resulted in separation, shame, guilt, and death (Isaiah 59:2, Daniel 9:8, Jeremiah 14:20). It had many other consequences, too.

A critical consequence is that sin warped human beings' view of God. Some people today, like Adam and Eve did, hide from God as a result of their sin (Genesis 3:8); they are afraid of God. Others, copying Cain, are consumed by their own sinful thoughts and feelings, disobey God, and become insolent and disrespectful toward him (Genesis 4:9). Some deny God altogether (Psalm 14:1) while others put idols in his place (Jeremiah 2:11, Romans 1:25). It isn't possible to have a good relationship with someone when you cannot even see the person clearly—when prejudice, negative feelings, and self-interest cloud your view.

While human beings broke the relationship with God, only God can restore it, which he did through his Son: "For Christ also suffered once for sins, the righteous for the unrighteous, that he might bring us to God, being put to death in the flesh but made alive in the spirit" (1 Peter 3:18). This is **justification**—*the state of being declared righteous before God through the work of Jesus Christ.*

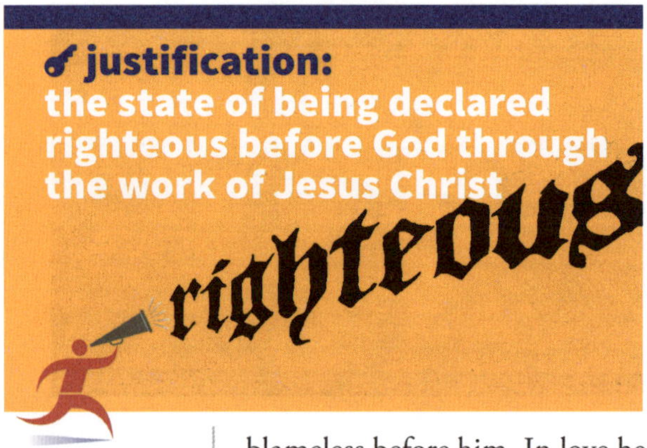

We cannot earn our own righteousness through good works. Being declared righteous is an act of God's grace, through faith (Ephesians 2:8–9). We are all guilty of sin, but are offered complete pardon by the Lord of the universe. However, we aren't just forgiven sinners. Christ restores us to the original relationship God had in mind. God chose us "before the foundation of the world, that we should be holy and blameless before him. In love he predestined us for adoption to himself as sons through Jesus Christ, according to the purpose of his will" (Ephesians 1:4–5).

We are children being brought into the home of a Father who loves us. The apostle Paul put it this way:

> For you did not receive the spirit of slavery to fall back into fear, but you have received the Spirit of adoption as sons, by whom we cry, "Abba! Father!" The Spirit himself bears witness with our spirit that we are children of God, and if children, then heirs—heirs of God and fellow heirs with Christ, provided we suffer with him in order that we may also be glorified with him. –Romans 8:15–17

The restoration of all things, including our relationship with God, means that if we have been reconciled to God through Christ, then we no longer have to be afraid of him, but can draw near to him (Hebrews 10:22). Even when we sin, we can come to him, knowing that he faithfully forgives (1 John 1:9). We can have confidence that we are his beloved children (1 John 3:1) and that he is completely for us. This is a message of hope that we have been called to share with others. Through Christ, we have been reconciled to God, and God has given us this very same message of reconciliation to share with the world (2 Corinthians 5:18–21).

7. Restored Relationship with Self

▸ **OBJECTIVE: You will be able to explain how God restores our relationship with ourselves and continues to transform us.**

The good news does not end with our justification. Restoration goes far beyond simply cleansing us of our sins so we can have a relationship with God. In addition to restoring our relationship with him, God restores to us our relationship with ourselves.

In describing sin's impact, Paul wrote: "I do not understand my own actions. . . . I have the desire to do what is right, but not the ability to carry it out. For I do not do the good I want, but the evil I do not want is what I keep on doing" (Romans 7:15, 18). All of us experience this tension of knowing what is good, but choosing to do wrong.

But God did not leave Paul, nor does he leave us, to simply struggle and feel wretched. Those who are in Christ Jesus are set free from sin's power (Romans 8:2). We no longer have to be alienated from ourselves, not understanding why we do the things we do. We can trust God, knowing that he is working to transform us and to give us the will and the ability that we need to live holy lives through the power of the Holy Spirit.

However, **sanctification**—*the process of becoming like Jesus*—takes time. Even though we received salvation immediately upon professing faith in Christ (Romans 10:9), Scripture says we are also *being* saved (1 Corinthians 1:18, Philippians 2:12–13) and *looking forward* to salvation (1 Peter 1:3–5). It's the already-but-not-yet nature of the kingdom of God once again.

The Christian life is one of continual growth. One author put it this way:

> Initial sanctification occurs instantly at the moment of salvation when we are delivered from the kingdom of darkness and brought into the Kingdom of Christ (Colossians 1:13). Progressive sanctification continues over time until we go to be with the Lord. [It] is implied throughout the New Testament epistles in all those instances where we are exhorted to grow, to change, to put off the deeds of the old man and put on godlike character, and so on.[12]

Sanctification is not easy. Letting go of destructive attitudes and habits is a daily challenge (Luke 9:23). Growth comes with growing pains (Hebrews 12:11). But the process is worth it! Jesus said that he came so that we might experience true life, abundance, love, and joy (John 10:10, 15:10–11). In Jesus, we are freed from the power of sin to be truly human. As one author put it:

The Incarnation takes all that properly belongs to our humanity and delivers it back to us, redeemed. All of our inclinations and appetites and capacities and yearnings and proclivities are purified and gathered up and glorified by Christ. He did not come to thin out human life; he came to set it free. All the dancing and feasting and processing and singing and building and sculpting and baking and merrymaking that belong to us, and that were stolen away into the service of false gods, are returned to us in the Gospel.[13]

Sanctification is not something we achieve on our own. We are encouraged to cooperate as the Holy Spirit works to bring restoration within us (Romans 8:12–14, Galatians 5:16). As we are restored to being who God created us to be, we can have a life of righteousness and peace and joy now, while anticipating even greater blessings in the future.

8. Restored Relationship with Others

▸ **OBJECTIVE:** **You will be able to describe how Christ's redemption provides the opportunity for restored relationship with others.**

Through Christ, we have a restored relationship with God and with ourselves. But the impact of Christ's death on the cross does not end there. Did you ever notice that a cross has *two* parts? The vertical beam can represent our relationship with God; the horizontal one, our relationships with others. People were created for relationships, and full redemption and restoration mean that we can appreciate others and freely enjoy love, friendship, and companionship with one another.

Jesus redeems us from sin, but most lists of sin in the Bible include far more than sins against God (such as idolatry) or sins against oneself (such as gluttony). They list sins against other people—sins of anger, envy, gossip, greed, sexual immorality, and more (for example, see Matthew 15:19 or Galatians 5:19–21). God wants our relationships to be characterized by love and other fruits of the Spirit (John 13:34, Galatians 5:22–23). Imagine restored relationships where sin is no longer an issue; where no one lies about you or misunderstands you or hates you; where love is sincere and people genuinely like and respect you; and where you, too, genuinely respect, like, love, and desire to serve others and spend time with them.

Restored relationships—with God, with ourselves, with others—are part of the hope that we have in Christ and are assigned to witness to throughout the world (Acts 1:8). We share the gospel, the good news that God sent his Son into the world to reconcile all creation to himself (Colossians 1:19–20). As we have seen, we are commissioned as ambassadors of reconciliation, encouraging every person to be reconciled to God (2 Corinthians 5:17–20). We also encourage people to seek reconciliation with each other (Matthew 5:9, James 3:18). In Christ, worldly divisions no longer matter (1 Corinthians 12:12–13, Galatians 3:28, Colossians 3:11). As God's ambassadors, we have been "entrusted with the gospel" (1 Thessalonians 2:4). We hope, with God's help, to show ourselves worthy of that trust.

Loving others is difficult, or impossible, without a spirit of reconciliation. Living in the Spirit means having a spirit of forgiveness, seeking always to be reconciled to others.

Jesus laid it out plainly in Matthew 6:14–15: "For if you forgive men their trespasses, your heavenly Father will also forgive you. But if you do not forgive men their trespasses, neither will your Father forgive your trespasses."

The Holy Spirit can give us the desire and tools to maintain healthy relationships and to mend them when they are strained or broken. He brings healing and wholeness to our lives. He helps us persevere in seeking peace (Romans 12:18). He gives us hope for the future (Galatians 5:5) where none of our relationships will suffer from sin. In the meantime, we proclaim the good news of reconciliation, looking forward to the day when there is no more war, division, or fear (Micah 4:3–4) and "the earth will be filled with the knowledge of the glory of the LORD as the waters cover the sea" (Habakkuk 2:14).

9. Restored Relationship with Creation

▸ **OBJECTIVE: You will be able to associate how redemption has implications beyond ourselves and extends to the restoration of all creation.**

Sin affected everyone and resulted in a curse on nature; Christ's death and resurrection brought about the hope of redemption for all people and nature. In Christ, "all things" will be reconciled and made new (Colossians 1:20). The Scriptures describe creation as rejoicing in God's righteous judgment (Psalm 96:10–13) and in its own restoration (Isaiah 11:6–9).

God cares about the physical world and every aspect of his creation. In God's final judgment, the material creation will continue, having been purified by fire and re-created, renewed, and perfected into a new heavens and Earth. People will have new, transformed bodies in the new creation, and God's purposes for creation will be fulfilled. He will reign supreme and we will reign with him (Daniel 7:18, Revelation 22:5).

However, we are not there yet. Through Christ's death, the price for the redemption of creation has already been paid, but we see that there is still death and decay in the world. Though our inner self is being renewed, our physical bodies waste away with the curse of death (2 Corinthians 4:16). Romans 8:19–22 describes how the creation was subjected to futility and groans under the weight of its bondage to corruption. The Holy Spirit is God's guarantee of the salvation that is yet to come, when "what is mortal may be swallowed up by life" (2 Corinthians 5:4–5), when all of creation will be made new and we will be given new, incorruptible bodies. This is good news, but what does the gospel mean for creation right now?

Some Christians worry that caring for creation is a distraction from sharing the gospel. Others think that the material world doesn't really matter because it will all be destroyed. But creation is central to God's plan. Christ's salvation is not intended to annihilate creation but to bring it to fruition. Being a good steward is a part of the gospel message because what God has done in Jesus is good news for the whole world. Until Jesus returns, we have the blessing to work to extend redemption to all facets of creation through wise stewardship of this planet, including its creatures and its resources.

Having a restored relationship with creation means changing the way we think about the natural world. Instead of seeing it as a tool to be used or exploited for our own purposes, we must see creation as God's gift to us.[14] This begins with noticing what is around us, pausing to see how God's glory is proclaimed in a tree or a river.[15] It means enjoying the creatures God has given and treating them well. It also means considering what impact our actions in agriculture, mining, and other industries have on the environment.

To be sure, we cannot fix the planet or make everything right, but this does not excuse us from responsibility now. Redemption saves us *for* life on Earth, not *from* it. We must care for Earth, where God dwells and will dwell with his people (Numbers 35:33–34, 1 Corinthians 6:19, Revelation 21:3). We must model the healing of all the relationships of creation as we wait for Jesus' return and the final restoration of all things.

10. Conclusion

Living in between Jesus' first coming and the final restoration of all things is not easy. On the one hand, God's kingdom has broken into the world, enabling us by the power of the Holy Spirit to become like Christ and to be the kind of people who love God and others.

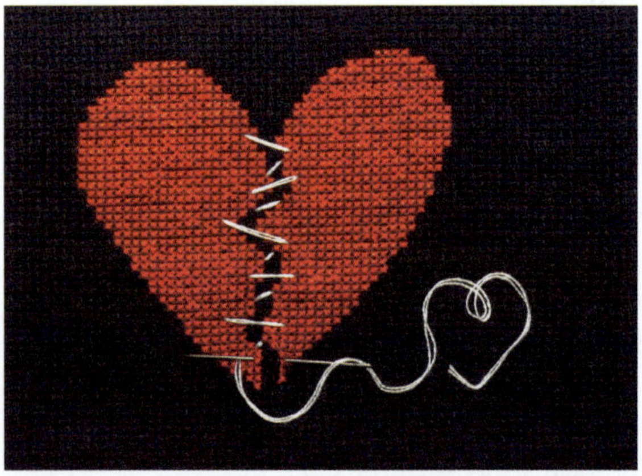

On the other hand, we see broken relationships, sin, evil, and death still running rampant. The kingdom is *already*, but *not yet*. Jesus' work on the cross is finished. He has defeated the powers of evil and rules the world as its true Lord. But not everyone acknowledges Jesus is Lord or believes his message.

That is where the church comes in. Through preaching the message of reconciliation, the church proclaims the good news and models the difference that knowing Jesus makes. Empowered by the Holy Spirit, the early Christians boldly shared their faith in the midst of a pagan culture. The writings of the apostles and other church leaders provided God's Word to the church and are still relevant for us today. For the last 2,000 years, Christians have been trying to live out and proclaim the gospel.

As we have seen, the gospel has implications for all our relationships. Jesus made it possible for us to be justified with God and sanctified through the work of the Holy Spirit. God's love and forgiveness transforms our relationships with him, with ourselves, and with others. The gospel also changes the way we think about the natural world, helping us to see it as a gift.

We have the opportunity to proclaim God's message of reconciliation and to live out; this can only be done in community. No Christian is meant to go it alone; we are all part of Christ's body (1 Corinthians 12:12–14). But there is no perfect church. Every church community is composed of broken people who are awaiting full restoration. This doesn't excuse sin, but it should cause us to be humble, recognizing the ways in which we may be contributing to the brokenness of our own community.

Sadly, the church can sometimes be a place where people fight, disparage, or ignore one another; where doubts, questions, and opinions are silenced; where creation is trampled; and where Christians use the Bible and religious practices to promote their own selfish desires rather than to serve God and others. But the church can, and should, be a place where we worship God, practice reconciliation, welcome others, and seek the welfare of our community and, ultimately, the world. It is where we learn what it means to be an ambassador for Christ first by being an ambassador of forgiveness to the person sitting next to us. Ultimately, the church's greatest witness is the way that believers love one another. "By this all people will know that you are my disciples, if you have love for one another" (John 13:35).

We have come a long way in the metanarrative of Scripture. It has brought us to the present day. Yet, there is still one more chapter of God's big story to come. That's what we'll explore in the next chapter of this book.

ENDNOTES

[1]Jeremy Bouma, "What Is the New Covenant?", zondervanacademic.com, https://zondervanacademic.com/blog/new-covenant.

[2]For a helpful discussion of the nature of the kingdom of God, see Robert H. Stein, *The Method and Message of Jesus' Teaching,* rev. ed. (Louisville, KY: Westminster John Knox Press, 1994), 60–81.

[3]Craig G. Bartholomew and Michael W. Goheen, *The Drama of Scripture: Finding Our Place in the Biblical Story* (Grand Rapids, MI: Baker Academic, 2004), 180.

[4]Paul's first journey is chronicled in Acts 13–14; a second journey, in Acts 16:1–18:22; and a third, in Acts 18:23–21:14.

[5]Andreas J. Köstenberger, L. Scott Kellum, and Charles L. Quarles, *The Cradle, the Cross, and the Crown: An Introduction to the New Testament* (Nashville, TN: Baker Academic, 2009), 391–394.

[6]See discussion in Gordon D. Fee and Douglas Stuart, *How to Read the Bible for All Its Worth*, 4th ed. (Grand Rapids, MI: Zondervan, 2014), 57–73.

[7]See Romans 12:5; 1 Corinthians 10:17, 12:12–13; Galatians 3:7–8, 26–28; Colossians 3:11, and Ephesians 2:13–22.

[8]See Justin S. Holcomb, *Know the Heretics* (Grand Rapids, MI: Zondervan, 2014), 23–32.

[9]See Romans 12:18, 1 Corinthians 1:10, Ephesians 4:1–6, James 3:13–18, and 1 Peter 3:8–9.

[10]Rodney Stark, *The Rise of Christianity: A Sociologist Reconsiders History* (Princeton, NJ: Princeton University Press, 1996), 73–94.

[11]Conrad Hackett and David McClendon, "Christians Remain World's Largest Religious Group, But They Are Declining in Europe," Pew Research Center, April 5, 2017, https://www.pewresearch.org/fact-tank/2017/04/05/christians-remain-worlds-largest-religious-group-but-they-are-declining-in-europe/.

[12]Jerry Bridges, *Transforming Grace* (Colorado Springs, CO: NavPress, 2008), 123–124.

[13]Thomas Howard, *Evangelical Is Not Enough: Worship of God in Liturgy and Sacrament* (San Francisco: Ignatius Press, 1984), 36–37.

[14]See Craig M. Gay, *Modern Technology and the Human Future: A Christian Appraisal* (Downers Grove, IL: InterVarsity Press, 2018), 136–147.

[15]For example, see Eugene H. Peterson, *Christ Plays in Ten Thousand Places: A Conversation in Spiritual Theology* (Grand Rapids, MI: Eerdmans, 2005), 49–129.

12

Act 6: Restoration Accomplished—New Creation

1. Longing for Restoration

▸ **OBJECTIVE: You will be able to relate redemption through Jesus Christ to the Christian hope of future restoration.**

In the last chapter, we learned about how God works through the church to proclaim the message of restoration. However, while the good news has been promised and proclaimed, it has not yet been fully realized. We still confidently await the fulfillment of many of God's great promises, trusting in him. Throughout Scripture, God is shown to be and declares himself to be a God of restoration.

He ***restores*** my soul. –Psalm 23:3

I will ***restore*** the fortunes of my people Israel, and they shall rebuild the ruined cities and inhabit them; they shall plant vineyards and drink their wine, and they shall make gardens and eat their fruit. –Amos 9:14

Return to your stronghold, O prisoners of hope; today I declare that I will ***restore*** to you double. –Zechariah 9:12

. . . until the time for ***restoring*** all the things about which God spoke by the mouth of his holy prophets long ago. –Acts 3:21

And after you have suffered a little while, the God of all grace, who has called you to his eternal glory in Christ, will himself ***restore***, confirm, strengthen, and establish you. –1 Peter 5:10

Ever since Adam and Eve rebelled in the garden, sin and death have plagued the world. In the Old Testament, God showed his faithfulness by making covenants with his people—saving, delivering, rescuing, forgiving, and healing them. However, sin and death continued to corrupt and ravage the world. That's why our redemption required that Jesus, "who knew no sin," die and rise again "so that in him we might become the righteousness of God" (2 Corinthians 5:21). Redemption required Jesus' holy life, his death, and his resurrection, which all showed God's power. Neither sin nor death will have the final say. As one writer put it, "All will be well, and you will see it yourself, that every kind of thing will be well."[1] This should give Christians great hope. Knowing that God has been faithful in the past and that his Spirit is with us gives us confidence as we look to the future when the new creation will finally arrive.

The full restoration of creation will involve the complete healing of the fractured relationships that we spoke of in Chapters 6, 7, and 11 (God, self, others, creation). However, it will not occur until death itself is fully defeated and Jesus "delivers the kingdom to God the Father after destroying every rule and every authority and power" (1 Corinthians 15:22–25). Creation will then be "set free from its bondage to corruption" (Romans 8:21) and all things will be made new (Revelation 21:5).

In this chapter, we will look at the last act of the biblical metanarrative—God's new creation. Naturally, we are curious about the details of God's restored world, and we will consider some of the passages that discuss the new creation. However, the Bible does not provide an in-depth analysis of what the new creation will be like. That's why approaching this conversation requires humility, since "no eye has seen, nor ear heard, nor . . . heart . . . imagined—what God has prepared for those who love him" (1 Corinthians 2:9). Let's begin with the book of Revelation.

2. Context of the Book of Revelation

▸ **OBJECTIVE: You will be able to explain the literary and cultural context of Revelation.**

The book of Revelation is the last book of the Bible. It was written by John, who was given a revelation about God's final restoration and the events leading up to it. Throughout history, Christians have puzzled over the meaning of the book, unsure of how to read it. In modern times, many have rejected the book because of its violent imagery. The philosopher Friedrich Nietzsche abhorred Revelation, calling it "the most rabid outburst of vindictiveness in all recorded history."[2]

There is no doubt that Revelation can be difficult to decipher, but as the final book in the Bible, it cannot be ignored. As we saw in Chapter 4, good interpretation begins with a work's literary and historical context. Considering the literary context, Revelation is an apocalypse, written by a prophet and distributed as a letter to churches in Asia Minor.[3]

The term **apocalypse** comes from a Greek word meaning *revelation, unveiling, or uncovering.* Apocalyptic literature is *literature that conveys meaning through symbols and metaphors to reveal reality and encourage God's people.* In apocalypses, someone generally sees a vision of an otherworldly realm. That vision reveals the true nature of reality. Apocalypses often include descriptions of judgment and God's eventual victory. One author says that apocalyptic literature's function is "to sustain the people of God, especially in times of crisis."[4]

Revelation contains many similarities to the writings of the Old Testament prophets. In fact, Revelation claims to be a prophecy (Revelation 1:3) and John draws heavily on prophetic books like Ezekiel, Isaiah, and Daniel. Recall from Chapter 8 that though prophets do sometimes predict the future, they most often call God's people to faithfulness and obedience. If you pay close attention, you will see many such calls to faithfulness in the book of Revelation (for example, Revelation 2:10, 13:10, and 14:12).

Revelation 2–3 consists of seven letters written to churches in Asia Minor. These letters provide encouragement and rebuke to specific churches, but they are also addressed to the church at large. The entire book is a letter of encouragement to the church, challenging Christians to remain faithful to Jesus.

Other elements of literary interest include John's use of common folk tales to illustrate the gospel (for example, Revelation 12); intentional contrasts between the Lamb and the dragon, Babylon and Jerusalem, and others; and the symbolic use of colors (white for victory, black for death, gold for beauty) and numbers (three for a particular group, four for the world, seven for perfection, twelve for the whole people of God), and so on.[5]

In considering the historical context, we must remember that John was living in the pagan Roman culture. Roman emperors were seen as divine. Many citizens worshipped them to gain their favor and the economic benefits that came with it. Many of the cities to which John addressed Revelation included great shrines to the emperor.[6] Rome was happy to tolerate other gods so long as one worshipped the emperor, but Christians' refusal to worship Caesar caused them to be seen as outsiders and potential threats to Rome's social unity.[7] Christians in John's day likely experienced sporadic persecution. Revelation frequently mentions martyrs and includes a possible reference to Nero, an emperor known for his cruelty to Christians. Thus, in the Roman world, followers of Jesus would have experienced enormous pressure to conform to societal norms by worshipping the emperor and participating in pagan religious festivals.

3. Worshipping God, Following the Lamb

▸ **OBJECTIVE: You will be able to describe the relevance of the Lamb in the book of Revelation.**

▸ **OBJECTIVE: You will be able to articulate the role of suffering in the Christian life.**

In Revelation, John was shown a vision of restoration and many things that will happen before God's new creation arrives. He also gave his readers a message of hope, challenge, and warning.

The central images in the book of Revelation are God on the throne[8] and the slaughtered Lamb. In Revelation 4–5, John is caught up to heaven (similar episodes occur in Isaiah 6 and Ezekiel 1). He views God's throne and his awesome power and glory. "Flashes of lightning, and rumblings, and peals of thunder" (Revelation 4:5) come from God's throne, reminding us of God's presence at Mount Sinai (Exodus 19:16). Before God's throne are seven flaming torches that represent God's perfection. Around God's throne are twenty-four elders and four strange beasts who cry out, "Holy, holy, holy is the Lord God Almighty, who was and is and is to come!" (Revelation 4:8).

Lamb of God mosaic, Saints Peter and Paul Basilica, Prague, Czech Republic

Then, a sealed scroll is brought out. The scroll represents God's plan for establishing his kingdom on Earth,[9] but sadly, there is no one who is worthy to open it. However, one of the elders tells John, "Behold, the Lion of the tribe of Judah, the Root of David" is worthy to open the scroll (Revelation 5:5). However, what John sees is not a lion, but a Lamb that has been slaughtered. This is a clear reference to Jesus and his crucifixion. Jesus is the Lamb of

God, the Messiah, the true Davidic Ruler who has conquered; but he has not conquered with a sword. Instead, he conquered by his righteous life, death, and resurrection. Jesus' atoning sacrifice is the way in which he defeated sin and death.

Christians living at the time were constantly told that Caesar was lord, the king of the world. Rome maintained its power through violence and coercion. John's vision, however, pulls back the curtain to reveal what is actually true—God is on the throne as the true Ruler of the universe. Unlike Rome, God does not rule through violence, but through sacrifice.[10]

John challenges his readers to follow the Lamb through suffering. He describes a great multitude of followers of the Lamb who have "washed their robes . . . in the blood of the Lamb" (Revelation 7:9–17). These believers have endured suffering and persecution for the sake of Jesus. They "follow the Lamb wherever he goes" (Revelation 14:4) even if that means death. Many Christians in the first century faced persecution and martyrdom at the hands of the Roman empire. What John offers them is a challenge and a promise. The challenge is to remain faithful to Jesus through suffering. The promise is that they will be vindicated, and their place is secure in God's coming kingdom.

Suffering is part and parcel of the Christian life. The way of the Lamb is the way of the cross (Luke 9:23). Those who follow the Lamb must follow him wherever he goes. We can do this knowing that God and the Lamb will rule the new creation (Revelation 22:1, 3). The key question of Revelation is "Whom do we worship?"[11] In other words, who really rules the world? Who deserves our allegiance? Is it God or Rome? God or the nation in which we live?

4. Judgment

▸ **OBJECTIVE: You will be able to defend the Christian view of God's final judgment.**

We have seen the message of hope and the challenge that John gives his readers. We must now turn to John's warning. The book of Revelation is famous for its intense scenes of violence and judgment. Four horsemen of the apocalypse ride over the earth bringing death and destruction; stars fall from the sky; the moon turns to blood; huge locusts terrorize those who are in opposition to God; a great dragon seeks to thwart God's plan of redemption; and two beasts make war on God's people.

Some see the judgments in Revelation as literal events reserved for a future time when God will pour out his wrath on the earth. Others see the judgments as symbolic, and part of the normal experience of life in the world as God gives people over to the consequences of their evil actions. Either way, the question is, how does violent judgment square with the image of the slaughtered Lamb in Revelation 5?

To begin with, note that at least some of the judgments described in the book of Revelation are not God striking people down as much as they are people experiencing the consequences of their actions or those of evil empires. As one biblical scholar put it:

> The judgment of the world originates in its failure to believe and be faithful to . . . God. When it creates its own deities, it suffers the natural consequences of deifying the non-divine. In this sense, judgment proceeds from the throne of God and from the Lamb (Revelation 6:16–17) because the rejection of the divine gift of life carries with it inherent deadly consequences.[12]

Ultimately, humans are dependent on God. He offers us life, but when we reject that life, we will inevitably experience the disastrous consequences. In Revelation 6, four horsemen ride over the earth, bringing war, famine, plague, and death. All of these are experienced in the world today, partly through human agency, including oppression, greed, and lack of ethical responsibility. Christians endure these trials like anyone else, but the difference is this: Christians will not be eternally lost. God does not promise to keep us from suffering (John 16:33), but he does promise that those who love him will always experience his nearness and that nothing will separate us from his love (Romans 8, Revelation 2–3).

Four Horsemen of the Apocalypse, illustration by German painter and printmaker Albrecht Dürer, 1498

The second thing to note is that judgment is not about God getting revenge on people he doesn't like. Rather, it is about God bringing justice on evil. God will not let evil run rampant forever. Revelation 11:18 declares judgment will come on those who have been destroying God's world. The city of Babylon is an important symbol in Revelation. It stands for Rome and its empire, which was then persecuting believers, and also for all evil empires who align themselves against God. Babylon was a city of immorality, economic exploitation, and greed. It trafficked in luxury items and also in slaves (Revelation 18:13). These and other sins are what God is coming to judge.

Finally, the judgments prepare the way for God's new creation to be revealed.[13] In order for humans to flourish there, the forces of evil must be eliminated once and for all. Only God can do this. John did not summon his readers to take up arms against their oppressors in the Roman empire. Instead, Christians win the victory by bearing faithful witness to the Lamb and following his example (Revelation 12:11). However, if we reject God and align ourselves with evil, we will experience judgment.

5. Hell

▸ **OBJECTIVE:** You will be able to clarify the truth about hell.

Discussion of God's judgment inevitably raises the question of hell. What is hell? **Hell** is *a place where all who reject Christ spend eternity excluded from God's presence.* It is a place prepared for Satan's judgment (Matthew 25:41) and for those who reject God (Revelation 21:8). The Bible describes hell as a "fiery furnace" where people weep and gnash their teeth, suffer, and experience regret and torment (Matthew 13:50, Luke 16:19–31). After God has consigned the devil to hell for eternity, those who are not found in the Lamb's book of life are cast into the lake of fire (Revelation 20:7–15).

Taken literally, the biblical images cause people to think of hell as a burning fire where the devil and his angels torture those who haven't trusted Jesus. However, considering the context of these passages, some of the imagery may be symbolic. This does not mean that hell is not a real place or somehow less horrible. As one scholar put it:

> The thing symbolized is not less horrible than the symbols, but more. Spiritual fire is worse than material fire; spiritual death is worse than physical death. The pain of loss—the loss of God, who is the source of all joy—is infinitely more horrible than any torture could ever be.[14]

The main idea to get about hell is this: to be in hell is to be outside, away from the presence of God, excluded from God's new creation. Ultimately, hell is more than just a place. As pastor Tim Keller wrote, "Hell . . . is the trajectory of a soul, living a self-absorbed, self-centered life, going on and on forever."[15]

It is common for people to think in terms of God sending people to hell. However, it may be that hell is more like God finally allowing people to experience eternity apart from him if that is what they truly want.[16] Hell is, in a sense, a place that people choose. That may sound odd, but consider this: If people want nothing to do with God in this life, is it likely that they will want to spend an eternity with him? Will God force those who reject him to live with him forever? Part of the dignity that God gives human beings is the ability to choose.

hell:
a place where all who reject Christ spend eternity excluded from God's presence

God has no desire for anyone to live outside of his presence. That's why his judgment is counterbalanced with patience. God is not quick to judge sinners. Instead, he is patient, longing for all people to come to repentance and faith (2 Peter 3:9). However, we do not have infinite time, and if we persist in turning away from God, we will find ourselves eternally outside. C. S. Lewis said it this way: "There are only two kinds of people in the end: those who say to God, 'Thy will be done,' and those to whom God says, in the end, 'Thy will be done.'"[17]

Whether or not the images of fire and brimstone are literal, one thing is certain: hell is a place of great anguish and regret (Matthew 18:8, 25:41). If we want nothing to do with

God, we may get what we want, but there will be no satisfaction in it. God is the Source of life, love, and joy. To be separated from him for all eternity will be the greatest possible loss. In the end, hell is an eternal turning away from God and the true life that he offers.

6. Heaven

▸ **OBJECTIVE: You will be able to discuss the eternal destiny of Christians.**

Many Christians have the impression that their eternal destiny is "up there" in the clouds somewhere. Perhaps you have heard about being "so heavenly minded that you are no earthly good." This complaint has commonly been lodged against Christians who believe that our only business on earth is to share the plan of salvation with people so they too can get to heaven. Everything else, including our daily work, social causes, and creation are too often neglected. Of course, sharing the plan of salvation with others is essential. Yet as we saw in the last chapter, the message of the gospel is much bigger than individual salvation. It is good news for all creation, and it makes some restoration possible beginning now.

The biblical metanarrative is not solely about people getting saved so they can go to heaven after they die. Rather, the great story reaches its fulfillment in God's new creation.[18] According to Revelation 21–22, we do not go to God at the end of all things. Rather, God comes to dwell among us. What has traditionally been called "heaven," then, is not our final destination. So, if heaven is not our final destination, what is it?

The Bible describes **heaven** as *the place God where dwells and is eternally worshipped.* After Jesus rose from the dead, he ascended to heaven, where he now sits at God's right hand (Mark 16:19). Revelation 4–5 reveals the endless worship of God and the Lamb that occurs in heaven. When we pray, "Your kingdom come, your will be done, on earth as it is in heaven" (Matthew 6:10), we are praying for the reality of heaven to be the reality on earth. Christians long for the day when everyone will give their worship and allegiance to the only One who is worthy.

But isn't it true that believers who die go to heaven? Yes. Until the restoration of all things, heaven is the place where believers who have died are present with Jesus. Revelation teaches that those who die in the Lord are present with him (Revelation 7:13–15, 14:13). In Philippians 1:23, Paul describes how he is torn between his desire to continue serving God in his mortal body and dying so he can "be with Christ, for that is far better." Yet, Paul "sees [heaven] as only a *temporary* state of affairs, an interim condition until Christ . . . return[s]."[19] When that happens, believers will be given new bodies that will no longer experience decay and death (1 Corinthians 15:35–58). We do not know what kind of body believers have in heaven between now and then. What we do know is that they are there, safe and secure in God's care.[20]

When the gospel writers used phrases like "the kingdom of God" or "the kingdom of heaven," they were talking about God's righteous rule over all creation. Our hope is not just that we will be in God's presence when we die, but that one day, God's kingdom will be fully established in the new heaven and the new earth (Revelation 21:1). The Holy Spirit in our hearts is the guarantee of God's promises about our future (2 Corinthians 1:22, 5:5; Ephesians 1:14) We do know we will be given new bodies to rule and reign with God for all eternity. This will be the final restoration of all things.

7. The Second Coming

▸ OBJECTIVE: You will be able to explain the significance of the second coming and what Christians should do while awaiting Christ's return.

The event that triggers the final restoration of creation is the return of Jesus Christ to Earth. Jesus told his disciples he would return at an unknown time in the future with great power and glory (Matthew 16:27, Mark 8:38, Luke 9:26). At the Last Supper, Jesus reaffirmed to the apostles that he would come again, and that in the meantime, he would send the Spirit (John 14:1–3, 16:7). He also told them about his death and resurrection many times, but they did not understand him until they saw him alive after his resurrection.

After his ascension from the Mount of Olives, an angel confirmed that Jesus would return:

> "Men of Galilee, why do you stand looking into heaven? This Jesus, who was taken up from you into heaven, will come in the same way as you saw him go into heaven."
> —Acts 1:11

The return of Jesus was the steadfast hope of the early church, and it continues to be the hope of believers today. *Jesus' personal and visible return from heaven to Earth* is known as the **second coming**.

Jesus taught that his return would come at a time no one would expect. He said his return would be like that of a thief in the night, a master away on business, or a delayed bridegroom (Matthew 24:30–31, 42–44, 45–50, 25:1–13).[21]

Paul wrote about Jesus' second coming, urging the Thessalonian believers to "encourage one another" while they waited for the Lord (1 Thessalonians 4:16–18). Peter, similarly, urged those he addressed as "beloved" to live "in holiness and godliness, waiting for and hastening the coming of the day of God," recognizing that the Lord wants people to repent and be saved (2 Peter 3:9–14).

Jesus' second coming will be good news for his church. Believers—both those still living and those who have already died—are called *the bride of Christ* and invited to the "marriage supper of the lamb" (Revelation 19:6–10). They will rule with him throughout eternity. However, the second coming will be bad news for those who reject Christ and persist in evil. John describes Jesus as returning on a white horse to bring final judgment. He will return as "King of kings and Lord of lords" (Revelation 19:11–21) and everyone will acknowledge that Jesus is Lord (Philippians 2:10–11). The last verse in the Bible affirms the promise of his return: "He who testifies to these things says, 'Surely I am coming soon.' Amen. Come, Lord Jesus!" (Revelation 22:20).

What then, are we to do as we wait for Christ's return? Throughout history, believers have waited in different ways. Some people, expecting the return of Jesus to happen in their lifetimes, have quit their jobs and gotten rid of all possessions. Others have constructed elaborate timelines or even predicted the exact date of Jesus' return. Still others have acted as if the urgency of sharing the gospel justifies their neglect of other God-given responsibilities. But none of these reactions is suggested by the Bible. Instead, the writers of the Bible urge us to remain faithful, share the good news that Jesus is King, preach the message of reconciliation, and work for the healing and restoration of this world as much as we can. We wait for Jesus' return not by speculating about when it will occur, but by living faithfully in obedience to Jesus every day, empowered by the Holy Spirit (Galatians 5:5, Titus 2:11–14, 1 John 2:28).

8. From the Garden to the City

▸ **OBJECTIVE: You will be able to compare and contrast the new creation described in Revelation with the first creation in Genesis.**

Besides promising Jesus' return, Revelation describes the coming of a city, "the New Jerusalem," that comes down from heaven (Revelation 21:1–2). The city is pictured as a giant cube, which doesn't refer to its actual dimensions, but rather to the city's perfection (Revelation 21:16). Its cubic shape also resembles the holy of holies,[22] signifying that it will be a place where God is personally present to his people. It is a city where God and humans will dwell together in harmony, with humans using their God-given abilities to the fullest.

In God's new creation, described in Revelation 21–22, the garden and the city come together.[23] We cannot fully comprehend the new creation, but there are remarkable parallels between the Bible's first three and last three chapters.

As you can see from the chart on the next page *(figure 12.a)*, the new creation will not simply be a return to Eden. The new creation will be a restoration of God's creation which was marred by the fall; it will be a reconciliation between God and all creation; and it will also be a more beautiful, gloriously new world where humans and creation can live in freedom with God. (Acts 3:20–21, Colossians 1:15–20, Romans 8:18–23). Death will be destroyed (1 Corinthians 15:26). Humans will have new, perfected bodies (1 Corinthians 15:22, 35–55). Harmony will be restored between animals, people, and God (Isaiah 65:25). The new earth will be characterized by God's intimate presence with humankind and with his creation. This state will persist into eternity (2 Peter 3:10–13).[24]

Genesis 1–3	Revelation 20–22
"In the beginning, God created the heavens and the earth." (Gen. 1:1)	"I saw a new heaven and a new earth." (Rev. 21:1)
"The darkness he called Night." (Gen. 1:5)	"There will be no night there." (Rev. 21:25)
"God made two great lights." (The sun and the moon, Gen. 1:16)	"The city has no need of sun or moon." (Rev. 21:23)
"In the day that you eat from it, you shall surely die." (Gen. 2:17)	There will be no more death or sorrow. (Rev. 21:4)
Satan appears as the deceiver of humankind. (Gen. 3:1)	Satan is sent away forever. (Rev. 20:10)
Humans are given a garden, into which defilement entered. (Gen. 3:6–7)	Redeemed humans are given a city, where nothing that defiles will ever enter. (Rev. 21:10, 27)
Human fellowship with God is disrupted. (Gen. 3:8–10)	Human fellowship with God is fully restored. (Rev. 21:3)
The serpent initially triumphs. (Gen. 3:13)	The Lamb ultimately triumphs. (Rev. 20:10; 22:3)
"I will surely multiply your pain." (Gen. 3:16)	There will be no more pain. (Rev. 21:4)
"Cursed is the ground because of you." (Gen. 3:17)	There will be no more curse on the earth. (Rev. 22:3)
Sin, death, and suffering enter the world through the fall of the first man, Adam. (Gen. 3:17–19)	Sin, death, and suffering are ended in the rule of the second Adam, Christ. (Rev. 21:6)
The first paradise is closed. (Gen. 3:23)	The new paradise is opened. (Rev. 21:25)
Access to the tree of life is cut off in Adam. (Gen. 3:24)	Access to the tree of life is reinstated in Christ. (Rev. 22:14)
Humans were driven from God's presence. (Gen. 3:24)	"They will see his face." (Rev. 22:4)

figure 12.a

9. All Things New

▸ **OBJECTIVE: You will be able to articulate details of the New Jerusalem.**

In Revelation 21:5, God declares, "Behold, I am making all things new." This promise echoes what God told Isaiah (Isaiah 65:17–19). God's new creation will be greater than anything we could possibly imagine. That's why Scripture uses vivid word pictures to describe it.

In the New Jerusalem, God will be fully present with his people without any physical walls or barriers. In the past, use of the inner court of the temple had been limited to Jewish men; only priests entered the sanctuary; and only the high priest could go into the holy of holies. In the New Jerusalem, the temple will be open to all. It will not be a physical structure; rather, the temple will be "the Lord God the Almighty and the Lamb" (Revelation 21:22). To be clear, God never abandoned his people; however, ever since the fall in Genesis 3, sin has come between God and humans. In the New Jerusalem, that barrier will be totally removed and we will flourish in God's presence.

The New Jerusalem is open to all followers of the Lamb. In the new creation, there will be open and unlimited access to God. People from every tribe, nation, and tongue will be there (Revelation 5:9, 21:24; Zechariah 2:11). There will be no more prejudice or division based on race, language, or culture. All will worship together in peace. Access to the tree of life will no longer be restricted; instead, the tree will be right in the middle of the city, and its leaves will be "for the healing of all nations" (Revelation 22:2).

In the New Jerusalem, God will wipe away all tears, "death shall be no more, neither shall there be mourning, nor crying, nor pain anymore" (Revelation 21:4). We will no longer be plagued by sinful desires, broken relationships, pain, or death (Isaiah 25:8). We will live without fear, knowing that nothing evil will ever enter there (Revelation 21:27). Satan and his minions will be banished and will never again wreak havoc in God's world (Revelation 20:10). There will be no more struggle, no more war, no more curse. People will turn their weapons into gardening tools (Isaiah 2:4).

The city will also be beautiful. The New Jerusalem has streets of gold (Revelation 21:21), the walls are covered with precious stones (Revelation 21:18–20), a river runs through the city, and the tree of life bears much fruit (Revelation 22:2). There will be no more night there, because God will be the light (Revelation 21:23). It will be more breathtaking than we can possibly imagine (Isaiah 65:17-19).

The city will be a place where God is worshipped and humans flourish. We will be praising God throughout eternity. This does not just mean singing in a choir (though one can definitely imagine beautiful songs of worship being sung there). Fully "transformed into [the Lord's] image with ever-increasing glory" (2 Corinthians 3:18), we will rule and reign with God, stewarding the world, using our creativity to its fullest extent, developing what God has given us, and bringing abundance out of what he has made. With bodies that no longer decay, we will experience life as it was meant to be lived in God's presence.

We look forward to all this because Jesus has won the victory over sin and death. We do not know when God's new creation will arrive, but Revelation encourages us to be ready: "He who testifies to these things says, 'Surely I am coming soon.' Amen. Come, Lord Jesus!" (Revelation 22:20)

10. Conclusion

In the last seven chapters, we have explored the grand metanarrative of Scripture. It is a story about God's good creation, how sin alienated us from God and corrupted creation, how God chose a people to be a blessing to the earth, how Jesus died and rose again to redeem sinful humanity, how the Holy Spirit empowers the church to share the gospel, and how one day, God will make all things new.

What makes the Bible's metanarrative unique? After all, as we saw in Chapter 5, there are many stories or worldviews on offer in the world today—such as secularism, new spirituality, and postmodernism, to name just a few. Each of these worldviews claims to tell the true story of the world and gives answers to life's biggest questions; however, the story of Scripture stands apart. In his book *A Walk Through the Bible*, British theologian Lesslie Newbigin explained why the biblical metanarrative is so special.[25]

Some worldviews, Newbigin said, invite us into something larger than ourselves. They say our lives will be meaningful if we contribute "to some historical project of civilization which in the end will lead to a perfect society in the future."[26] But you and I will not get to share in the future utopia. We will be long gone before it arrives.

Instead of building for a future in which we will not share, many seek meaning in personal fulfillment—through power, money, or fame. In this way of thinking, the world as a whole does not matter and there is no metanarrative that can make sense of everything: there is only me and my story.

Newbigin pointed out that the biblical metanarrative, by contrast, calls us out of selfish individualism. It encourages us to work for God's kingdom, culminating in the new creation in which all believers will share. We have been invited into God's story. We labor with him and with one another, which provides meaning for our individual stories and gives us community. The Bible's vision, said Newbigin, "enables us to see the whole human story and each of our lives within that story as meaningful . . . [It] therefore invites us through Jesus Christ to become responsible actors in history."[27]

In other words, we have a place in the biblical metanarrative *today*: the "filming" is still taking place; we are actors on the set as the story resolves. We can exercise our gifts, talents, and passions for God's glory and in the service of others, as we anticipate the full restoration of God's kingdom on Earth.

In the last seven chapters, we have only briefly surveyed the metanarrative of Scripture. It makes sense of the grand sweep of history, explains our place in the world, and invites us to participate in God's mission. However, there are many details we did not have space to discuss. You can't do any better than to go and read the Bible for yourself. As you do, you may just find yourself caught up in God's great story. In the next few chapters, we'll take a deeper dive into Scripture as we consider the nature of God and humans.

ENDNOTES

[1]Julian, *Julian of Norwich: Showings*, trans. Edmund Colledge, and James Walsh, (Mahwah, NJ: Paulist Press, 1978), 305.

[2]Friedrich Nietzsche, as quoted in Michael J. Gorman, *Reading Revelation Responsibly: Uncivil Worship and Witness—Following the Lamb into the New Creation* (Eugene, OR: Cascade Books, 2011), 2.

[3]Mitchell G. Reddish, "The Genre of the Book of Revelation," in *The Oxford Handbook of the Book of Revelation*, ed. by Craig R. Koester (Oxford: Oxford University Press, 2020), 21–35.

[4]Gorman, *Reading Revelation Responsibly*, 15.

[5]Gorman, *Reading Revelation Responsibly*, 17–19.

[6]N. T. Wright, *Revelation for Everyone* (Louisville, KY: Westminster John Knox Press, 2011), 10–41.

[7]For a thorough treatment of how Romans viewed Christians, see Robert Louis Wilken, *The Christians as the Romans Saw Them* (New Haven, CT: Yale University Press, 1984). See also Larry W. Hurtado, *Destroyer of the Gods: Christian Distinctiveness in the Roman World* (Waco, TX: Baylor University Press, 2016), 52–62.

[8]Paul Spilsbury, *The Throne, the Lamb, & the Dragon: A Reader's Guide to the Book of Revelation* (Downers Grove, IL: IVP Academic, 2002), 51.

[9]Richard Bauckham, *The Theology of the Book of Revelation* (New York: Cambridge University Press, 1993), 80.

[10]Spilsbury, *The Throne, the Lamb, & the Dragon*, 72.

[11]Spilbury, *The Throne, the Lamb, & the Dragon*, 51–65.

[12]Gorman, *Reading Revelation Responsibly*, 140.

[13]Spilsbury, *The Throne, the Lamb, & the Dragon*, 127–128.

[14]Peter Kreeft, "Hell," Crossroads Initiative, January 15, 2021, https://www.crossroadsinitiative.com/media/articles/hell-peter-kreeft/.

[15]Tim Keller, *The Reason for God: Belief in an Age of Skepticism* (New York: Riverhead Books, 2008), 79.

[16]Keller, *The Reason for God: Belief in an Age of Skepticism,* 78–79.

[17]C. S. Lewis, *The Great Divorce* (New York: HarperCollins, 1946), 75.

[18]For a thorough treatment of this topic, see N. T. Wright, *Surprised by Hope: Rethinking Heaven, the Resurrection, and the Mission of the Church* (New York, NY: HarperCollins, 2008).

[19]Ben Witherington III, *Revelation and the End Times: Unraveling God's Message of Hope* (Nashville: Abingdon Press, 2010), 45.

[20]Wright, *Surprised by Hope*, 171–172.

[21]Some scholars take these verses to refer to the destruction of the temple in AD 70 and interpret the destruction of the temple as the vindication of Jesus. However, many proponents of this view still affirm that Jesus will come again at the end of history, though they argue that these verses do not refer to that event. See for example, N. T. Wright, *Jesus and the Victory of God* (Minneapolis, MN: Fortress Press, 1996), 360–365.

[22]Craig R. Koester, "Revelation's Vision of New Jerusalem: God's Life-Giving Reign for the World," *Word & World* 40, no. 2, (Spring 2020): 115.

[23]Koester, "Revelation's Vision of New Jerusalem: God's Life-Giving Reign for the World," 119.

[24]Zachary Klein and Hannah Klein, "Effects of the Fall on the Physical Creation: A Biblical Analysis," *Answers Research Journal* 13, (August 12, 2020):95–111, https://answersingenesis.org/sin/effects-of-the-fall-on-the-physical-creation-a-biblical-analysis/.

[25]What follows is a summary and modification of Newbigin's insights on pages 82–85 of Lesslie Newbigin, *A Walk Through the Bible* (Louisville, KY: Westminster John Knox Press, 1999).

[26]Newbigin, *A Walk Through the Bible*, 82.

[27]Newbigin, *A Walk Through the Bible*, 84–85.

13

Who God Is

1. Four Gods

▸ **OBJECTIVE: You will be able to categorize four ways in which people view God.**

What do people mean when they say they believe in God? According to research shared in the book *America's Four Gods*, most Americans—about 95 percent—believe in God. They usually fall into one of four categories.

- 31 percent believe in an *authoritative* God who is engaged in human affairs and also judgmental, punishing or rewarding us now.

- 24 percent believe in a *benevolent* God who is engaged and nonjudgmental, rescuing or providing alternatives in crises.
- 16 percent believe in a *critical* God who is disengaged and judgmental, not interfering in human affairs now but planning to judge us in the afterlife.
- 24 percent believe in a *distant* God who is disengaged and nonjudgmental.[1]

How we view God is no small matter. Theologian A. W. Tozer emphasized in his classic book *Knowledge of the Holy* that "what comes into our minds when we think about God is the most important thing about us."[2] Our view of God both affects and is affected by the way we live.

Theology is *the study of God*—his nature and actions and everything that relates to him. Most of us are engaged in some form of theological reflection on a regular basis; almost everyone has thoughts about who God is. We can truly say that everyone is, in this sense, a theologian. A theologian is someone who thinks about God and God's relation to the world. All of us, even atheists, think about God.

Window in Victoria Legislative Building, Victoria, British Columbia, Canada

So, what does the average US Christian think about God? According to one study:

> [About] 93 percent of (US) Christians believe God loves all people, regardless of their faults. Nearly nine-in-ten (87 percent) say that God knows everything that happens in the world. And about eight-in-ten (78 percent) believe God has the power to direct or change everything that goes on in the world. In total, three-quarters of US Christians believe that God possesses all three of these attributes—that the Deity is loving, omniscient and omnipotent.[3]

What are these beliefs based on, though? In this chapter we'll talk about whether we can discover who an infinite God is. We'll then look at who God reveals himself to be and his nature as Father, Son, and Holy Spirit.

If God "is there and he is not silent,"[4] as the philosopher and pastor Francis Schaeffer put it, can we actually *know* him?

2. Can We Really Know an Infinite God?

▸ **OBJECTIVE: You will be able to conclude it is possible to know God as he reveals himself to us in scripture.**

Nearly a thousand years ago, a Benedictine monk and philosopher named *Anselm of Canterbury* defined God as "that than which none greater can be conceived,"[5] adding we must think of God as "the greatest possible being, an individual exhibiting maximal perfection."[6] **Perfect being theology** is *a view that defines God as the greatest possible being.*

According to Anselm, it is impossible even to imagine a being that is greater than God. Since God is infinite, our ability to understand him is limited and he is greater than any of our definitions. Because we are finite, all of our thinking about God is to be characterized by humility, with the recognition that we cannot possibly ever have all the answers.

perfect being theology: a view that defines God as the greatest possible being

Some people fall into the trap of thinking that because they cannot know *everything* about God, they cannot know *anything* about God. But that conclusion isn't true. As one researcher phrased it, "While we cannot know God *exhaustively*, we can know him *truly*. The finite human mind cannot fully comprehend the nature of an infinite God . . . but we can grow in our understanding and experience of God as he has *revealed* himself in creation, Scripture, and through Jesus Christ."[7]

The apostle Paul wrote in Romans 11:33, "Oh, the depth of the riches and wisdom and knowledge of God! How unsearchable are his judgments and how inscrutable his ways!" Even as we marvel at how far God is above our understanding, Scripture also assumes we can know him truly. Jeremiah 9:23–24 says: "Let not the wise man boast in his wisdom, let not the mighty man boast in his might, let not the rich man boast in his riches, but let him who boasts boast in this, that he understands and knows me."

God has chosen to reveal himself in how he created the world and by giving us the Scriptures. However, the fullest way we know God is through Jesus Christ (Hebrews 1:1–2). The Holy Spirit teaches us about Jesus (John 14:26). Not only can we know God, but we can know him well enough to obey him and to love him (Deuteronomy 29:29, 1 John 5:3).

God reveals himself in both word and action. He wants to be known, and through the Bible he has given us information to understand him as he wants to be understood.

3. Who God Reveals Himself to Be—Part 1

▸ OBJECTIVE: You will be able to determine that God is self-existent, personal, spirit, and incarnate in Jesus.

We previously discussed God's transcendence (he is above and outside his creation) and immanence (he is within and among his creation). But there is much more that we can know about God! In this and the next two sections, we will look at a dozen more of his characteristics.

1. God is self-existent. Theologians use the word **aseity** (from the Latin *a se*, "from oneself") to describe *God's self-existent and self-sufficient nature.* As philosopher William Lane Craig describes, "God doesn't just happen to exist, as if by accident. Rather God exists by a necessity of his own nature; it is impossible for him not to exist. Moreover, God does not depend upon any other being for his existence. God alone is self-existent, and everything else depends on Him."[8]

As a self-existent being, God alone can cause everything else to exist and can sustain its existence: Everything that exists does so only because God exists first (Genesis 1:1, Job 33:4, Romans 11:36, Colossians 1:16–17). God's existence makes sense of the origin of the universe because it makes sense of the universe's design. Design, after all, must have a designer. Moreover, because God exists apart from nature, he can provide a foundation for objective moral values.

2. God is spirit and incarnate in Jesus. Some people think of God as an old man in the sky who likes to spoil his children, or as a Zeus-like figure holding a lightning bolt waiting to strike us when we sin. But the Bible affirms that God is not a physical being. Rather, he is pure spirit (John 4:24). He is not bound by space or time. John 1:18 affirms that "no one has ever seen God." It also asserts that Jesus, who was God in the flesh, made God known to us. Jesus became a human being so that we might know God. God makes himself known to us by becoming human, like us.

This truth about God reveals two important things about the nature of reality. First, both spirit and matter exist. The physical world is not all that exists (as materialism teaches), nor is the world only spiritual (as pantheism teaches). Second, both the physical and the spiritual are good and valuable, demonstrated by God's actions in revealing himself to us.

3. God is personal. For 53 percent of people surveyed by the authors of *America's Four Gods*, God is not a person but a "cosmic force,"[9] like the force in *Star Wars*. However, God is a person to be known, rather than a force to be used. The entire Bible is the story of God interacting as a person. It records some of his conversations with Adam and Eve (Genesis 3:16–19), Abraham (Genesis 17:1–22), Moses (Exodus 3), and many others. It tells about how he delights in his people or is disappointed by them (Deuteronomy 30:9, Zephaniah 3:6–8). It tells about his longing for a relationship with us (Ephesians 1:4–5, Revelation 21:3–4) and his thoughts and plans for us (1 Corinthians 2:9). The very idea of personhood comes from God—he made human beings in his image.

4. Who God Reveals Himself to Be—Part 2

▸ **OBJECTIVE: You will be able to discuss God's eternality, omniscience, omnipotence, omnipresence, and immutability.**

4. God is eternal. To say God is *eternal* is to say that he has always existed. There never was a time when he was not, and there will never be a time when he will not be. Psalm 90:2 tells us, "Before the mountains were brought forth, or ever you had formed the earth and the world, from everlasting to everlasting you are God." Jude 1:24–25 acknowledges God's eternal nature: "Now to him who is able to keep you from stumbling and to present you blameless before the presence of his glory with great joy, to the only God, our Savior, through Jesus Christ our Lord, be glory, majesty, dominion, and authority, before all time and now and forever. Amen."

5. God is all-knowing. We use the word *omniscient* to describe God's unique and unbounded capacity for knowledge. God knows everything possible and actual. He possesses complete knowledge of the past, present, and future. A passage we looked at earlier, Romans 11:33, affirms: "Oh, the depth of the riches and wisdom and knowledge of God! How unsearchable are his judgments and how inscrutable his ways!" Isaiah 46:9–10 says: "I am God, and there is no other; I am God, and there is none like me, declaring the end from the beginning and from ancient times things not yet done, saying, 'My counsel shall stand, and I will accomplish all my purpose.' "

Engraving by German painter Julius Schnorr von Carolsfeld

6. God is all-powerful. We use the word *omnipotent* to say that God is perfect in power. God possesses the power to do anything he desires. "Ah, Lord GOD! It is you who have made the heavens and the earth by your great power and by your outstretched arm! Nothing is too hard for you" (Jeremiah 32:17). In Mark 10:27, Jesus told his disciples, "With man it is impossible, but not with God. For all things are possible with God." This does not mean, however, that God *will* do anything. God will not do the illogical for him, such as make a squared circle or a married bachelor, nor will he act contrary to his nature.

7. God is present everywhere. We use the word *omnipresent* to say that God is eternally present—in all places, at all times. Jeremiah 23:23–24 says, "Am I a God at hand, declares the LORD, and not a God far away? Can a man hide himself in secret places so that I cannot see him? declares the LORD. Do I not fill heaven and earth? declares the LORD." Psalm 139:7–10 says, "Where shall I go from your Spirit? Or where shall I flee from your presence? If I ascend to heaven, you are there! If I make my bed in Sheol, you are there! If I take the wings of the morning and dwell in the uttermost parts of the sea, even there your hand shall lead me, and your right hand shall hold me."

8. God is unchanging. God's character is *immutable*—constant and unchangeable. He is the same yesterday, today, and forever (Hebrews 13:8). Numbers 23:19 says, "God is not man, that he should lie, or a son of man, that he should change his mind. Has he said, and will he not do it? Or has he spoken, and will he not fulfill it?" Psalm 33:11 concurs: "The counsel of the LORD stands forever, the plans of his heart to all generations." God's constancy is a source of protection for his people. "For I the LORD do not change; therefore you, O children of Jacob, are not consumed" (Malachi 3:6).

5. Who God Reveals Himself to Be—Part 3

▸ **OBJECTIVE:** You will be able to explain that God is holy, wise, righteous, and loving.

9. God is holy. To be *holy* means to be set apart. God is set apart from everything and everyone. No one is like him. He is absolutely pure. Scripture repeatedly affirms this. Exodus 15:11 asks, "Who is like you, O Lord, among the gods? Who is like you, majestic in holiness, awesome in glorious deeds, doing wonders?" Revelation 4:8b says, "'Holy, holy, holy, is the Lord God Almighty, who was and is and is to come!'" Even though no human being can be as holy as God, he makes us holy through his Holy Spirit. 1 Peter 1:16 says, "You shall be holy, for I am holy."

10. God is wise. To say God is wise is to say he knows all the implications of his actual and potential actions, bringing about no unintended consequences. Scripture directly affirms God's wisdom more than 200 times. Job 12:13 affirms, "With God are wisdom and might; he has counsel and understanding." Psalm 104:24 says, "O Lord, how manifold are your works! In wisdom have you made them all; the earth is full of your creatures." People are seen to be wise when God's wisdom is in them, and to be fools when knowledge of him is absent. "The fear of the Lord is the beginning of knowledge; fools despise wisdom and instruction" (Proverbs 1:7).

11. God is righteous. God's *righteousness* refers to his justice and moral purity. Deuteronomy 32:4 says he is a "God of faithfulness and without iniquity, just and upright is he." Psalm 89:14 says, "Righteousness and justice are the foundation of your throne." This is good news in a corrupt world. God will always do right. He can't be bribed and he won't lie. He is in the business of righting wrongs. Part of that business means he rights what is wrong in us, too. On the cross, Jesus gave us his righteousness, so that when God looks at us, he sees us as holy and blameless in his sight (Colossians 1:22). Our righteousness is not our own, but a gift from God when we are justified by faith in Christ.

Moses and the Burning Bush, painting by Gebhard Fugel, c. 1920

12. God is loving. Love is so central to God's character that to misunderstand it is to not even know God. The apostle John says this quite clearly: "Anyone who does not love does not know God, because God is love" (1 John 4:8). God is "merciful and gracious, slow to anger, and abounding in steadfast love and faithfulness" (Exodus 34:6).

It is God's nature to love. And here's some stunning news: because of the power of the Holy Spirit, we can love this way too. Romans 5:5 says God's love has been "poured into our hearts through the Holy Spirit who has been given to us." It is this kind of love of which the apostle Paul speaks in his famous passage on love:

> Love is patient and kind; love does not envy or boast; it is not arrogant or rude. It does not insist on its own way; it is not irritable or resentful; it does not rejoice at wrongdoing, but rejoices with the truth. Love bears all things, believes all things, hopes all things, endures all things. –1 Corinthians 13:4–7

doctrine of the Trinity:
the Christian belief that God is one Being in three Persons: Father, Son, and Holy Spirit

6. The Triune God

▸OBJECTIVE: You will be able to summarize the doctrine of the Trinity and argue that tritheism and modalism are false beliefs.

On the surface at least, all of the above qualities are not too difficult to grasp, even if it's a bit hard to imagine a being possessing all these qualities. But there is a doctrine about God that has confused people for centuries and still confuses people today. The **doctrine of the Trinity** is *the Christian belief that God is one Being in three Persons: Father, Son, and Holy Spirit.* In the Trinity, "one divine Being eternally exists as three distinct centers of consciousness, wholly equal in nature, genuinely personal in relationships, and each mutually indwelling the other."[10]

The book *Life's Biggest Questions: What the Bible Says about the Things That Matter Most* gives this helpful summary:

> The biblical teaching on the Trinity is summarized with four essential affirmations: (1) There is one—and only one—true and living God, (2) This one God eternally exists in three persons—God the Father, God the Son, and God the Holy Spirit, (3) These three Persons are completely equal in attributes, each having the same divine nature, and (4) While each Person is *fully* and *completely* God, the Persons are not identical.[11]

Before we set out what Scripture says about the Trinity, let's first look at some common incorrect ideas about the Trinity. Some people say it is like an egg with a shell, a white, and a yolk, all together. But this is incorrect. Each part of an egg is a separate and distinct part. To say the Trinity is like an egg is to flirt with **tritheism**, which is *the belief that the Trinity is composed of three separate and distinct gods.*

But Scripture teaches there is only one God (1 Corinthians 8:6), not three. The doctrine of the Trinity is *not* claiming there is *one* God with three different parts, or that there are *three* gods. The Trinity teaches *one* God and *three* Persons (One *What* and Three *Whos*).

tritheism:
the belief that the Trinity is composed of three separate and distinct gods

Others say the Trinity is like the three states of water: liquid, solid, and gas. That comparison gets close to a false belief that denies the "three-ness" of the Trinity. Think about it like this—water is one thing; yet, a sample of water cannot exist in its liquid, solid, gaseous forms at the same time. For example, if a sample of water is liquid, then it cannot at the same time be in the form of a solid or a gas. Similarly, **modalism** is *the belief that the Trinity is composed of one God who over time presents himself in three different modes (Father, Son, and Holy Spirit).* According to modalism, God cannot be Father, Son, and Holy Spirit at the same time; he can only be one person at a time.

In contrast, Scripture indicates that God is one essence in three distinct persons who exist in relationship with one another. John 1:1 states that Jesus (the Word) was with God at the beginning of creation, and Genesis 1:2 describes the Spirit of God hovering over the waters at creation. So, Father, Son, and Holy Spirit existed simultaneously as three distinct persons before the world began. Furthermore, Matthew 3:13–17 shows that all three persons—Father, Son, and Holy Spirit—were present and active at Jesus' baptism. If modalism were true, such an episode would make no sense. God does not appear in three different modes (as in, sometimes he shows up as Father, sometimes as Son, sometimes as Holy Spirit). Rather, the one God is three separate and distinct Persons—Father, Son, and Holy Spirit.

modalism: the belief that the Trinity is composed of one God who over time presents himself in three different modes (Father, Son, and Holy Spirit)

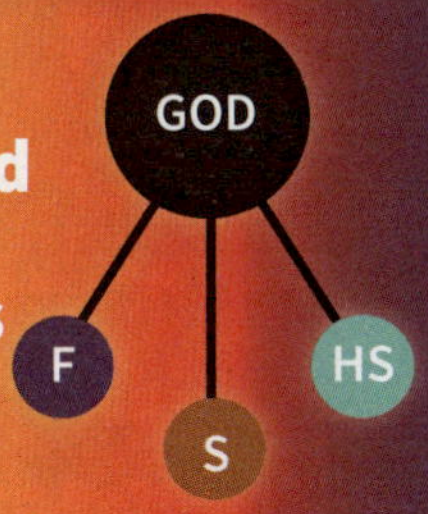

It might surprise you to know that the word *Trinity* isn't in the Bible. The term was first used by Tertullian, an African theologian who lived between AD 150 and 220, to describe the "three and yet one" nature of God. But the doctrine of the Trinity is not one person's clever invention; it is rooted in biblical teaching, which is why the church continues to teach it today. Let's consider how the three Persons of the Trinity are described as God in the Old and New Testaments.

7. The Trinity in the Old Testament

▸ OBJECTIVE: You will be able to use Old Testament verses to support that God is three Persons in one.

We already quoted several verses in the Old Testament that show God referring to himself as singular. Yet, God also refers to himself in the plural in passages such as Genesis 3:22, 11:7, and Isaiah 6:8. The names we learned for God from Genesis 1 and 2, *Yahweh* and *Elohim*, also teach the singular and plural nature of God. In the Old Testament, each member of the Trinity—Father, Son, and Holy Spirit—is called God and displays the attributes of deity.

The Old Testament reveals God as Father. God called the nation of Israel his children and wanted them to call him Father: "I said, 'How I would set you among my sons, and give you a pleasant land, a heritage most beautiful of all nations. And I thought you would call me, My Father, and would not turn from following me" (Jeremiah 3:19). And at times, they did call him Father (Isaiah 63:16, 64:8).

Isaiah is also the prophet through whom God told the world he would send God the Son to redeem humankind: "Therefore the Lord himself will give you a sign. Behold, the virgin shall conceive and bear a son, and shall call his name Immanuel" (Isaiah 7:14).

Immanuel means *God is with us*. Isaiah 9:6 adds, "For to us a child is born, to us a son is given; and the government shall be upon his shoulder, and his name shall be called Wonderful Counselor, Mighty God, Everlasting Father, Prince of Peace."

Isaiah wrote about God the Holy Spirit as well: "And the Spirit of the LORD shall rest upon him, the Spirit of wisdom and understanding, the Spirit of counsel and might, the Spirit of knowledge and the fear of the LORD" (Isaiah 11:2). This Spirit would rest on the coming Messiah, the Son of God: "The Spirit of the LORD GOD is upon me, because the LORD has anointed me to bring good news to the poor; he has sent me to bind up the brokenhearted, to proclaim liberty to the captives, and the opening of the prison to those who are bound" (Isaiah 61:1). Jesus quoted this verse about himself in Luke 4:18.

The Holy Spirit was active in creation: "In the beginning, God created the heavens and the earth. The earth was without form and void, and darkness was over the face of the deep. And the Spirit of God was hovering over the face of the waters" (Genesis 1:1–2). The Spirit dwells in God's servants: "Cast me not away from your presence, and take not your Holy Spirit from me" (Psalm 51:11). This same Spirit would be poured out on all people in a coming day, according to the promise made in Joel 2:28–29.

These verses about the deity of the three Persons of the Trinity can appear contradictory and confusing without the light shed on them in the New Testament, which we will consider next.

8. The Trinity in the New Testament

▸ OBJECTIVE: You will be able to identify New Testament verses that confirm God is Father, Son, and Holy Spirit.

Several passages in the New Testament mention all three Persons of the Trinity together, such as Matthew 28:19–20, John 14:26, 2 Corinthians 13:14, Hebrews 9:14, 1 Peter 1:1–2, and Jude 1:20–21. One of the clearest accounts of all three Persons being present together is the baptism of Jesus. "And when Jesus was baptized, immediately he went up from the water, and behold, the heavens were opened to him, and he saw the Spirit of God descending like a dove and coming to rest on him; and behold, a voice from heaven said, 'This is my beloved Son, with whom I am well pleased'" (Matthew 3:16–17).

In addition to presenting the three Persons of the Godhead all together, in the New Testament the Father, Son, and Holy Spirit are each individually called God and display the attributes of deity.

The Father is God: Jesus refers to God the Father in passages such as John 5:17, "But Jesus answered them, 'My Father is working until now, and I am working,'" And again, one chapter later, "Do not work for the food that perishes, but for the food that endures to eternal life, which the Son of Man will give to you. For on him God the Father has set his seal" (John 6:27). God the Father is mentioned often in Acts (1:4, 2:33, 10:38) and the epistles (1 Corinthians 8:6, Galatians 4:6, Ephesians 1:17, 2:18, 1 Peter 1:2, 2 Peter 1:17).

The Son is God: Jesus was called *God* from before his birth. "All this took place to fulfill what the Lord had said through the prophet: 'Behold, the virgin will conceive and bear a son, and they shall call his name Immanuel, (which means God with us)" (Matthew 1:22–23). John 1:1 introduces Jesus as the Word, "And the Word was with God, and the Word was God." Thomas called Jesus, "My Lord and my God" (John 20:28). In the epistles Jesus is recognized as "God over all" (Romans 9:5). Titus 2:13 talks about "waiting for our blessed hope, the appearing of the glory of our great God and Savior Jesus Christ." And Hebrews 1:3 says, "He is the radiance of the glory of God and the exact imprint of his nature, and he upholds the universe by the word of his power."

The Holy Spirit is God: The Gospels contain references to the Holy Spirit in conjunction with the Father and the Son, but they also show the Holy Spirit is himself God. Scripture shows the Holy Spirit manifesting God's attributes: omnipresence (Psalm 139:7), omniscience (1 Corinthians 2:10–11), and omnipotence (Job 33:4). In Acts 5:3–4, Ananias, the man who lied about his offering, is asked by Peter why he allowed Satan to fill his heart to deceive the Holy Spirit. Peter added, "You have not lied to man but to God." To the church in Corinth, Paul writes, "Do you not know that you are God's temple and that God's Spirit dwells in you?" (1 Corinthians 3:16) and "But you were washed, you were sanctified, you were justified in the name of the Lord Jesus Christ and by the Spirit of our God" (1 Corinthians 6:11).

Dove of the Holy Spirit, Chiesa Spirito Santo dei Napoletani, Rome, Italy

9. Why the Trinity Matters

▸ **OBJECTIVE: You will be able to give reasons why the Trinity is important to the Christian faith.**

We have seen that the Trinity is one Being (one God) in three distinct Persons (Father, Son, and Spirit), each of whom is fully God. We've also seen how both the Old and New Testaments affirm this doctrine. But so what? What possible difference could it make to your Christian faith that God is a Trinity? According to theologian Michael Reeves, the Trinity makes all the difference in the world. In fact, the Trinity is "what makes Christianity absolutely distinct."[12] Let's consider three ways in which the Trinity makes a difference to your faith.

For starters, consider that a solitary God, defined primarily by his power, wouldn't have anyone to love or any reason to love. But God's trinitarian nature means that before all of creation, the Father was sharing life and love with the Son and the Holy Spirit. God created us, not because he needed us to be who he is, but because it is in his nature to share life and love.[13]

Secondly, the Son, being in perfect harmony with the Father and Spirit, shares the life of the Trinity with us in unique ways. Through Jesus we can know God truly (John 1:18) and be saved (John 14:6). 1 John 4:9 says that the Father showed his love for us by sending "his only Son into the world, so that we might live through him." Jesus not only shows us what God is like, he shows us what it means to be truly human. He models how we can do the works of the Father (John 5:17) in the power of the Spirit (Luke 4:14). Jesus shows us what a truly life-giving, others-centered life can look like. He invites us to receive God's love through faith and give it out again to others.

Finally, the Trinity provides the model for Christian community. In the Trinity, there is both diversity (three distinct Persons) and unity (one God). The members of the Trinity are separate Persons, yet they are all united in a perfect relationship of love and harmony. Christian community should also be characterized by unity and diversity. The members of our Christian community come from many different backgrounds (Romans 10:12, Galatians 3:28, Colossians 3:11). Even though each member has specific characteristics and gifts, all receive the same Spirit and are part of the same body (1 Corinthians 12:4–7, 12–13; Ephesians 4:4–6). The gospel does not demand that we ignore our differences, but it does call us all to unity (1 Corinthians 1:10, 2 Corinthians 13:11, Philippians 2:2–3, Colossians 3:13–14). As we love one another and strive for peace and reconciliation, we reflect the harmonious relationship of Father, Son, and Holy Spirit.

Even though the Trinity can be challenging to understand, it makes all the difference to our view of God, salvation, and community.

10. Conclusion

Our discussion of God's nature and character in this chapter can be summarized in this statement by the late theology professor Gordon R. Lewis:

> God is an invisible, personal, and living Spirit, distinguished from all other spirits by several kinds of attributes: metaphysically, God is self-existent, eternal, and unchanging; intellectually, God is omniscient, faithful, and wise; ethically, God is just, merciful, and loving; emotionally, God detests evil, is longsuffering, and is compassionate; existentially, God is free, authentic, and omnipotent; relationally, God is transcendent in being, immanent universally in providential activity, and immanent with his people in redemptive activity.[14]

This can all seem pretty complicated. But the goal of theology is not merely to learn more or think more accurately about God. Instead, we want to know God personally and *love* him with all of our mind and heart, as Jesus stated in Matthew 22:37. As we grow in our love for God, we will also grow in our desire to know his thoughts and values. The best theology is more than an academic discipline; it is a way of loving, of knowing, and of cherishing God. Good theology is an act of worship of the very highest sort.

The proper response to the God of the Bible is worship. We bow down in humble awe and reverence to the perfect, utterly trustworthy, only wise, self-existent, personal, completely unselfish, great, good God—Father, Son, and Holy Spirit. In the next chapter, we'll see how getting to know this God leads to a loving relationship with him and an outward flow of love to others.

ENDNOTES

[1]Paul Froese and Christopher Bader, *America's Four Gods: What We Say about God & What That Says about Us* (New York: Oxford University Press, 2010), 33–34.

[2]A. W. Tozer, *Knowledge of the Holy* (New York: HarperCollins, 1961), 1.

[3]"When Americans Say They Believe in God, What Do They Mean?" Pew Research Center, April 25, 2018, https://www.pewforum.org/2018/04/25/when-americans-say-they-believe-in-god-what-do-they-mean/.

[4]Francis A. Schaeffer, *He Is There and He Is Not Silent* (Carol Stream, IL: Tyndale House Publishers, 1972).

[5]Quoted in Thomas V. Morris, *Our Idea of God: An Introduction to Philosophical Theology* (Downers Grove, IL: InterVarsity Press, 1991), 35.

[6]Anselm quoted in Morris, *Our Idea of God*, 35.

[7]Jonathan Morrow, "Can We Truly Know an Infinite God?" *Think Christianly* (blog), December 29, 2012, http://www.thinkchristianly.org/can-we-truly-know-an-infinite-god/.

[8]William Lane Craig, *Dr. Craig's What Is God Like? God Is Self-Sufficient. The Attributes of God for Children* (Self-published, CreateSpace, 2012), back cover copy.

[9]Froese and Bader, *America's Four Gods*, 5.

[10]J. Scott Horrell, "The Eternal Son of God in the Social Trinity," in *Jesus in Trinitarian Perspective: An Introductory Christology*, eds. Fred Sanders and Klaus Issler (Nashville: B&H Academic, 2007), 47–48.

[11]Erik Thoennes, *Life's Biggest Questions: What the Bible Says about the Things That Matter Most* (Wheaton, IL: Crossway, 2011), 71–72.

[12]Michael Reeves, *Delighting in the Trinity: An Introduction to the Christian Faith* (Downer's Grove, IL: InterVarsity Press, 2012), 15.

[13]Reeves, *Delighting in the Trinity*, 19–38.

[14]Gordon R. Lewis, "Attributes of God," in *Evangelical Dictionary of Theology*, ed. Walter A. Elwell (Grand Rapids: Baker Academic, 2001), 492.

1. Being Human

▸ **OBJECTIVE: You will be able to explain what being human means and why we have a need for God.**

Who am I? Who do I want to be? These are just two of the many questions that we ask ourselves on the road to self-discovery. Knowing ourselves is essential to living well in the world. Learning more about our personalities, temperaments, and deepest desires is important. But have you ever stopped to ask, "Who does God want me to be?" Answering this question is essential to understanding our true identity.

An accurate picture of ourselves must begin with the fact that we are all human. In Genesis 1:26–27, we discover that humans are made in God's image. We are not an accident, trash, a mistake, or a cruel experiment. Being made in God's image means that we have dignity and worth right from the get-go. We are so valuable that Christ gave his life for us so that we might become God's children and share in all his blessings (John 1:12–13, Galatians 4:1–7, 1 John 3:1–3).

In Genesis 2:18, we discover that humans are made for relationships. Human life is defined by our relationships with God, ourselves, others, and creation. God gave us the capacity to make choices and to love others. While we are not able to do these things perfectly, like God can, we are still called to imitate him (1 John 2:6, 1 Peter 2:21). We also learn from Scripture that humans have responsibility in God's world, to rule over it (Genesis 1:26, 28; Psalm 8:3–6).

Though we have a privileged place in God's creation, we are not gods. We are limited beings, dependent on God (Acts 17:28, 1 Corinthians 8:6). Without him, we (and everything else) would cease to exist. Compared with God, we are quite limited; compared with the universe, we are small. Yet, our limitations are not meant to hold us down or to keep us from achieving our potential. Rather, they cause us to realize our need for God and others, and so drive us out of ourselves to seek relationships.

It's also clear from Scripture that humans have a major problem. But the problem is not that we are human, but that our humanity has been corrupted, hijacked by the curse of sin. As descendants of Adam and Eve, we have all inherited a sin nature, which has crippled our ability to do what is right (Psalm 14:2–3, Romans 5:12). Through our sinful thoughts and actions, we rebel against God, hurt other people, abuse ourselves, and disregard God's creation. In trusting Jesus, we begin the process of sanctification, but the battle against sin is one that we must fight our whole lives. C. S. Lewis summarized this well at the end of his book *Prince Caspian*. To be descended from Adam and Eve, Aslan says, "is both honour enough to erect the head of the poorest beggar, and shame enough to bow the shoulders of the greatest emperor on earth."[1]

Because of sin, another of our present limitations is that our lives are mortal. Over time, our bodies decay and eventually die. In trusting Jesus, we have been given eternal life. But until the kingdom comes, we live in the time of already and not yet. We are confident that God will transform our sinful natures and grant us new bodies that will never die.

Humans are not perfect now, but they have the hope of being perfected in the future. Being human is not a problem; it is an incredible gift. It is who God made us to be.

2. Living in the Here and Now

▸ **OBJECTIVE: You will be able to express that because Jesus was fully human, he is a model we can follow for holy living in this world.**

We have said that being human is not the problem. There is no clearer evidence of this in Scripture than the fact that Jesus himself was fully human (God incarnate). He is the model of everything that humans were meant to be—the one who submitted to the Father's will, loved without reservation, and gave of himself for the sake of others. If we are to become who God made us to be, we must learn to follow Jesus.

The Gospel writers are united in affirming that Jesus was a living, breathing human being—that Jesus "became flesh and dwelt among us" (John 1:14). The four Gospels are based on eyewitness testimony from those who knew Jesus while he walked on earth.[2] Jesus' humanity was also affirmed by Paul, who wrote about how Jesus appeared, when he had been "manifested in the flesh" (1 Timothy 3:16). As a human, Jesus had a physical body. He would have experienced headaches, tiredness, and stubbed toes; and the need to eat and drink, to use the bathroom, and to sleep. He also would have been subject to all kinds of temptations—including temptations to steal, lust, cheat, or lie (Hebrews 2:17–18).

You may be used to thinking about Jesus in this way, but the idea of God becoming human would have been scandalous in Jesus' time. For the Jews, a human being claiming to be God was blasphemy (John 10:33). Certainly, no one was expecting God to come as a helpless child born of a virgin, but this is exactly what happened (Matthew 1:23). For Gentiles, the idea of God becoming human was simply foolishness. Appalled by the idea that God would reveal himself as a lowly human, some people rejected the humanity of Christ altogether. Instead, they taught **Docetism**, which is *the heretical teaching that Jesus was completely divine and only appeared to be human*. This belief was ultimately rejected by the church as a heresy.[3]

As a human, Jesus was in the closest possible relationship with the Father (John 1:18). He knew himself as God's beloved Son (Matthew 3:17), sent to bring salvation (Luke 19:10). Unlike all other humans, Jesus chose to submit himself totally to God, rejecting all temptation and never sinning (Hebrews 4:15, 1 Peter 2:22). Unlike other humans, Jesus did not play favorites. Jesus did not select a few privileged people and teach them how to withdraw from the world by contemplating secret spiritual knowledge. Instead, Jesus ministered on the streets and in the towns to all, including the poor, oppressed, and downtrodden. He came into our mess and walked around in it. Frequently, he invited people to follow him (Luke 18:22).

Jesus does not call us to withdraw from society or escape the world; nor are we to denigrate the material creation in favor of more "spiritual" concerns. If we are to follow

Jesus, we must deal with the here-and-now of earthly life. This means not just tolerating, but loving the frustrating and difficult people in our lives. It means looking for ways to worship God in our physical work and in the humdrum moments of everyday life. To follow Jesus is to follow him into the mud and muck of the human experience. But it is also to share in the joy and wonder of what God is doing and who he is making us to be.

3. Becoming Like God and Glorifying Him

▸ **OBJECTIVE: You will be able to infer that as we follow Jesus, our character is gradually transformed so we can glorify God.**

The call to follow Jesus is a call to be more human, but it is also a call to imitate Jesus and ultimately to become more like him. To be clear, we do not become God; rather, we become *like* him through the transforming work of the Holy Spirit. As this happens, we are not absorbed into God, nor do we become indistinguishable look-alikes or miniature copies of Jesus. Rather, in becoming like Jesus, we become the individuals we were created to be—loving people who glorify God in everything we do.

In Matthew 5:48, Jesus said: "You therefore must be perfect, as your heavenly Father is perfect." Throughout the rest of the Bible, we find similar statements. God commanded the people of Israel to be holy, "for I the Lord your God am holy" (Leviticus 19:2); and later, Peter told Christians the same thing (1 Peter 1:16). If you're like many people, these commands sound impossible, even absurd. However, being "perfect" here does not mean that we will never sin again. The word used for "perfect" in Matthew 5:48 is the Greek word *telios*. It refers to a goal, to something or someone that is complete, perfect, or spiritually mature.

We are to grow up into maturity by following Jesus. This means that we draw our standard for living from God's character, not what culture tells us. But fulfilling Jesus' directive isn't only up to us. We can expect God's help, being confident that he will one day complete his work in us (Philippians 1:6). Thus, "be perfect" is "a command, a promise, and statement of hope."[4] As we follow Jesus, we are transformed into who God wants us to be, so that we may glorify God.

What does it mean to glorify God, though? Does it mean we only watch certain movies, pray before every meal, or make sure that every event we take part in has an evangelistic focus? While these can all be good things, these kinds of actions by themselves do not communicate what glorifying God is all about. Something that has "glory" has weight or value. In glorifying God, we ascribe weight or value to him, giving him the honor of which he is worthy. To **glorify God** is *to make God famous by worshipping him and attesting to his goodness through holiness and acts of love.*

Glorifying God is about mirroring God's character and priorities in all we do. It means living our lives in such a way that God can be known in and through us. That's another reason why Jesus is our model. Throughout his life, Jesus made God famous through holiness and acts of love. He did not seek to glorify himself (John 8:50); rather, he desired that the Father would be glorified through him (John 17:1–3). Jesus emptied himself of his own glory, so that others might see the Father. Jesus' sacrificial death was the ultimate act that brought glory to the Father and salvation to the world. This is the example we are called to imitate (2 Corinthians 8:9, Philippians 2:3–8, 1 Peter 2:21).

4. Participating in the Divine Life

▸ **OBJECTIVE: You will be able to describe the benefits of being in union with Christ.**

Jesus' invitation to follow him in becoming more like him is an invitation to share in the divine life of God. In 2 Peter 1:4 we read that God has given us "great promises" so that "through them you may become partakers of the divine nature." What can this possibly mean?

To understand what Peter is talking about, we must look at Jesus, who was fully human and fully God (Colossians 2:9). Jesus said or implied this many times, and it got him into trouble with the religious leaders (Matthew 9:1–7; John 1:1, 5:18, 10:33). Jesus was not just another human leader or a good teacher. He was God himself. This can be a difficult concept to accept; that's why some people instead taught that Jesus was not God, but rather a divine being created by God. This is known as **Arianism**, which is *the heretical teaching that Jesus was only a divine being created by the Father*. Arianism was also rejected as heresy by the church.[5]

Arianism: the heretical teaching that Jesus was only a divine being created by the Father

As God, Jesus shows us what the divine life of God is all about—love, generosity, goodness, holiness, justice, peace, and so on. We do not naturally live like God does because we are slaves to sin (John 8:34, Romans 6:19). Only God can break the power of sin; that's why Jesus' divinity is so important. When we trust Jesus, we become participants in the divine nature. We are no longer bound by our sin nature but instead are alive to God in Christ Jesus (Romans 6:6–7, 11). Through the Holy Spirit, we are empowered to resist temptation and live holy lives.

Through Jesus, we have been united to God. We were buried with him in death—that is, through the cross, Jesus has conquered sin so that we can die to sin—and we have been raised to new life in Jesus. Our old self has died so that the new self (who we were made to be) can come alive (Romans 6). This is union with Christ.

In being united to Christ, we become participants in the life of God. We do not become mini-gods or God's equals. Nor are we absorbed into God. Rather, we remain distinct from

God, yet we are invited into the joyous life of Father, Son, and Holy Spirit. We are invited to become more like Christ in character and action. This process begins now, and will be completed when Jesus returns at the end of all things. Then we will be glorified (2 Corinthians 3:18, Philippians 3:20–21, 1 John 3:2). **Glorification** is *the doctrine that all believers will be finally freed from sin, restored, and given new, eternal bodies.*

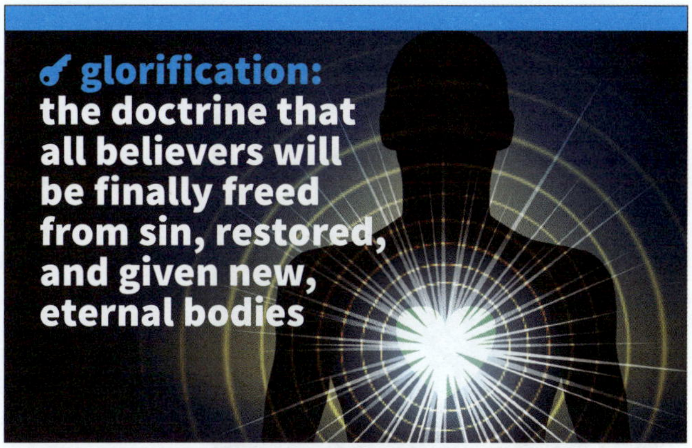

As we await our glorification, we can begin growing in holiness now. We do this by walking in the Spirit, following Jesus' commands, learning to say no to sin, and giving of ourselves for the sake of others. Though it may not always be evident to us, as we grow we gradually learn to abide more in Christ (John 15:4–5).

5. Becoming a Servant

▸ **OBJECTIVE:** You will be able to conclude that following Jesus requires serving others.

In Philippians 2:3–4, Paul wrote to the church, "Do nothing from selfish ambition or conceit, but in humility count others more significant than yourselves. Let each of you look not only to [your] own interests, but also to the interests of others." Most of us do not consider others first. We tend to operate out of our own needs and wants. We spend a lot of time trying to get ahead, often seeking fame, power, and popularity at the expense of others. However, Paul called Christians to be servants.

The Greek word for servant in the New Testament is *doulos*, which can also mean *slave*. The word *slave* rightly makes us uncomfortable given the evils of slavery we have witnessed throughout history. But to be a slave of God (Romans 6:22) is not the same as being forced into subjugation by another. Instead, it is to imitate Jesus, the one who willingly "emptied himself, by taking the form of a servant, being born in the likeness of men. And being found in human form, he humbled himself by becoming obedient to the point of death, even death on a cross" (Philippians 2:7–8).

Though he was God, Jesus didn't come to earth to show off his power, nor did he expect everyone to grovel before him, attending to his every desire. He came as a servant (Luke 22:27) "to seek and save the lost" (Luke 19:10). When Jesus wanted to show his disciples what God was really like, he didn't call fire down from heaven or lead them in a charge against the Romans. He got down on his hands and knees and washed their feet (John 13:1–17). This was the lowest of all jobs, reserved only for the lowest of slaves.[7] Yet Jesus did it gladly, and he told his disciples to follow his example.

To be a servant is to be others-centered, seeking their benefit and well-being before your own. This kind of service requires humility, but humility does not mean talking down about yourself or feeling like you are worthless. Those who are truly humble recognize that God has gifted them; instead of using their talents to boost their ego or get power, they use their gifts in the service of others. They recognize how gracious God has been to them and wish to share that grace with everyone. For a true servant, no job is too low, no person unworthy.

Serving others, like Jesus did, doesn't necessarily mean that we never hold positions of leadership; it means that when we do have authority, we use it for others' benefit. Jesus warned his disciples about "lording" it over each other. Leadership for Jesus isn't defined by being in charge and telling other people what to do, but rather by serving. If we want to be great in God's kingdom, Jesus says, we must become servants (Mark 10:42–45).

We serve others by providing for their needs (James 1:27); comforting them in sorrow (Romans 12:15); giving of our time, talent, and treasure (2 Corinthians 9:6–15); submitting to one another (Ephesians 5:21); bearing each other's burdens (Galatians 6:2); and sometimes, even giving our lives (John 15:13). We are called to serve others no matter who they are, what they look like, what they say, and what they do. In giving of ourselves to others, we are not less; instead, we become most truly who we were created to be.

Gace (Basse-Normandie, France)

6. Picking Up the Cross

▸ OBJECTIVE: You will be able to discuss how following Jesus requires us to pick up our cross daily and be willing to face suffering and persecution for his sake.

One day, Jesus was speaking with his disciples about how he was going to be persecuted and ultimately killed by religious and political leaders. Alarmed, Peter took him aside and told him that such things could never happen to him. But Jesus sharply rebuked Peter and told his disciples, "If anyone would come after me, let him deny himself and take up his cross and follow me. For whoever would save his life will lose it, but whoever loses his life for my sake will find it" (Matthew 16:21–25). If we are to find true life, we must deny ourselves and follow Jesus into suffering.

This is perhaps Jesus' least-liked teaching. After all, no one wants to experience pain, suffering, or persecution. Much of our time is spent trying to avoid these altogether, but that's not the way of Jesus. He did not avoid trouble by telling people what they wanted to hear; rather, he boldly confronted religious leaders for their sin, even though he knew it would cost him his life. He refused to sidestep the suffering of the cross. He willingly went right into it. In giving his life, Jesus offered us true life.

Following Jesus does not lead to ease, comfort, or material prosperity. Jesus promised his disciples that they would experience trouble in this world (John 16:33). As Jesus was persecuted, so too would his followers be persecuted (John 15:20). Jesus' disciples could expect to be hated, dragged before councils, imprisoned, tortured, and sometimes even put to death (Matthew 24:9, Mark 13:9, Luke 21:12). For followers of Jesus, suffering is not so much a matter of *if*, but *when*.

When persecution comes, we may be tempted to think that God has forgotten us. Yet, Jesus promises that he will be with us (Matthew 28:20); he will never abandon us (Hebrews 13:5). Having experienced suffering himself, he knows what it is like and sympathizes with us (Hebrews 4:15). He is stronger than evil, and ultimately, he will bring justice for all those who suffer for his name (Revelation 6:10–11, 11:18). Jesus said that those who suffer for righteousness' sake will be blessed. They are not left out or abandoned but will inherit the kingdom of God (Matthew 5:10–12).

However, experiencing persecution does not automatically mean that we are following Jesus faithfully. If as believers we are persecuted for being rude, uninformed, ungenerous, or hateful, this cannot be called suffering for Christ. Peter said Christians should be characterized by love, gentleness, and respect, always repaying evil with good (1 Peter 3:8–22). If we experience suffering for living like Christ, we are blessed, but not if we experience suffering for doing evil. When we truly experience suffering for Christ, we can have joy by entrusting ourselves to God's loving care (2 Corinthians 4:17, 1 Peter 4:12–19).

Ultimately, suffering for Christ prepares us for future glory. The suffering we experience here cannot even begin to compare to the future glory that will be revealed when we are remade (Romans 8:18). We can be confident that in all things, God is working for our good, so that we can become the people he created us to be (Romans 8:28–30). Nothing—not "trouble or hardship or persecution or famine or nakedness or danger or sword"—can separate us from God's love (Romans 8:31–39).

7. Living in Hope

▸ **OBJECTIVE: You will be able to differentiate Christian hope from optimism and pessimism, and explain why believers can have such hope.**

Following Jesus is not always easy. It will sometimes feel like we are wasting our time or missing out on the fun. Yet through the centuries, Christians have continued to follow Jesus, even when it led to persecution and suffering, or when everything seemed to be going wrong, or when it seemed that God was silent. Why did they do this? The answer is that they had hope.

Christian hope is not optimism. The optimist tends to look on the bright side, minimizing negative feelings and experiences. In the face of evil and suffering, the optimist simply asserts that things will get better. This makes it difficult to deal with real problems.

Christian hope is not pessimism. A pessimist views a situation in the most negative light possible. Seeing everything that is wrong with the world, the pessimist despairs of the possibility of redemption or restoration. Even in the face of good, the pessimist refuses to believe that things can get better. The pessimist's despair offers no motivation for addressing what is wrong.

Neither optimists nor pessimists look accurately at reality. In contrast to both, Christian hope honestly acknowledges the pain, suffering, and evil in our world, and instead of despairing, it prays for guidance and works to change things.

When we hope, we hope in something or someone. For Christians, the object of our hope is Jesus. Hope looks backward to what Jesus has done on the cross and forward to his second coming. The Bible describes Jesus in his resurrection as the "firstfruits" of those who have died (1 Corinthians 15:20, 23). Because of Jesus' resurrection, Christians can have hope that death does not have the final say and that one day, they too, will rise again (John 11:25, Romans 6:5). When Jesus comes again, the Bible promises that he will finish off sin and death once and for all, establish his kingdom, and make all things new (Revelation 20–22). A Christian's hope is "a resolute, unwavering hold on something that *has happened* and *will happen*."[8] **Christian hope** is *trusting in what Jesus has done and will do.*

Christian hope implies waiting, but it is not simply sitting around until Jesus comes back. Rather, Christian hope is a kind of "loyalty."[9] It is an allegiance to Jesus. It is trusting that as we await his kingdom, he is working through us even now to bring hope to the world. Instead of causing us to put up our feet and letting things be, hope motivates Christians to get busy serving God (1 Corinthians 15:54–58). Because we hope in Jesus, we can do good and be generous (1 Timothy 6:18), live in strength and joy (Isaiah 40:31), endure trials (1 Thessalonians 1:3), and lay down our lives for others (1 John 3:16–18). Even when all the odds are against our success, hope motivates us to persevere. We keep sharing the love of Jesus because no situation is hopeless; no person is beyond God's reach. All this we do as we await our "blessed hope, the appearing of the glory of our great God and Savior Jesus Christ" (Titus 2:13).

8. Growing in Christlikeness

▸ **OBJECTIVE: You will be able to give biblical examples of growing in Christlikeness.**

In Christ, we are new creations (2 Corinthians 5:17), empowered by God's Holy Spirit to live lives that glorify him. But becoming like Christ is a lifelong journey, and along the way we will continue to wrestle with our sin nature. Thankfully, Jesus is ready to give us grace and forgiveness (1 John 1:9). Growth in Christlikeness happens as we walk in the Spirit, learning to say *yes* to God, to imitate his character, and to be obedient to his commands. We do this together with others in all our relationships with family, friends, mentors, and more. Let's consider three people who grew in Christlikeness.

One of Jesus' first and most famous disciples was Peter. Peter could be hotheaded, overzealous, overeager, foolish, and unthinking. The Gospel writers tell of his many blunders. He spoke when he should have been silent (Mark 9:4–7), refused to believe that Jesus would suffer (Matthew 16:21–23), resisted Jesus' offer to wash his feet (John 13:6–10), used violence when Jesus was arrested (John 18:10), and ultimately denied Jesus three times (Luke 22:54–62). Yet Peter was one of Jesus' closest friends. After Jesus' resurrection, Jesus restored Peter and told him to lead God's people (John 21:15–19). Peter became a leader in the early church. He boldly preached in front of crowds (Acts 2:14–36), healed a lame man (Acts 3), and refused to stop preaching Jesus even when threatened (Acts 4:1–22). Peter continued to grow. At one point, Paul confronted Peter for acting hypocritically (Galatians 2:11–21). Peter humbly accepted Paul's rebuke and later he commended Paul's writings (2 Peter 3:16). Eventually, Peter was martyred in Rome for his witness for Christ.

Martha, the sister of Mary and Lazarus, was also close to Jesus. When he first visited her house, Martha was too busy with preparations to sit and listen to him. She complained to Jesus that Mary wasn't helping her. But Jesus compassionately told Martha that though she was worried about many things, Mary had chosen what was better—listening at Jesus' feet (Luke 10:38–42). This must have been hard for Martha to hear. We can imagine her frustration. Sometime later, Lazarus died. This time, Martha went to meet Jesus before he arrived, and listened to him. She boldly professed her faith in Jesus as God's Messiah. She was confident that God would give Jesus whatever he asked for (John 11:17–27). We do not know exactly what happened to Martha after this, but some traditions say that she shared the gospel in what is now southern France.[10]

After being radically converted, the apostle Paul became one of Jesus' most influential followers (Acts 9). He endured great suffering for Christ (2 Corinthians 11:16–33) and was eventually martyred in Rome. But before that, Paul became a spiritual guide for many believers. He called others to follow him as he followed Christ (1 Corinthians 11:1). Paul acted as a mentor to his younger colleague Timothy. Paul called Timothy his "true child in the faith" (1 Timothy 1:2) and wrote two letters to encourage him in his pastoral ministry at the church in Ephesus. Because Timothy was so young, he may have been intimidated by older believers and false teachers, but Paul urged him to be confident in using his gifts (1 Timothy 4:12). This mentoring relationship encouraged growth in both Paul and Timothy.

9. Growing Together

▸ **OBJECTIVE: You will be able to summarize why it is necessary for believers to be in community.**

Having experienced God's grace in their lives, Peter, Martha, Paul, Timothy, and many others sought to become like him and live for his glory. But they did not do this alone.

Growing in Christlikeness is something that happens in community. Following Jesus isn't about you, Jesus, and a Bible only. As we learned in Genesis 1–2, humans were created for relationships with other people, so to be most fully who God created us to be, we must join with others as we follow Jesus.

Following Jesus in community can provide companionship, encouragement, and protection. However, being in community can be challenging. The church is filled with people like ourselves who are struggling with sin, trying but often failing to follow Jesus. Faced with this, many choose to bail on the church. Yet, the New Testament is clear. We are to bear with one another (Colossians 3:13), seek fellowship with one another (1 John 1:7), and meet together to encourage each other (Hebrews 10:24–25). There are no solo Christians. In fact, much of what Jesus and the apostles taught is practically impossible to live out unless you are in community.

The New Testament churches provide a clear picture of the joys and challenges of following Jesus in community. It is easy to idealize the early churches, but these churches were just as broken and messed up as our own churches today. The first-century churches were filled with people from all different backgrounds and social statuses, and there was a lot of fighting. Here is a brief snapshot of the problems faced by some of the early Christians communities.[11]

- **Rome:** This church had an issue with unity, especially between Jews and Gentiles. Paul taught them that the gospel welcomed both Jews and Gentiles.
- **Corinth:** Among other things, this church had problems with popularity contests around particular leaders and had at least one case of sexual misconduct. Paul challenged the believers to follow Christ and to take sexual integrity seriously.
- **Galatia:** This church was plagued by people who were teaching that it was necessary to follow Jewish customs in order to be saved. Paul argued that this was a false gospel and urged the church to reject it.
- **Thessalonica:** This church was experiencing persecution and uncertainty about the return of Christ. Paul wrote to strengthen their convictions and give them hope about Christ's return.
- **Churches of the Diaspora (those scattered around the empire):** These churches may have struggled to "walk the talk." James encouraged them to live out their faith through action, not just words.
- **Churches of Asia Minor:** These churches were in danger of compromising their faith and worship. John challenged them to remain faithful to Jesus even in the midst of persecution.

Following Jesus together is not easy, but it is necessary. We should not be surprised at the problems that arise in church communities because we are all sinners. In fact, one author put it this way, "If the group is totally nice, that is a sure sign that something has gone wrong. For here are the foolish, weak, lowly, and despised of the world, whom God has chosen . . ."[12] This motley group of people is brought together by God's Spirit. And throughout history, they have had an incredibly positive impact on society—fostering education, art, and science; providing relief to the poor and aid to the suffering; and promoting equality, justice, and hope. The church has sought to bring the light of Christ into the darkest places. All this has been possible because of God's Spirit working in and among the community of believers who, together, encourage one another to become more like Christ.

10. Conclusion

Perhaps you have experienced the pressure of someone trying to force you to be someone you are not. Sometimes, even with good intentions, our parents, pastors, teachers, and coaches put pressure on us to be the people *they* want us to be. Sometimes we choose to be someone that we are not simply to fit in with others. We say things we don't mean, dress in a way that we don't like, or do things we normally wouldn't so others will like us. All of this can be very damaging, making it hard to become who God wants us to be.

The good news is this: God is not trying to get you to be someone you are not. God made you "fearfully and wonderfully" with the characteristics, personality, and gifts that make you unique (Psalm 139:13–17). God does not create us a certain way and then try to bend us into a totally different shape. God made every one of us in his image and he loves us just as we are. God also knows we are broken and sinful, but he will not leave us there. God's salvation is more than just a rescue. It's about God restoring us to who we were made to be, and ultimately making us like his Son, Jesus. God desires our well-being and longs for us to reach our full potential as human beings.

At the end of the Bible, the church is pictured as the bride of Christ, invited to the great marriage supper of the Lamb (Revelation 19:6–9). Fully glorified, we will be free from sin, unleashed to glorify and worship God in all we do. In Ephesians 5:25–27, Jesus is pictured as a husband, who gives himself for the church so that "he might sanctify her, having cleansed her . . . so that he might present the church to himself in splendor, without spot or wrinkle or any such thing, that she might be holy and without blemish." For those who follow Jesus, this is our destiny.

However, be warned. God's love is so strong that he will not give up on us until we have reached that goal. That means that sometimes he will get our attention in loud ways, going against our selfish plans and calling us out of our apathy. Furthermore, the life he calls us to will not be easy. If we follow the way of Jesus, we must count the cost. Following Jesus will require service and sacrifice, living in hope and clinging to God's promises even when it seems that all has gone wrong. But following Jesus also leads to a life of fullness and joy (Psalm 16:11, John 10:10). As we become more like Christ, we experience more and more of what God intended for us. This is the path that leads to true self-discovery and glorification as we are conformed to Christ.

So then, God invites us to follow Jesus and be like him, so that we can glorify God in all we do. But how do we do this? How do we become who God made us to be? As we have said, this is primarily the work of the Holy Spirit in us. But God invites us to participate in that work. In the next chapter, we'll explore some practices that can help form us into people who truly love God and others.

ENDNOTES

[1]C. S. Lewis, *Prince Caspian: The Return to Narnia* (New York: HarperCollins, 1951), 218.

[2]See Richard Bauckham, *Jesus and the Eyewitnesses: The Gospels as Eyewitness Testimony*, 2nd ed. (Grand Rapids, MI: Eerdmans, 2017).

[3]Justin S. Holcomb, *Know the Heretics* (Grand Rapids, MI: Zondervan, 2014), 55–61.

[4]Michael J. Wilkins, *The NIV Application Commentary: Matthew* (Grand Rapids, MI: Zondervan, 2004), 254–55. See also R. T. France, *The New International Commentary on the New Testament: The Gospel of Matthew* (Grand Rapids, MI: Eerdmans, 2007), 228–29.

[5]For an account of Jesus' way of leadership, in contrast to the ways of the world, see Eugene H. Peterson, *The Jesus Way: A Conversation on the Ways that Jesus Is the Way* (Grand Rapids, MI: Eerdmans, 2007).

[6]Holcomb, *Know the Heretics,* 87–98.

[7]Andreas J. Köstenberger, *Encountering John: The Gospel in Historical, Literary, and Theological Perspective*, 2nd ed. (Grand Rapids, MI: Baker Academic, 2013), 132.

[8]Jay Y. Kim, "Hope Is an Expectant Leap," *Christianity Today*, November 20, 2020, https://www.christianitytoday.com/ct/2020/november/advent-hope-is-expectant-leap.html

[9]G. K. Chesterton, *Orthodoxy* (Peabody, MA: Hendrickson, 2006), 61–76.

[10]Robin Gallaher Branch, "Martha: A Remarkable Disciple," Biblical Archaeology Society, June 21, 2021, https://www.biblicalarchaeology.org/daily/martha-a-remarkable-disciple/

[11]The letters of the New Testament were originally addressed to specific communities facing specific issues. The writers do not always spell out exactly what the issues were. For this reason, scholars try to infer from the letters what the situation was at each church, but the solutions are not always clear or definitive. For introductory information about each of these churches see, Andreas J. Köstenberger, L. Scott Kellum, and Charles L. Quarles, *The Cradle, the Cross, and the Crown: An Introduction to the New Testament* (Nashville: B&H Publishing Group, 2009).

[12]Dallas Willard, *The Divine Conspiracy: Rediscovering Our Hidden Life in God* (New York: HarperCollins, 1997), 125.

15 Walking with God

1. Spiritual Disciplines—For What?

▸ **OBJECTIVE:** You will be able to explain the purpose of spiritual disciplines.

Throughout the centuries, Christians have placed great value on spiritual disciplines like Bible reading, prayer, worship, and fasting—to name just a few. **Spiritual disciplines** are *habits and practices that help form us to be more like Jesus.* They are actions that invite us into a deeper relationship with God so that we can know God more intimately. Central to this is the truth that God desires a loving relationship with each person (Ephesians 3:14–19, 1 Peter 3:18, 1 John 3:1). Spiritual disciplines help us in our journey to know God more truly and shape us into the people he created us to be—that is, people who are like Jesus, loving God and others.[1]

Spiritual disciplines are worthwhile, though they can be mistaken for a measuring stick to tell how good a Christian someone is. For example, you might think you're a good Christian if you pray for fifteen minutes and read at least three chapters of the Bible every day. If you don't do these things regularly, you might start to feel guilty or think that you are a bad Christian. But spiritual disciplines are not about doing more stuff or trying to make God happy by tireless effort. Ephesians 2:8–9 is clear that salvation is a free gift of God's grace—so practicing spiritual disciplines won't help us earn salvation. God already loves each of us more than we could ever fathom (Romans 5:8, 8:38–39)—so we don't need to somehow win God's love or favor.

Scripture is also clear that believing the gospel isn't simply about getting a pass into eternal life. If you are a believer in Jesus, you are destined to rule with him throughout eternity (Revelation 5:10). God's kingdom has already broken into the world through Jesus (Matthew 12:28, Mark 1:15, Luke 11:20), so eternal life begins now! Even as we anticipate the full arrival of God's kingdom, we are to actively prepare for it—loving one another, forgiving those who wrong us, sharing the good news about Jesus, and bringing *shalom* to our communities.

Some people might think that being a Christian saps the joy or fun out of life. But Jesus said that he came so that people might "have life and have it abundantly" (John 10:10). To live an abundant life is to live life to the fullest, enjoying God's good creation, becoming all that we were created to be, fulfilling our role as stewards, and bringing glory to Jesus in all our actions. Paul was clear in his letter to the Ephesians that he didn't want Christians to remain babies in the faith. He wanted them to grow and mature so that they could become like Christ (Ephesians 4:11–16). As Christians, that is our destiny (Romans 8:29).

Spiritual disciplines are the kind of practices that help form us into people who can live well and rule well in God's kingdom. It will take discipline and hard work on our part, but the good news is that becoming this kind of person is not ultimately up to us. By practicing spiritual disciplines, we are simply putting ourselves in a place where God can work on our hearts. We come to God with open hands, but it is the Holy Spirit who works in us and transforms us into people who are more like Jesus (Romans 12:1–2; Galatians 5:19–26; Philippians 1:6, 2:13).

2. Solitude, Silence, Listening, and Self-Examination

▸ **OBJECTIVE: You will be able to differentiate between Christian spiritual disciplines and Eastern religion transcendence practices.**

Right now, your life is probably dominated by your school schedule, extracurricular activities, and spending time with friends. If you are bored, you can pop on headphones and tune out the world, browse social media, or text your friends. Many people are so addicted to these activities that they would be totally lost without them. Perhaps the reason we are so uncomfortable without any background noise, entertainment, or distractions is because silence forces us to confront our inner self—our fears, sins, failures, and unmet desires. We don't often like what we find when we look inside ourselves.

Christ in the Wilderness, by British painter Briton Rivière, 1898

But if we are to be transformed into the image of Christ, we must begin by being honest about who we are. It helps to begin with solitude and silence, but the Christian practices of solitude and silence are not "me time," self-isolation, or a self-help project that liberates you to live in any way that you feel. Nor is the goal to help you transcend yourself or achieve higher consciousness, as in some Eastern religions. Rather, silence and solitude are about taking the time to step away from the chaos of life to listen to the Holy Spirit through the Word and to spend time in loving relationship with God through prayer. The goal is to put aside distractions so one can focus on knowing God more, and be transformed into his image, "filled with all the fulness of God" (Ephesians 3:19). One author called solitude "the furnace of transformation," the place where our sinful tendencies are continually put to death and we are remade to be like Christ.[2]

Jesus modeled these disciplines by regularly separating himself from the crowds to be alone with the Father (Matthew 14:23–24, Mark 1:35, Luke 5:16). You can practice these disciplines by finding a quiet place where you can be alone without distractions. You want to give God your full attention. Try leaving your phone on silent or shutting it off during this time. Many people find that being outside in creation helps to focus their mind on God. Practicing these biblical disciplines will not be easy at first, but remember that God wants to spend time with you.

Practicing silence and solitude also gives you space to practice two other spiritual disciplines—listening and self-examination. In listening, you are not necessarily listening for the audible voice of God; rather, you listen by reflecting on how God is leading you. He may speak through Scripture, guide you through the counsel of others, or the circumstances in your life. Pay attention to the conviction, encouragement, comfort, or challenge of the Holy Spirit. Look for the ways that God is with you throughout your day.

As you open your heart to God in this way, the Holy Spirit may remind you of the truth about who God is and the truth about your identity as his beloved child (John 14:26).

Self-examination involves asking the Holy Spirit to help you discern ways you have sinned and failed to love God and others throughout your day. It is recognizing your brokenness and confessing your sins to God, praying for the strength to change. It also involves hearing the words that God forgives you (1 John 1:9), has already forgiven you through Jesus (Ephesians 4:32), and does not condemn you (Romans 8:1). So even as you confess your sins, remember that God is patient with you. He remembers that you are dust (Psalm 103:14)—as one book puts it, we are "beloved dust."[3]

3. Prayer

▸ **OBJECTIVE:** You will be able to give examples of various approaches to prayer.

▸ **OBJECTIVE:** You will be able to explain the Lord's Prayer as a model for prayer.

Prayer is vital to the life of every Christian. Yet for many believers (including people like Martin Luther and Teresa of Avila[4]), it is a struggle to pray at all. Perhaps this is because prayer may not always offer immediate rewards, make us feel better, or provide a sense of accomplishment.[5] We can't see God with our eyes. We might doubt that God even hears our prayers at all, but we can know that he does (I John 5:14-15).

But prayer is not just another thing to do. Prayer is about being in relationship with God. Through Jesus, Christians have been adopted into God's family (John 1:12–13, Galatians 4:4–5). The Holy Spirit gives us confidence to approach God the Father as we would a parent (Romans 8:14–17) with our needs and requests (Hebrews 4:16). And when we do not know how to pray, the Spirit prays for us (Romans 8:26). Ultimately, prayer is not just something that we do, but something God uses to shape our hearts. Just as Jesus relied on the Father in prayer (John 11:41–42, 17), so too, as we offer our requests and listen patiently, we learn to depend on and trust God.

When the disciples asked Jesus how to pray, he gave them this prayer:

> "Our Father in heaven,
>   hallowed be your name.
> your kingdom come,
> your will be done,
>   on earth as it is in heaven.
> Give us this day our daily bread,
> and forgive us our debts,
>   as we also have forgiven our debtors.
> And lead us not into temptation,
>   but deliver us from evil." –Matthew 6:9–13

From this prayer, often called *the Lord's Prayer*, we learn that God wants us to address him as a loving parent, while recognizing his utter holiness. We learn to seek what God desires and conform to his will. We learn to trust God for our daily needs and to seek forgiveness, as well as to forgive those who have wronged us. Finally, we learn to ask God to bring us safely through trials and temptations.[6] Try praying this prayer and pausing after each line to offer your own words to God.[7]

The Lord's Prayer, painting by James Tissot

The apostle Paul encouraged believers to "pray without ceasing" (1 Thessalonians 5:17). This doesn't mean we mutter nonstop prayers. Rather, it means we are continually in a posture of prayer—recognizing our total dependence on God and paying attention to the ways he is present throughout our day. We can pray this way by saying simple prayers such as, "Thank you, Father," "Help me, Jesus," or "Have mercy on me, a sinner."

Written prayers are a rich way of expressing ourselves to God. The Psalms teach us how to talk to God in times of joy, thanksgiving, lament, frustration, anger, and grief. No matter how you're feeling, there is a prayer for it in the Psalms. In addition, *The Book of Common Prayer* (from the Anglican tradition) and *The Valley of Vision* (from the Puritan tradition) include many short prayers of devotion.[8] Your own church or denomination may have similar resources.

Some people find it helpful to pray in the morning or evening for a set time. Others pray the hours, a liturgical practice that involves stopping two to four times a day to reflect on God's presence and lift up requests to him. Some Christians "say grace" before every meal as a way of thanking God for his many blessings. You might find it helpful to make a list of people and circumstances that you want to pray for on a regular basis or simply offer what is on your heart and pray as the Spirit leads you.

Many people involve their bodies in prayer. God will hear us in any position that we pray, but praying on one's knees or lying prostrate before him can express humility before God. Some pray with their palms up to express their desire to receive what God wants to give them; others raise their hands or place them on their heart as a gesture of surrender to his will. Another way to pray with your whole self is to try a prayer walk, which involves walking through a neighborhood and praying for the people around you, or to dance before the Lord.[9] However you pray, remember that prayer is spending time with God!

4. Worship

▸ **OBJECTIVE: You will be able to describe various forms of Christian worship.**

To *worship* is *to show reverence or adoration for someone or something.* Who or what we worship is the person or thing that commands our utmost attention, service, and loyalty.

For Christians, the object of our worship is the triune God of love—Father, Son, and Holy Spirit—the Creator and Sustainer of all things, the perfect Judge, the humble Redeemer and Restorer. Our worship of God is our response to who he is, what he has done, and what he is doing.

One way to worship God is through praise. After God answered her prayer for a son, Hannah offered a prayer of praise (1 Samuel 2:1–10). In response to God's power and glory, David praised God, singing and lifting up his hands (Psalm 63:2–4). At the dedication of the temple, Solomon offered praise and worship to God for his faithfulness (1 Kings 8:12–66). Even Jesus offered worship through song. In Matthew 26:30, Jesus participates in singing a hymn, and in Hebrews 2:12, he sings a song of praise.[10]

The Psalms provide templates for how to praise God (see Psalms 34, 100, and 145). The church also has many great hymns and praise songs. Some people begin their time of worship by singing; others listen to worship songs. You might even try writing your own song or poem of praise. Think about an aspect of God's character that you are grateful for and try expressing your praise to God through song.

Another way to worship God is through adoration, which may include praise, but goes beyond it.[11] To express adoration for God is to be reverent before him, seeking to love him with our whole selves, and offering our lives to him for his glory and service. In Isaiah 6, Isaiah finds himself in the presence of God. He realizes his own unworthiness, is purified by God, and offers his life for God's service. Jesus also showed reverence for the Father by submitting to his will (Luke 22:41–44) and offering his life (Hebrews 9:14).

Ultimately, our whole lives are meant to be an act of worship. In the Old Testament, the Hebrew word meaning *work* (*'abad*) often refers to sacred service offered to God. So, when God put humans in the garden of Eden "to work it and keep it" (Genesis 2:15), their work was to be an act of worship to God.[12] Similarly, what we do can show reverence and love for our Creator. It should be done for his glory (1 Corinthians 10:31), reflecting his excellence, goodness, and creativity. Brother Lawrence, author of *The Practice of the Presence of God*, believed that all of our actions, including washing dishes and cleaning a room, could be acts of worship to God.

We may not always feel like worshipping God. Worshipping him does not mean we pretend everything is okay. God can handle our doubts and confusion. In Psalm 73, Asaph begins by complaining the wicked seem to get off so easily, but when he comes into God's presence, he is able to finish his psalm with praise, expressing trust in God's justice and wisdom. As we spend time in worship and adoration, our understanding of who God is can be transformed so we love him more, growing in gratitude for all his works.

5. Reading, Memorizing, Meditating on, and Contemplating Scripture

▸ **OBJECTIVE: You will be able to incorporate Christian meditation and Christian contemplation into personal Bible study.**

The Bible is the great story of what God has done, is doing, and will do. Through it, we learn who God is, who we are, and what part we have to play in God's world.

There are many plans available to help you read through the Bible in a year. This can be a good challenge, but it's easy to get behind and then feel hopeless about catching up. Perhaps you tried to read through the Bible, but found yourself getting bogged down in Leviticus and just giving up. Here's a word of advice: if you miss a day, you don't have to catch up. It's not a bad thing if it takes you three or four years to get through the whole Bible. The important thing is to read it regularly. Some people find it helpful to read a little bit every day; others like to read large chunks or whole books at a time. However you choose to do it, remember that it's not about checking a box.[13]

Memorization helps you to internalize God's Word. The book of Luke tells how 12-year-old Jesus astounded Israel's teachers with his knowledge and understanding. Memorizing Scripture was a significant part of the spiritual education of Jewish children, so we can assume that Jesus knew the Scriptures well. Luke says that Jesus asked questions of the teachers and grew in wisdom (Luke 2:46–47, 52). Because Jesus knew God's Word well, he was prepared to combat the devil's lies and temptations (Matthew 4:1–11). The Bible is like a lamp that lights our path and helps protect us in times of temptation (Psalm 119:11, 105), so we do well to have it ready at hand. Try picking a favorite passage and reading through it every day for a month. Then slowly work on memorizing it line by line until you know it by heart.

Christian meditation: reflecting on God's Word

Meditating on and contemplating Scripture are other ways to internalize it. **Christian meditation** is *reflecting on God's Word* and **Christian contemplation** is *resting quietly in the presence of God and his infinite love.* When we meditate, we do not empty our minds as in Eastern religions; we use our minds to reflect on what a passage reveals about God and what he desires for our lives. In contemplation, we reflect on what God wants to do in our lives by opening our heart to God and allowing his Word to take root. The goal is to know God more deeply and personally as he is revealed in Scripture.

One very old practice that brought meditation and contemplation together is *Lectio Divina*, which simply means *divine reading*. To practice it, pick a short passage of Scripture, perhaps from one of the four Gospels. Before you begin, take a moment to sit quietly and ask the Holy Spirit to guide you. Then follow these four steps:[14]

3. **Read:** Slowly read the passage several times. What catches your attention?
4. **Meditate:** Reflect on the meaning of the passage. What questions does it raise about the passage? What does the passage reveal about God? What might it be teaching you?

Christian contemplation: resting quietly in the presence of God and his infinite love

3. **Contemplate:** Sit in silence and just be with God, allowing his Word to permeate your heart and soul. How does it make you feel? Does it prompt you to praise God? To repent from sin? To worship God in awe?
4. **Pray:** Talk to God about what you are reading. What is your reaction? How would you like God to work in your heart and your life? Thank God for his Word. Enjoy his presence.

When reading the Bible, remember the lessons we learned in Chapter 4 on how to avoid taking a passage out of context or miss the meaning all together. Careful reading and study of Scripture combined with prayerful meditation and contemplation, provide an avenue for God to speak powerfully to you through his Word.

6. Further Reading and Exploration

OBJECTIVE: You will be able to evaluate the merits of reading from a variety of authors including those you disagree with.

Scripture challenges us to love God with our whole selves, including our minds (Mark 12:30). Proverbs instructs us urgently to seek wisdom and understanding (Proverbs 4:5–9). In other words, we don't just believe things because someone told us to. Instead, we are to take our faith seriously, seeking to understand it and learning from others how to live it.

For Christians, the key source of wisdom and knowledge is the Bible. Through it, the Holy Spirit speaks to us today, showing us how we can be redeemed and remade into people who truly love God and others. But the Bible does not cover every topic exhaustively, and some passages can be hard to understand. That's why, for over 2,000 years, Christians of all walks of life have been writing about the faith, trying to understand the meaning of Scripture, and helping us think about how to live as Christians in our own time. Their works are a rich treasure we can learn from.

It can be helpful to read some books by authors we don't necessarily agree with. We need to hear the voices of other Christians—Christians from other parts of the world, other traditions, and other eras. C. S. Lewis advised people to read one old book between every new book. His reason? We tend to become trapped in the mindset of our own age and culture. We neglect the wisdom of thinkers throughout history, and we often assume that whatever is the latest is the best. Reading old books and books written from other perspectives challenges us to think more carefully.[15]

We should recognize that non-Christians also have valuable things to teach us. John Wesley said, "To imagine that none can teach you but those who are themselves saved from sin, is a very great and dangerous mistake. Give not place to it for a moment."[16] Reading non-Christian authors can help us understand the culture we are living in so that we can more effectively communicate the gospel. Paul offered us a model for this when he spoke to the Greeks at Athens. He quoted two of their own philosopher-poets—Epimenides and Aratus—in his argument that Jesus was the unknown God whom they were seeking to worship (Acts 17:16–34).[17]

Think of reading as an exercise where you invite the author to have a conversation with you. Ask careful questions, make a generous effort to understand the author's perspective, challenge the author where appropriate, and treat the author with respect even when you don't agree.[18]

This exercise can be done with all kinds of genres—including fiction. For example, Jane Austen, author of *Pride and Prejudice*, was a master of understanding human personality. Her stories can give us insight into and compassion for the people in our own lives.[19] The best fiction echoes elements of the true story—creation, fall, redemption, restoration—and illuminates our own experiences.[20]

Jesus is a good example for us. We know that even as a boy, Jesus was actively learning and growing. He had a solid understanding of the Scriptures, but on more than one occasion, he quoted cultural proverbs (Matthew 16:2–3, Luke 4:23). He also understood the power of fiction and used parables to teach about the kingdom of God.

To practice this spiritual discipline, you might start by asking your pastor, parent, or teacher for some recommendations. If reading isn't something you enjoy very much, start slow. Try reading one book every two months or listen to the audio version. You can also learn a lot through sermons, podcasts, videos, and other resources.

7. Fasting and Abstinence

▸ **OBJECTIVE: You will be able to distinguish between three different types of fasts and describe appropriate fasting.**

To *fast* is *to intentionally abstain from food and drink, or to abstain from certain foods and drinks, for a set period of time.* Numerous examples of fasting can be found in the Old Testament (1 Samuel 7:6, Daniel 10:2–3, Ezra 8:21–23). Jesus also practiced fasting (Luke 4:1–13) and assumed that those who followed him would fast as well (Matthew 6:16–18). Fasting was a common practice in the early church, though it might seem odd to us today.

Fasting is not a display of holiness for the spiritually elite. Jesus said that when we fast, we shouldn't go about broadcasting it to everyone (Matthew 6:16–18). Fasting is not an attempt to get God to do something for us, nor does it earn his forgiveness.

One theologian categorizes fasts under these three headings:[21]

1. **Defining Moment Fast:** Fasting when we recognize that God is doing something new in our lives, or in response to a defining moment in our relationship with God.
2. **Turning from Sinful Choices Fast:** Fasting when we realize we're living in sin, grieving over our actions, and repenting before God.
3. **Tragic Calamity Fast:** Fasting in response to tragedy and asking God to redeem it or to bring justice.

Dieting is not fasting. By fasting we acknowledge that we need more than food to live (Matthew 4:4)—that ultimately, it is God who sustains us. By going without food for a time, we come to realize how great a gift it is, and we grow in gratitude. Fasting is thus a response to what God is doing in our lives, our awareness of sin, and the brokenness of the world.[22]

Consider the three categories above and think about when it might be appropriate for you to take a fast. A word of caution: if you are considering a fast, it is wise to consult your parents and your pastor first. If you have a medical condition that would make it dangerous, you should not practice fasting.

Similar to fasting is the practice of abstinence. To *abstain* is simply *to refrain from doing something.* In the fourth century, thousands of men and women went into the deserts to practice abstinence from worldly pleasure and follow Jesus in more focused discipleship. They became known as ascetics. *Asceticism* is *the practice of avoiding all forms of indulgence.*

You may have heard stories about wild ascetics who sat on top of pillars for years, beat themselves with whips, or severely damaged their bodies through starvation (see Chapter 16). Such extreme cases and practices are not consistent with Scripture (1 Timothy 4:3-5). For most Christians, abstinence is a helpful discipline in battling sin and sometimes giving up something good to pursue God more intensely.[23]

How can we practice abstinence today? Ask what things in your life distract you. They might not be bad things, but perhaps God is inviting you to abstain from them for a time so that you can follow him in greater discipleship. Try abstaining from social media or video games for a week and see what happens.

8. Giving, Stewardship, and Simplicity

▸ **OBJECTIVE: You will be able to articulate the biblical view of simplicity and stewardship.**

For many people, the goal of life is comfort, success, and upward mobility—we work to earn money so we can be secure, have a nice house, nice car, nice career, and extra left over to spend on our pleasures.

For a Christian, there is a very different motivation for earning money. Paul instructed the Ephesians to do "honest work" so that each person "may have something to share with anyone in need" (Ephesians 4:28). God's heart is compassionate toward those in poverty (Leviticus 19:9–10, Proverbs 31:8–9, Luke 6:20–21). Jesus himself became poor for our sake (2 Corinthians 8:9), and early followers of Jesus were marked by their concern for the poor and needy.[24]

Generous giving should be a part of every Christian's life. Christians do well to support their local church[25] and charitable organizations,[26] but being generous is more than simply giving money. In fact, sometimes giving money can make things worse for the people we are trying to help.[27] Therefore, we must also be willing to give generously of our time and expertise to help others.

For a Christian, giving is tied directly to the idea of stewardship. A *steward* is *one who cares for and manages what belongs to another.* Everything that we have is a gift from God, so giving to those in need is a way of faithfully stewarding God's resources—time, talent, and treasure. Being generous stewards might mean that we have to cut back on our personal pleasures or hobbies. It might mean not getting the latest piece of technology. Ultimately, this calls us to the spiritual discipline of **simplicity**—*the practice of living simply so that we can seek God's kingdom first* without being enslaved by material possessions.

Jesus told us not to store up treasures here on Earth (Matthew 6:19–20). He modeled this himself by living simply (Luke 8:1–4, 9:58) and focusing on his mission of spreading the good news of God's kingdom.

> **simplicity:**
> **the practice of living simply so that we can seek God's kingdom first**

Living simply doesn't mean that all of us are called to live in poverty, nor that having wealth is bad. Rather, it means trusting our needs to God, recognizing that he will take care of us. It means finding our primary joy in God and not in our possessions; holding what we have as belonging to God and using it for his glory; and trusting that our identity comes from being God's children, not from what we possess. Our disposition is to be one of generous giving and wise stewardship of God's creation.

Here are a few practical ways to live simply and steward God's creation:[28]

- Reject the need to always have the latest and greatest.
- Practice regularly giving to others.
- Spend time enjoying God's creation. Consider how you could help protect and preserve it through eating better or using environmentally friendly products.
- Think about ways you can reduce damage to creation by reusing and recycling instead of simply throwing things out.

- Think about who or what is being harmed by the products you buy. Try to find ethically sourced products.
- Reevaluate any hobby or material possession that keeps you from seeking God's kingdom first.

9. The Example of the Saints

▸ **OBJECTIVE:** You will be able to consider how the stories of faithful believers can encourage Christians to grow spiritually.

As we seek to practice these spiritual disciplines, we look to Jesus, our ultimate Example and Teacher. Throughout history, many of Jesus' followers have also practiced these disciplines. Their example provides encouragement and support for our journeys

- **Monica of Hippo (331–387):** Regarded as an exemplary wife and mother, she faithfully prayed for her family members for many years. Eventually, Monica's husband and mother-in-law accepted Christ, as did two of her three sons. Her oldest son, Augustine, resisted for many years. After he came to faith, he became an influential bishop who said his mother's unfailing love and persistent prayers influenced his life for Christ.
- **Benedict of Nursia (c. 480–547):** Benedict founded the Benedictine order. His rule for the monks under his care provided for regular reading of and meditation on Scripture. Benedictine monks helped to preserve Scripture and other writings for future generations.[29]
- **Clare of Assisi (1194–1253):** Born into a noble family, Clare vowed not to marry and gave away her inheritance to the poor in order to follow Jesus. A disciple and friend of Francis of Assisi, Clare helped found an order for women ("the Poor Clares") that focused on simple living and voluntary poverty.[30] Like Francis, she had a deep respect for creation.
- **John Wycliffe (1330–1384):** This theologian, philosopher, and writer used his skills to promote ideas leading to the Reformation. However, it was his devoted study of the Bible that led to his most notable and lasting contribution, the first English translation of the Bible.
- **Susanna Wesley (1669–1742):** As the mother of John and Charles Wesley, Susanna's impact on their lives, as well as the Methodist movement, is noteworthy. Susanna ran the Wesley household, bore 17 children, and provided for their academic, religious, and moral education, including weekly one-on-one time with each child.[31] She worshipped God and prayed through all that she did.

Dietrich Bonhoeffer (1906–1945)

- **Dietrich Bonhoeffer (1906–1945):** A German Lutheran pastor and theologian during WWII, Bonhoeffer encouraged believers to practice regular times of solitude and silence, noting these times were essential for Christians to live together in healthy community.[32] Bonhoeffer stood up to Hitler and was eventually executed by the Nazis.

- **Luis Palau (1934–2021):** Palau was a beloved Argentinian evangelist, author, and radio preacher. He left an important legacy of humility, endurance, and obedience to God. Palau carefully studied the Bible and shared the gospel message all over the world. He was known for being honest about his mistakes and spoke of the role of repentance in the Christian life. Palau encouraged many people to pursue a passionate and rooted Christian faith.

Each of these believers desired something more than surface-level faith. They wanted to know and love God intimately and to offer their whole selves in his service. The goal of listing them here is not for us to compare ourselves to them (2 Corinthians 10:12). Paul instructed his fellow Christians to follow him as he followed Christ (1 Corinthians 1:11). So, we follow the example of others who have followed Christ. These believers are part of the "great cloud of witnesses" that have gone before us (Hebrews 11:1–12:1). Their lives witness not to extraordinary abilities, but to the power of God's Spirit working through all who faithfully seek him.

10. Conclusion

As the title of this chapter suggests, practicing these disciplines is a lifelong journey of walking with God. It is a journey that leads us deeper into knowledge of God and ourselves, so that through the power of the Holy Spirit we can imitate Jesus and become the people the Father created us to be. In this lifetime, we will not complete the journey, but we can be confident that Christ is renewing us day by day (2 Corinthians 4:16–17) and will one day complete the work of sanctification that he began in us (Philippians 1:6).

Maybe talking about all these spiritual disciplines has left you feeling a little overwhelmed. You might be regularly practicing only one or two of these disciplines, or maybe you have a hard time practicing any of them at all. Don't be discouraged. Remember that this is not a giant to-do list. Instead, the spiritual disciplines are an invitation to experience relationship with God at a deeper level. He wants you to know him as he truly is, and he is for your good. Even when you fail, he is patient, longing for you to return to him so that you can experience true life.

If you struggle to practice any of these disciplines, don't start tomorrow by trying to practice all of them. Instead, ask God to show you what he is inviting you to do. Choose one or two that you think you could start practicing regularly. Maybe that means just taking off your headphones for 15 minutes every day and reading the Bible. Maybe that means stopping to pray and reflect on your day before bed. It might mean fasting from a meal, reading a book about faith, or taking a meal to your neighbor.

There will be seasons of life in which you feel like you aren't getting anything out of the disciplines. You might feel God is silent or doesn't hear you; you may feel like you aren't making any progress. During these times, you may be tempted give up, thinking that there must be something wrong with you. But the testimony of numerous Christians over the centuries is that this is a normal experience in the Christian life. In such dry times, God is working on you in ways that you cannot see. It is during these seasons that God invites you to trust him while he works silently to transform you.

A final word of caution. This chapter could give the impression that being a Christian is a private, individual affair, exclusively between you and Jesus. It is true that the gospel is for *you* as an individual. It is an invitation to enter a personal relationship with Jesus. But no one was ever meant to live the Christian life alone. In fact, Scripture warns us not to isolate ourselves from other believers (Hebrews 10:25). It challenges us to build one another up (1 Thessalonians 5:11). The Christian life is to be lived out in community. In the next chapter, we'll learn how to practice spiritual disciplines in community, so that together with our Christian brothers and sisters we can grow to become more like Jesus.

ENDNOTES

[1]For a more in-depth study of how to know God. pray, and meditate on his Word, see A.W. Tozer, *The Knowledge of the Holy* (New York: Harper Collins, 1961).

[2]Henri Nouwen, *The Way of the Heart: The Spirituality of the Desert Fathers and Mothers* (New York: HarperCollins, 1981), 25.

[3]Jamin Goggin and Kyle Strobel, *Beloved Dust: Drawing Close to God by Discovering the Truth about Yourself* (Nashville, TN: Nelson Books, 2014).

[4]See Michael Reeves, *Enjoy Your Prayer Life* (Leyland, England: 10Publishing, 2014), 15–16 and Teresa of Avila, *Book of Her Life*, in *The Collected Works of Saint Teresa of Avila: Volume 1*, trans. Kieran Kavanaugh, O.C.D and Otilio Rodríguez, O.C.D. (Washington, DC: ICS Publications, 1987).

[5]Goggin and Strobel, *Beloved Dust*, 3.

[6]For possible meanings of Matthew 6:13, see "3 Things 'Lead Us Not into Temptation' Might Mean—and Which Fits Best," Logos Blog, https://blog.logos.com/4-things-lead-us-not-into-temptation-might-mean-and-which-fits-best/.

[7]See C. S. Lewis, *Letters to Malcolm: Chiefly on Prayer* (New York: Houghton Mifflin Harcourt, 1964), 24–28.

[8]*The Book of Common Prayer* can be found online here: https://www.bcponline.org/; excerpts from *The Valley of Vision* are available at https://banneroftruth.org/us/devotional-series/the-valley-of-vision-devotional/.

[9]See Exodus 15:20; 2 Samuel 6:14; Psalm 149:3, 150:4.

[10]Rony Reinke, "Jesus Sings," Desiring God, https://www.desiringgod.org/articles/jesus-sings.

[11]"What Is Adoration in the Bible?", Got Questions, https://www.gotquestions.org/adoration-in-the-Bible.html.

[12]For discussion of the word *'abad*, see John H. Walton, *Genesis: The NIV Application Commentary* (Grand Rapids, MI: Zondervan, 2001), 172–174.

[13]Ben Keiser, "Spiritual Disciplines: Reading Scripture," Summit Ministries, April 6, 2020, https://www.summit.org/resources/articles/reading-studying-scripture/

[14]This is a modified form of *Lectio Divina*. Technically, *Lectio Divina* follows the pattern "read," "meditate," "pray," "contemplate," but prayer and contemplation are often intermingled. The *Lectio Divina* was first developed by Benedict of Nursia for the Benedictine monasteries, and the four-step process was outlined by French monk Guigo II the Carthusian in *Scala Paradisi* or *The Ladder of Paradise*.

[15]C. S. Lewis, "Introduction" in St. Athanasius, *On the Incarnation* (Crestwood, NY: St. Vladimir's Seminary Press, 1996), 4–5.

[16]John Wesley, *A Plain Account of Christian Perfection* (London: Epworth Press, 1952), 87, as quoted in J. P. Moreland, *Love God with All Your Mind* (Colorado Springs, CO: NavPress, 2012), 54.

[17]Mark Allan Powell, "Acts 17:27–28—Paul Quotes the Pagans," supplement to *Introducing the New Testament*, 2nd ed. (Ada, MI: Baker Academic, 2018).

[18]Alan Jacobs, *Breaking Bread with the Dead: A Reader's Guide to a More Tranquil Mind* (New York: Penguin Press, 2020), 27.

[19]Ben Keiser, "The Enduring Popularity of Jane Austen," Summit Ministries, February 21, 2020, https://www.summit.org/resources/reflect/jane-austen-good-literature/.

[20]Jerram Barr, *Echoes of Eden: Reflections on Christianity, Literature, and the Arts* (Wheaton, IL: Crossway, 2013), 67.

[21]Tim Mackie, "Practicing Faith Part 2: Feasting and Fasting," Episode 26, Exploring My Strange Bible Podcast, September 11, 2017, https://bibleproject.com/podcast/practicing-faith-part-2-feasting-fasting/.

[22]Mackie, Episode 26.

[23]See James E. Goehring, "Alone in the Desert?" Christian History Institute, https://christianhistoryinstitute.org/magazine/article/alone-in-the-desert.

[24]Rodney Stark, *The Triumph of Christianity: How the Jesus Movement Became the World's Largest Religion* (New York: HarperCollins, 2011), 105–119.

[25]Many Christians give to their local churches in the form of a tithe. In 2 Corinthians 9:7, Paul says, "Each one must give as he has decided in his heart, not reluctantly or under compulsion, for God loves a cheerful giver." Further, Paul affirms that the preaching of the gospel is real and valuable work for which it is right for one to receive compensation (1 Corinthians 9:7–11; Galatians 6:6).

[26]Christians do not all agree on giving directly to charitable organizations. The kind of charities that exist today were not around in the ancient world, so we should not expect to find specific verses directing us to give or not give in these ways. Some churches partner with local charities so that some of their regular funds go to those who work directly with people in need. All Christians must seek to be wise stewards of their resources and to share God's concern for the poor, giving generously—whether that be directly, through the church, or through charities.

[27]See Steve Corbett and Brian Fikkert, *When Helping Hurts: How to Alleviate Poverty Without Hurting the Poor . . . and Yourself* (Chicago: Moody Publishers, 2012).

[28]Richard J. Foster, *Celebration of Discipline: The Path to Spiritual Growth* (New York: HarperOne, 1988), 90–95. For a note on Foster's approach to spiritual disciplines, see Douglas Groothuis, "Apologetics as Spiritual Formation," Equip.org, https://www.equip.org/articles/apologetics-as-spiritual-formation/.

[29]Bruce L. Shelley, *Church History in Plain Language*, ed. Marshall Shelley, 5th ed. (Grand Rapids, MI: Zondervan, 2021), 154–58.

[30]Ingrid Peterson, "Francis's Tenacious Lady," Christian History Institute, https://christianhistoryinstitute.org/magazine/article/francis-tenacious-lady.

[31]Elesha Coffman, "Faith of Our Mothers," Christian History Institute, https://christianhistoryinstitute.org/magazine/article/faith-of-our-mothers.

[32]Dietrich Bonhoeffer, "The Day Alone" in *Life Together* (New York, NY: HarperCollins, 1954), 76–89.

16 Walking with God in Community

1. The Christian Life in Community

▸ **OBJECTIVE: You will be able to critique Simeon Stylites' model of spiritual solitude in relation to the Christian's need to be in community.**

In the fifth century, in Syria, a man named *Simeon Stylites* often found people getting in the way of his spiritual practice. He might have said, like many people do today, "I love Jesus, but not the church." Simeon was known for his extreme religious devotion, but he often inflicted punishments on his body and nearly starved himself to death because he

ST. SIMEON STYLITES, HERMIT OF THE PILLAR

wrongly thought this would make him more like Christ. The people around him objected to these practices, so he was asked to leave his monastery.

Simeon set out on his own, but it was not long before crowds of people came to observe his religious fervor and ask his advice. Seeking to escape them and have more time to pray, Simeon ascended a pillar that he found among some ancient ruins. He built a small platform on top of the pillar and remained there for the next 37 years of his life, coming down only occasionally to receive food or to raise the pillar even higher (eventually reaching at least 50 feet high). Fully exposed to the elements, standing constantly to pray, and eating only once a week, Simeon soon attracted large crowds who gathered around his pillar to hear his sermons and learn from him. He became famous and many people set out to imitate him.[1]

If you think about it, Simeon's methods in search of solitude are not consistent with Scripture. By leaving the monastery, he wouldn't have to listen to other believers or figure out how to live with difficult people in community. He wouldn't be troubled by the problems of his next-door neighbor. He would also seem to have a clear way of measuring his own spirituality. Yet Simeon soon discovered that he couldn't escape people. Notable as Simeon's devotion to Christ was, any form of Christian spirituality that encourages us to permanently withdraw from others or to inflict harm on ourselves is dangerous and shortsighted.[2] Tempting as it may be to try and escape people, it is only with them that we can become the people Christ has called us to be (John 13:34–35).

In the last chapter, we surveyed several spiritual disciplines or practices that help us develop as Christ followers. These practices are important for each of us individually, but each is also meant to be practiced in community or to prepare us for our life in community. In this chapter, we want to explore how we become like Christ side by side with other Christians. As we go along, we'll see that following Jesus in community—that is, being part of the life of a local church—matters. Because the church is filled with sinful people, we might sometimes feel it hinders our growth. But the church is the training ground where we may be sanctified and formed to be like Christ. It can be a place where we give and receive encouragement, comfort, and support to one another as we seek to follow Jesus.

2. Worship in Community

▸ **OBJECTIVE: You will be able to describe the elements of Christian worship in community.**

Since the earliest days of the church, it has been common for believers to gather at least once a week to worship God together. The term *worship* is often used as a synonym for this weekly gathering. Though most Protestant churches meet on Sunday, Scripture is not particular about which day of the week we meet (Romans 14:5); but it is particular that Christians gather on a regular basis (Hebrews 10:25).

Justin Martyr, Great St. Mary's Church, Cambridge, United Kingdom

The form of many modern church services is derived from ancient tradition. The second century Christian apologist Justin Martyr described a typical worship service:

> And on the day called Sunday, all who live in the cities or in the country gather together in one place and the memoirs of the apostles [the gospels] or the writings of the prophets are read. . . . The president [leader or pastor] verbally instructs, and exhorts to the imitation of these good things. Then we all rise together and pray. . . . When our prayer is ended, bread and wine and water are brought, and the president . . . offers prayers and thanksgivings . . . and there is a distribution to each. . . . And they who are well-to-do, and willing, give what each thinks fit; and what is collected is deposited with the president, who . . . takes care of all who are in need.[3]

Though Justin did not specifically mention singing, Pliny, a non-Christian writer from the same era, noted that Christians gathered on a specific day to recite a hymn (which may refer to a creed or psalm) and say an oath.[4] In the next several sections, we'll explore how each of the elements listed by Justin and Pliny plays a role in forming believers in Christlikeness. Let's begin with worship.

Upon entering a church building, one is often confronted with various symbols, banners, images, and artwork. These elements are designed to draw our attention to some aspect of God's character, beauty, holiness, or majesty; an event in biblical history; or the example of a faithful Christian witness. In addition, some churches are designed to direct our attention toward God (arches are a common way of achieving this). Through architecture and art, "the entire building" can be "a book in which the mysteries of faith [are] reflected,"[5] drawing us into the worship and adoration of God.

Most church services include worship through song. Expressing praise, thanksgiving, petitions, and lament to God through song has its grounding in the Old Testament. In addition to the psalms (many of which were composed for congregational worship), there are numerous instances of God's people breaking out in song in response to something God did (Exodus 15:1–21, Deuteronomy 32:1–43, 2 Chronicles 20:21).

Christians today are also inheritors of a rich tradition of hymn writing from people like Charles Wesley and Fanny Crosby. In the last fifty years, many new songs have been written for modern worship.

The songs we sing in church should express heartfelt adoration for God, sound Christian theology, praise, thanksgiving, and honest lamentation. Worship is about *responding* to what the Spirit is doing, not about how we look doing so. Some worshippers will lift their hands, clap, or sway, while others who are less expressive simply stand and sing. Worshipping with other believers helps form us in Christlikeness by inviting us to remember and reflect on who God is and what he has done for us as a community. Worshipping helps us to grow in gratitude and thankfulness.

3. Studying Scripture in Community

▸ OBJECTIVE: You will be able to discuss the value of worship services and small groups.

Today, many people have easy access to a Bible. This is a great gift, but it also comes with a potential hazard. If we are not careful, our Christian faith can become a private affair—just me, Jesus, and the Bible. But no one is an infallible interpreter of Scripture. As we read the Bible, we will inevitably make mistakes, misunderstand, or read our own ideas into the text. This is why it is so important to read and study Scripture in community.

In the earliest days of the church, most people's only access to Scripture was through public readings during the worship service, which would have included the letters of the apostles. Such readings allowed people to hear God's words directly. Many churches today continue this tradition by including a specific time during the service to read passages from the Old and New Testaments.

The reading of Scripture is often followed by the preaching of a sermon, also called *a message* or *homily*, to help the congregation understand God's Word and live it out (see Nehemiah 8, Acts 2:14–41). The pastor or speaker's job is not just to talk *about* the Bible, but to help people hear and respond to the voice of God in Scripture.[6] For this reason, the sermon is not a one-way communication. It is a communal activity that requires our pondering, investigation, and response (Acts 17:11).

Throughout Scripture, God's people are called to keep his word present with them at all times—to meditate upon it and to use it to teach one another (Joshua 1:8, Psalm 1:2, Colossians 3:16). One way of doing this is through small groups, also known as *cell*, *community*, or *fellowship groups*. Small groups usually meet as Sunday school classes at church or in members' homes. They gather on a regular basis to discuss a book of the Bible, the latest sermon, or another Christian book. These meetings offer encouragement and support as people seek to understand and apply God's Word. Small groups can also provide an opportunity for us to meet with people who can challenge our thinking and help us read and interpret better. While most small groups take place as part of the ministry of a local church, those offered by parachurch ministries in various settings bring people with different perspectives together to study the Word.

By studying the creeds of the church and the confessions, catechisms, doctrines, or statements of faith of churches or denominations, you can see the results and benefits of Scripture study in community. Creeds help Christians grasp fundamental aspects of the faith; confessions clarify what a particular group teaches about various biblical doctrines; and catechisms provide short, memorable questions and answers about Christian truth (accompanied by Scripture references). In addition to these, thousands of books have been written about Scripture, which can help illuminate how Christians throughout time and place have interpreted God's Word.

As we read and study Scripture together, we can grow in humility, patience, and charity. We recognize that those who have gone before us and those around us have valuable things to teach us. Together, we have a much better chance of interpreting correctly, internalizing, and living God's Word. And as we read our "family story," we discover our true identity and what a Jesus-following community should look like.

4. Prayer in Community and Exercise of Spiritual Gifts

▸ **OBJECTIVE: You will be able to explain the importance of prayer and the appropriate use of spiritual gifts.**

Prayer was one of the hallmarks of the early church (Acts 1:14, 2:42). Praying together with others is a powerful expression of our faith in God and shapes us in profound ways. As we pray together, we grow in unity with one another (it is difficult to be angry with someone that you are regularly praying with or for). Praying helps us practice putting the needs of others before our own. It teaches us to depend on God and pay attention to how he is at work in our communities and in the world at large.

Community prayer can happen in small groups where individuals regularly meet to encourage and pray for each other. Community prayer can also happen during the church service through prayers read together by the congregation or through open time for spontaneous prayers. Some churches allow for time in which people can share their prayer requests with the whole church. Together, we should pray for those who are lost (Romans 10:1), those in positions of authority (1 Timothy 2:1–4), the sick (James 5:14–16), those sharing the gospel abroad (2 Corinthians 1:11), and all believers (Ephesians 6:18).

Another way that we grow in Christ is by serving one another with our spiritual gifts. A **spiritual gift** is *a God-given ability or strength exercised for the encouragement and building up of believers.*

Some of the spiritual gifts listed in Scripture are prophecy, service, teaching, encouragement, generosity, leadership, mercy (Romans 12:3–8); wisdom, knowledge, faith, healing, miracles, discernment, speaking in tongues, and interpreting tongues (1 Corinthians 12:1–11, 28–31); and apostleship, evangelism, and shepherding (Ephesians 4:7–12). There are four things that Scripture emphasizes about these spiritual gifts.

First, each gift is exactly that—a gift. Though we can cultivate them, they are not abilities that we develop through our own strength. "They are," as one ancient theologian said, "visible signs that the grace of the Holy Spirit is at work in the faithful."[7]

Second, spiritual gifts are not given for self-promotion, showing off, or private indulgence. They are to be used for the encouragement and building up of the church (Ephesians 4:12, 1 Corinthians 12:7).

Third, every Christian has one or more spiritual gifts, and no one spiritual gift is more important than another. In 1 Corinthians 12, Paul explains that each person in a church is like a part of the body. Just as the body needs each part in order to function properly, the body of Christ needs each individual member. Some will exercise their gifts in public in preaching, teaching, singing, or leading, while others will exercise them behind the scenes through acts of mercy or service. But all have their gifts from the same Spirit and are to use them in service of one another.

Finally, spiritual gifts must be exercised in an appropriate, loving, and orderly fashion (1 Corinthians 14). This doesn't mean there is no room for spontaneity, but that there should be order to ensure spiritual gifts do not distract people but instead build them up.

By praying together and exercising our spiritual gifts for the sake of the church, we grow up in maturity. We learn together what it looks like to be a community that loves one another, and in so doing, proclaims the gospel to the world.

5. Confession, Accountability, Mentoring

▸ **OBJECTIVE:** You will be able to relate the significance of confession, accountability partners, and spiritual mentors.

In Christ, we are new creations (2 Corinthians 5:17), being renewed daily by God's Spirit (2 Corinthians 4:16). However, because we are not yet perfect, we need confession and repentance. To *confess* is *to acknowledge our sin and be honest about the ways that we have failed to love God and others.* To *repent* is *to turn from our sin and follow a different way.*

Turning from sin can be slow, hard work. That's why we need the support and encouragement of other believers. James urges us to confess our sins and to pray for one another (James 5:16), while Hebrews calls us to encourage one another so that no one becomes hardened in sin (Hebrews 3:13). It is important to bring our sins into the light; otherwise, we can become trapped in them. As long as our sin is concealed, we cannot get help (Proverbs 28:13). Confessing our sins to each other allows us to repent and seek accountability.

accountability partner: a person who commits to listen, pray, encourage, ask hard questions, and share spiritual concerns

Some churches make space for individual confession before Sunday worship. Others incorporate time in the Sunday service for corporate confession. In corporate confession, people usually confess their sins silently to God. This is then followed by a prayer said aloud by the whole congregation.

We all need spiritual companions to aid us in our battle against sin. One relationship that many people find helpful is that of an **accountability partner**—*a person who commits to listen, pray, encourage, ask hard questions, and share spiritual concerns,* such as questions about your struggles, and sometimes sharing his or her own struggles also.

An accountability partner should be someone of your same gender who is trustworthy, will listen carefully to you, and commit to pray with you on a regular basis. Members of a small group can commit to being accountability partners. But accountability meetings should not be like a visit to the doctor's office where your accountability partner simply ticks off several embarrassing questions: Did you lust this week? Have you lied today? While an accountability partner should challenge you in your walk with Christ, they should not shame you for sinning but help you by asking more inviting questions: How have you been experiencing temptation? How is your relationship with your mom going? An accountability partner can be a peer, but it is also wise to seek out older Christians who have greater wisdom and experience.

Another important relationship is that of a **spiritual mentor**—a person, usually of the same gender as you, who is *an older companion who provides wisdom and encouragement in a specific area.*

Mentors can help you to grow in a spiritual discipline, understand a job or career, or learn more about a particular subject. The best mentors are good listeners, not just people who like to dish out advice. Mentoring relationships should not be entered into hastily. First, discuss with your parents and pastor who might be someone in your congregation that could be a good mentor

spiritual mentor: an older companion who provides wisdom and encouragement in a specific area

for you, then ask that person if he or she would be willing to meet with you to discuss the possibility of forming a mentoring relationship with clear boundaries.[8]

God wants us to grow in community. We worship, study, and pray together; serve each other with spiritual gifts; and challenge each other to grow in church, in small groups, and through accountability partners and spiritual mentors. There is wisdom in having many counselors (Proverbs 11:14, 15:22, 27:17) and in seeking, together, to grow (Galatians 6:1–10, Ephesians 4:15–16).

6. Baptism and Communion

▸ **OBJECTIVE: You will be able to explain the purpose of baptism and communion.**

Two significant ways that we worship God together are through the sacraments of baptism and communion. (Some churches call these *ordinances* rather than sacraments.) At their most basic level, baptism and communion tell a story about what God has done, is doing, and will do. By participating in them we proclaim our faith to one another and experience God's grace afresh. That is why Augustine called them "visible form[s] of an invisible grace."[9] Sacraments are powerful representations of God's grace and goodness in our lives.

In Matthew 28:19–20, Jesus told his disciples to go into the whole world, making disciples, "baptizing them in the name of the Father and of the Son and of the Holy Spirit." **Baptism** is *a sacrament that symbolizes dying to sin and rising wih Christ.* The word *baptism* comes from the Greek word *baptizo*, which means *to dip* or *submerge.* Those being baptized are dipped in the water, or water is poured or sprinkled over them. Baptism also hearkens back to the story of the Exodus when God rescued the people of Israel from slavery and took them through the waters of the Red Sea (Exodus 14). Like the Israelites, Christians have been freed from slavery to sin and brought through the water into new life in Christ (Romans 6:3–7).

Baptism retells the salvation story and is a public declaration of our new identity as God's people.[10] It is not just a ritual. It is the beginning of our journey of following Jesus, the defining moment proclaiming our true identity.[11] In a sense, baptism is a daily affair. Each day, through the power of the Holy Spirit living inside us, we die to sin and rise again to our new life in Christ.

Communion is also known as *the Eucharist* (from the Greek *eucharistia*, meaning *thanksgiving*) or *the Lord's Supper*. On the last night before his arrest, Jesus held a meal with his disciples. He took bread and wine, blessed them, and declared that they were his body and blood, broken and poured out for the forgiveness of sins (Matthew 26:26–28). Jesus instructed his disciples to take **communion**, which is *a sacrament to commemorate the body and blood of Jesus given for the forgiveness of sins.* Paul said that in taking communion we proclaim Christ's death (1 Corinthians 11:23–26). By giving his body and blood for us on the cross, Jesus opened the way to eternal life. That is why he can say that his body and blood are truly food and drink (John 6:55–58).

communion: a sacrament to commemorate the body and blood of Jesus given for the forgiveness of sins

Last Supper, 1816 mosaic by Giacomo Raffaeli imitating Leonardo da Vinci's work, Vienna, Austria

Normally, communion happens in church on a weekly or monthly basis. Believers receive a small piece of bread and a sip of wine or grape juice (symbolizing the body and blood of Christ). Communion is a time of solemn remembrance, but it is also a celebration in which we receive God's loving grace. Taking communion assumes that we are in communion (or fellowship) with other Christians. If we are willfully living in sin against God or our neighbor and still taking communion, we are not taking Jesus' sacrifice seriously. That is why communion is typically preceded by a time for the confession of sin (1 Corinthians 11:28). One good reason for taking communion often is to encourage forgiveness and reconciliation in the church.

7. Giving and Service

▸ **OBJECTIVE:** You will be able to express how giving and serving meet the needs of our community.

One of the distinctive marks of early Christian communities was generosity. Acts 2:44–45 describes how Christians shared all their possessions, even selling their property and using the money to give to those who were in need. The apostles also collected funds to distribute to widows and other impoverished people. For example, while Paul was traveling, he visited several churches and collected funds for poor Christians in Jerusalem. Those who had plenty, he said, should gladly supply those in need; and if circumstances changed, those who received should also give back. Paul's goal was for self-sacrificing generosity to be standard among the believers, but he did not coerce anyone to give. He encouraged them to give cheerfully out of the fullness of their hearts. He promised that those who gave would also receive—that God would supply all their needs (1 Corinthians 16:1–4, 2 Corinthians 8:1–9:15, Romans 15:14–32).

Since that time, it has been common for churches to collect tithes and offerings. The tithe has its grounding in the Old Testament, when Abraham gave 10 percent of the goods he won in battle to the priest Melchizedek (Genesis 14:18–20). This tithe preceded the Law given to Moses, which specified tithes for the priesthood (Numbers 18:21), feasts (Deuteronomy 14:22–27), and the poor (Deuteronomy 14:28–29), as well as other offerings. Following Jewish custom, many Christians tithe 10 percent of their income, yet this amount is not specifically mandated in the New Testament. Of greater importance is our mindset when we give. James wrote that every good gift is from God (James 1:17). We are to be generous with the gifts God has given to us, freely giving to those in need.

The church must steward tithes and offerings responsibly. In Paul's collection, trustworthy individuals were selected by the church to distribute the gifts (2 Corinthians 8:16–24). It is just as important today for the church to have wise and qualified people overseeing the use of funds so that there is no mismanagement. Church funds can be used in various ways—paying the pastors and staff (1 Corinthians 9:7–11, Galatians 6:6), funding church programing and the upkeep of church property, supporting church planting and missionaries, and giving to local charities or community organizations that help the poor.

There are many more ways to give than simply offering money. Assuming only money is necessary can be destructive and condescending to the people we are trying to help.[12] Instead, we can look for ways to help others develop their own skills and talents, bolstering their self-confidence and restoring their sense of self-worth and dignity. In addition to money, we can give of our time and abilities. We can advocate for others and use the influence we have on their behalf.

Meeting the needs of our community provides the opportunity for all of us to use our God-given gifts to serve one another. We do this in different ways. In the early church, the apostles appointed deacons to oversee the needs of the community, especially those of widows and others who could not provide for themselves (Acts 6:1–7). Many churches today have special ministry teams, which mobilize individuals to use their gifts to help others. Some examples include: spending time with those who need comfort or encouragement, doing yard work for the sick or elderly, visiting people who are in the hospital or stuck at home, or volunteering to help with community service.

In giving of ourselves and stewarding God's gifts wisely, Christians participate in God's story, growing together and modeling God's redemptive love to the world.

8. Sharing the Gospel

▸ **OBJECTIVE:** You will be able to give examples of how to share the gospel.

After every worship service, the congregation is sent back out into the world to be a light for Christ. Every believer is called to make disciples (Matthew 28:19–20). We do this individually at home, school, and work, but also together with other believers. How exactly do we do this? St. Francis is often credited with saying, "Preach the gospel, and when necessary, use words." Though it is unlikely that St. Francis actually said this, the statement has some merit. The point is that we can also preach the gospel through our actions.

The way we live our lives with other believers should be attractive to those outside the faith. In fact, Jesus explicitly said that unbelievers would be able to identify Christians by their love for one another (John 13:35). In other words, the way that we treat other Christians—being generous, serving, and forgiving one another—should be a testimony to the transforming love of Jesus at work in our communities. We love because he first loved us (1 John 4:19). The early church father Tertullian wished that unbelievers would look at Christians and say, "Look [at] how they love one another . . . and how they are ready to die for each other." [13]

Our lives should demonstrate love not only toward believers, but to everyone around us, including our enemies (Matthew 5:44). Jesus taught that we are to treat everyone as we ourselves would like to be treated (Luke 6:31). One way to love others and share the gospel with them is by serving your neighborhood and community. Many churches do this by offering meals and shelter to the homeless, providing aid to refugees, and organizing community service days. By doing these things, we show that the gospel is not just about the afterlife. We show that God cares about neighborhoods and communities, as well as every individual person.

Giotto's fresco of St. Francis speaking to the birds in the Basilica of San Francesco in the heart of Assisi

While our actions on their own can raise the curiosity of unbelievers, they need to be accompanied by words. Ultimately, faith comes through hearing the message about Jesus (Romans 10:17), so we must offer that message to others. Christ's love compels us to do this (2 Corinthians 5:14). We can use our words to share about Jesus and then invite others to follow him. The best way to go about this is to make friends with those outside the faith. Invite them into your house, get to know them, and show genuine interest in them. We don't do this to try and convert them, but to show them the love that Jesus showed us. We cannot save anyone. It is the Holy Spirit who does the work of conversion in a person's heart. But he empowers us to share our testimony with others (Acts 1:8).

The privilege of sharing the gospel is enormous, but the opportunities are endless. That's why various parachurch organizations have been created. These Christian organizations come alongside the church and assist in sharing the good news. For example, the Salvation Army provides relief for the homeless, Compassion International supports children in impoverished countries, Gideons International distributes Bibles all over the world, The Navigators aid Christians in sharing their faith, and Summit Ministries provides worldview and apologetics training to help students defend and commend the faith. Many others could be listed.

As we have seen throughout this book, the gospel is indeed our personal salvation, yet it also includes the eventual restoration of all creation. That's why the gospel must be proclaimed in word *and* deed. Both are necessary for faithful Christian witness.

9. The Positive Impact of the Church on Society

▸ OBJECTIVE: You will be able to identify four specific ways the church has positively impacted society.

When the Spirit is at work among believers who are seeking to follow Jesus together, incredible things can happen. Throughout the centuries, the church has had a positive impact on society. Let's highlight four ways in which this has happened.

Caring for the Sick and Impoverished. When plagues hit Rome in the second and third centuries, many pagan priests and doctors fled the city, leaving the sick to die. But Christians cared for their sick neighbors—even those who did not believe in Jesus.[14] The church became known for its good deeds, which were shocking to the Romans. In AD 362, the emperor Julian complained to a pagan priest that Christians "support not only their poor, but ours as well."[15] During the Middle Ages, the Christian concern for the poor and downtrodden led to the founding of many hospitals and shelters. Today, Christians continue to be heavily involved in medical care and poverty relief.

Honoring and Protecting Women and Children. In ancient Roman culture, men had absolute power in the household. They could divorce their wives, force them to have abortions, and even have them killed. Male children were prized, so families often kept only the oldest female child (other girl babies would be left on the streets to die). In this situation, the Christian teaching that both women and men are God's image-bearers was revolutionary. Christians rejected abortion and infanticide. Instead, they took in abandoned infants.[16] Because the church valued them, women converted to Christianity at a far higher rate than men and served in positions of leadership.[17] The church also required that husbands be faithful to and love their wives (1 Corinthians 7:1–16, Ephesians 5:25).

Promoting Culture and Education. The Christian duty to love God with all one's heart, soul, mind, and strength (Luke 10:27) has fueled the desire for learning and education. Throughout the centuries, monks and nuns gathered together in monasteries and convents to devote themselves to God. They helped preserve ancient writings, both Christian and otherwise. During the Middle Ages, numerous schools and universities were opened for the study of theology and philosophy. Christian scholars also laid the groundwork for the endeavors of modern science. In addition, Christian artists were inspired to create for God's glory, leaving behind some of the most magnificent examples of artwork, sculpture, music, and architecture in the world.

Pursuing Racial Unity. Ever since the fall, wherever there have been people, there has been prejudice of one kind or another. Sadly, this has even happened in church settings. But the belief that all people bear God's image has led Christians to fight against prejudice (Romans 10:12–13, Galatians 3:28, Colossians 3:11). One example of this was in Rwanda in 1994, when racial prejudice between the Hutu and Tutsi people in that country led to a genocide of the Tutsi people. Almost 30 years later, Rwanda has demonstrated to the world the incredible power of forgiveness and the possibility of unity and healing. The Rwandan church plays a key role in this process.[18] Another example is from the United States. In 2015, a White supremacist murdered nine Black people during a Bible study at the Emanuel African Methodist Episcopal Church in Charleston, South Carolina. Confronting the murderer later in court, many members of the church openly forgave him and expressed how they were praying for him.[19] Though there is still much to be done, this tragedy has led to attempts to heal racial divides in the churches in Charleston.

These examples show how Christians have followed Jesus together and have left the world a better place. In and through them, the power of the gospel was evident to all. May the same be said of us.

10. Conclusion

Every week, Christians all over the world gather together in fields, homes, and church buildings to worship God through song, study of Scripture, preaching, prayer, confession, communion, and giving. Your school may have worship services too. In many of these gatherings, people regularly confess the Nicene Creed, which includes this line: "I believe in one holy catholic and apostolic church." (The word *catholic* here refers to the *universal* church.) The idea of the universal church is this: despite the multiplicity of denominations, doctrinal variations, and cultural expressions, there is ultimately only one church, composed of all those who follow Jesus and confess him as Lord (1 Corinthians 1:2, 12:12–13). No believer is excluded from God's community, no matter where they live in the world, the color of their skin, their gender, social status, or ethnicity. All who trust Jesus are a part of God's community.

In the church, the Holy Spirit calls together broken people—sinners in need of redemption—and transforms them into a new people who love God and others. It is inevitable that in diverse communities of fallen human beings there will be problems, challenges, and frustrations. Discouraging as these can sometimes be, growth in the life of faith happens primarily in fellowship with other believers (Proverbs 27:17, Hebrews 10:24–25). The nature of Scripture itself indicates this—from the Old Testament to the New, God spoke through prophets, kings, evangelists, and apostles directly to a community, whether it was Israel, a particular nation, or a church.

Our life in community influences the way we engage with God and others on an individual level. By learning from other believers and worshipping together with them, we discover new ways to follow Jesus more faithfully ourselves. In the same manner, each individual spiritual discipline that we talked about in Chapter 15 prepares us for our life in community. As we are growing individually, we come together to help and encourage one another to grow as well (Ephesians 2:19–21; 4:15–16). Through God's Spirit, we grow up together in Christ, becoming the people we were intended to be—that is, people who live holy lives and glorify God in everything.

However, like anything else, community can become an idol. We can gather together with others who are just like us and use community as a way of excluding others. Another temptation is to search for the perfect community where your gifts and talents are appreciated, where the music suits your taste, and the pastor is dynamic and interesting. But such a quest is dangerous and illusive; it can cause us to become calloused toward other Christians and resistant to the work of the Holy Spirit. We must remember that God can always form us right where we are—even when our church is less than ideal.

It is in the less-than-ideal places where it is often most difficult to follow Jesus' two greatest commands—love God and love your neighbor. So, before we close this book, we need to explore what love means and what it looks like when we live it out.

ENDNOTES

[1]"Simeon Stylites," *New World Encyclopedia*, https://www.newworldencyclopedia.org/entry/Simeon_Stylites.

[2]Simeon's excesses do not invalidate all monastic endeavors. In the fourth century, faced with increasing corruption in church and society, many Christians fled to the deserts to seek God in solitude and engage in more intense discipleship. They practiced *asceticism*, though occasionally to an extreme, unhealthy degree. However, it quickly became apparent that solitude, though an important practice, was not a good condition in which to live permanently. For this reason, small communities of men and women formed in order to foster greater devotion to God. Even among solitary monks, it was common to gather together at least once a week.

[3]Justin Martyr, *The First Apology in Ante-Nicene Fathers Volume 1*, 3rd edition, ed. Philip Schaff (Eternal Sun Books, 2017), 160.

[4]Pliny (the younger) in *Documents of the Christian Church*, 4th edition, ed. Henry Bettenson and Chris Maunder (Oxford: Oxford University Press, 2011), 4.

[5]Justo L. González, *The Story of Christianity Volume 1: The Early Church to the Dawn of the Reformation* (New York: HarperCollins, 2010), 384.

[6]Harold L. Senkbeil, *The Care of Souls: Cultivating a Pastor's Heart* (Bellingham, VA: Lexham Press, 2019), 225–26.

[7]Theodoret of Cyr, as quoted in *Ancient Christian Commentary on Scripture: 1–2 Corinthians*, ed. Gerald Bray (Downers Grove: IVP Academic, 2006), 115.

[8]For more information about mentoring, see Jeff Myers, Paul Gutacker, and Page Gutacker, *Cultivate: Forming the Emerging Generation through Life-on-Life Mentoring* (Dayton: Passing the Baton International, 2010), and *A Mentoring Guide: Christ, Conversation, Companionship* (Sioux Falls, SD: VantagePoint3 Ministries, 2019).

[9]St. Augustine, as quoted in Edwin Oliver James, "Sacrament," Encyclopedia Brittanica, https://www.britannica.com/topic/sacrament.

[10]N.T. Wright, *The Way of the Lord: Christian Pilgrimage Today* (Grand Rapids, MI: Eerdmans, 1999), 25–33.

[11]Wright, 31.

[12]Steve Corbett and Brian Fikkert, *When Helping Hurts: How to Alleviate Poverty Without Hurting the Poor . . . and Yourself* (Chicago: Moody Publishers, 2012), 139.

[13]Tertullian, as quoted in J. Warren Smith, "See how these Christians love one another," Christian History Institute, https://christianhistoryinstitute.org/magazine/article/see-how-these-christians-love.

[14]Rodney Stark, *The Rise of Christianity: A Sociologist Reconsiders History* (Princeton, NJ: Princeton University Press, 1996), 73–94.

[15]Julian, as quoted in Stark, 83–84.

[16]"Doing Life Together," Summit Ministries, reproduction rights granted by Charles Moore. September 9, 2009, https://www.summit.org/resources/articles/doing-life-together/.

[17]Stark, 128.

[18]Jonatán Soriano, "Rwanda: 25 years building forgiveness and reconciliation," Evangelical Focus, https://evangelicalfocus.com/world/4393/rwanda-25-years-of-forgiveness-and-reconciliation.

[19]Mark Berman, "'I forgive you.' Relatives of Charleston church shooting victims address Dylann Roof," *The Washington Post*, June 19, 2015, https://www.washingtonpost.com/news/post-nation/wp/2015/06/19/i-forgive-you-relatives-of-charleston-church-victims-address-dylann-roof/.

17 Loving God and Others

1. The Two Greatest Commandments

▸ **OBJECTIVE: You will be able to discuss the importance of keeping the two greatest commandments.**

"Teacher, which is the great commandment in the Law?" a lawyer once asked Jesus. His response: "You shall love the Lord your God with all your heart and with all your soul and with all your mind. This is the great and first commandment. And a second is like it: You shall love your neighbor as yourself. On these two commandments depend all the Law and the Prophets" (Matthew 22:36–40).

The apostle Paul said something similar:

> Owe no one anything, except to love each other, for the one who loves another has fulfilled the law. For the commandments, "You shall not commit adultery, You shall not murder, You shall not steal, You shall not covet," and any other commandment, are summed up in this word: "You shall love your neighbor as yourself." Love does no wrong to a neighbor; therefore love is the fulfilling of the law.
>
> –Romans 13:8–10

Just imagine if humanity actually kept these two great commandments. Loren Cunningham, the founder of Youth with a Mission (YWAM), spent a few pages describing what this would look like in *The Book That Transforms Nations*. Here's part of his list:

- A majority would honor God and respect each other, viewing life as God's gift.
- Every mother would treasure her unborn child, and every father would provide the loving stability his child needs.
- Racism would be rare. Reconciliation and unity would bring all races and ethnic groups together.
- We wouldn't have to fear violence or theft.
- Most people would protect the environment, practicing good stewardship over God's creation.

- Child abuse and spousal abuse would all but disappear.
- Divorce would be extremely rare.
- Politicians, officials, and judges would be public servants, not abusers of power.
- Empty prisons would be demolished or repurposed for other uses.
- People would speak the truth in love.
- Profanity and slander would become the exception, not the norm.
- Road rage would be a peculiar phenomenon for history scholars to ponder.[1]

This all sounds great, yet creating such a world is not as simple as getting everyone to obey two commands. In fact, we are entirely incapable of bringing about the world described above. Standing in our way is the problem of sin. Each and every one of us has failed to love God and others as we ought, so we all contribute to the ongoing mess of our world. In order to truly love God and neighbor, we need something more than an iron will to do good or a strong commitment to obey; we need a transformed heart. Here's the good news: through Jesus, believers have been given new hearts and commissioned to witness to the power of God's love to heal and transform the world. Only God can bring about the world we long for, but he wants us to anticipate that world by demonstrating his love through the power of the Holy Spirit. In this chapter we'll look at what the Bible says about loving God and our neighbor and how that can make a difference in our world.

2. What Love Is

▸ OBJECTIVE: You will be able to distinguish between four types of love.

The Bible was written mostly in two languages: Hebrew and Greek. Both of these languages tell us about what love is and is not.

The Old Testament uses the Hebrew word for love, *ahava*. It is related to the root word *hav*, "which means *to give*. This Hebrew word contains a tremendous truth: giving is fundamental to loving. . . Love is not something that simply happens to us but something that we create through our actions when we give of ourselves to others."[2]

Greek, the language that the New Testament was written in, specifies different types of love by giving each type its own word. Four Greek terms for love are *philia*, *storge*, *eros*, and *agape*. *Philia* is *love of family, friends, and community.* This type of love refers to affectionate regard for another in a nonsexual way. *Storge* means *natural affection*, such as the love of parents for their children. It might also be used for love of country or a sports team. *Eros* means *romantic love and sexual desire.* It borrows its name from the Greek god of love and sensual passion. From *eros* we get the word "erotic." The Bible uses the word *agape* to describe the kind of love that comes from God. *Agape* love is *selfless, self-giving love.*

The word *agape* is used more than 200 times in the New Testament. "Charity means love," wrote C. S. Lewis. "It is called *agape* in the New Testament to distinguish it from *eros* (sexual love), *storge* (family affection), and *philia* (friendship). So, there are four kinds of love, all good in their proper place, but *agape* is the best because it is the kind God has for us and is good in all circumstances."[3]

Lewis went on to explain that *eros*, *philia*, and *storge* can all become corrupted if they are not caught up in *agape*. Unless our loves are tempered by *agape*, they can become selfishness, jealousy, bitterness, anger, and hatred. Love that does not seek the good of another is not really love at all. That's why love is ultimately defined by God himself. God is love, and he demonstrated to us what love really looks like. John 3:16 says that "God so loved the world, that he gave his only Son . . ." God's love is proactive and self-giving. Before he was crucified, Jesus told his followers that people would know they were Christians by the *agape* love they had for one another (John 13:35).

What does agape look like in practice? Paul famously explained this in 1 Corinthians 13:4–7. Love, he said, is patient and kind, not envious, boastful, proud, dishonoring, self-seeking, or easily angered. It does not keep a record of wrongs or delight in evil. It rejoices in truth and always protects, trusts, hopes, and perseveres. In Scripture, love is more than just a feeling, It takes work. It is a commitment to loving action for the good of another.

3. Loving God

▸ **OBJECTIVE:** You will be able to explain how to love God.

It is God's nature to love (1 John 4:8). When he decided to create human beings, he did so in love, in order to adopt us through Jesus Christ (Ephesians 1:4–5). God created us to be in relationship with him. He is a Person who cares for us, who knows our thoughts and even how many hairs we have on our head. He desires fellowship with us (1 Peter 5:7, Psalm 139:1–4, Matthew 10:30, Revelation 3:20). Our love for God is grounded in the fact that he loved us first (1 John 4:19).

So, how do we go about loving God? We begin by responding to him, by seeking him out and enjoying his company. Loving God means delighting and rejoicing in him (Psalm 37:4, Philippians 4:4). We learn to love God by just being with him, spending time in his presence.

Some people are concerned that they don't really love God because they seldom have warm feelings for him. Others worry that they don't really love God if they are mad at him or are confused because their prayers are not answered the way they hoped. Though our feelings toward God can vary (just as they vary in any other relationship we have), loving God is not just a matter of feelings. It involves our whole self, including our actions toward others. Loving God goes hand in glove with loving other people (1 John 4:7–8). John even goes so far as to say that if we don't love others, we can't possibly say that we love God (1 John 4:20). Loving God also means being obedient to his commands (John 14:15, 21, 23). All of us will inevitably fail to love and obey at times, yet God is gracious, ready to forgive us and to enable us to try again.

When we love God, we recognize his true worth and put him first in our lives. We don't allow other things to crowd in and deprive us of time with him. In short, we reject idolatry, which is the sin of worshipping anyone or anything other than God.

Idolatry is vividly portrayed in Scripture after God led the children of Israel out of Egypt. While Moses received the Ten Commandments, his brother Aaron fashioned a golden calf and other idols. Then, he announced, "These are your gods, O Israel, who brought you up out of the land of Egypt!" (Exodus 32:4). How had Aaron and the Israelites so quickly forgotten the Lord?

We might think we are superior to the Israelites because we don't usually bow down before physical images. However, we also construct idols out of things like money, sex, or status. One of the direst consequences of idolatry is that we end up resembling the idols we have created.

Adoration of the Golden Calf, 1633 painting by Nicolas Poussin, National Gallery, London, United Kingdom

> The idols of the nations are silver and gold,
>   the work of human hands.
> They have mouths, but do not speak;
>   they have eyes, but do not see;
> they have ears, but do not hear,
>   nor is there any breath in their mouths.
> Those who make them become like them,
>   so do all who trust in them. –Psalm 135:15–18

When we trade God for idols, we not only forget God but become shallow, unstable, unthinking, and uncaring—just like the things we worship. We are rescued from idolatry when we respond to the Holy Spirit's urging to turn from sin and to recognize who God is and what he has done for us.

4. Accepting God's Love for Us

▸ **OBJECTIVE: You will be able to relate receiving God's love to the ability to love others.**

Our love for God and others is a response to God's love for us. This means that before we can love others, we must first receive God's love for ourselves. As one pastor explains:

> The only reason you can love God or love anybody else is because God first loved you. He showed that love by creating you. He showed that love by everything you have in life; it's all a gift of God's love. And he showed that love by sending Jesus Christ to Earth to die for you. Once we're secure inside God's unconditional love, we'll start showing others more grace. We won't be as angry as we've been. We'll be more patient. We'll be more forgiving. We'll be more merciful. We'll give others grace. But you cannot give others something you haven't received yourself. . . . It's impossible to love others until you really feel loved yourself.[4]

When Jesus said, "You shall love your neighbor as yourself" (Mark 12:31), he assumed that we do, in fact, love ourselves. Most people do love themselves. Loving ourselves is natural, though self-love waxes and wanes like other feelings do. But some people believe they are too broken or sinful to be loved, or that they are worthless compared to others, or that they are not lovable. Yet the truth is that God loves us more than we could possibly imagine (Romans 5:8).

Romans 12:3 says that we are not to think of ourselves more highly than is warranted, but neither are we to think of ourselves as less than God has made us. We are to acknowledge our sinfulness while resting in our true identity as God's beloved children. We can also ask God to help us be humble and teachable, to give us a more accurate perception of our own character, abilities, and gifts, and to help us gain a deeper knowledge of his love.

As we receive God's love and are transformed by it, we can begin to give that love to others. This is about more than just doing acts of love. It's about becoming the kind of person whose natural response is to love unselfishly. One of the ways this happens is through our habits. We can cultivate a life of love through what we habitually do. We can spend time with God, experiencing his care for us and learning to receive his love. We can practice seeing ourselves as God sees us. He sees all our flaws, and yet he has compassion on us. We can also consider others' interests in addition to our own and put them first (Philippians 2:3–4).

John Stonestreet, president of the Colson Center, recommends asking four questions to connect our love for God with the life habits that will personally help us to flourish:

- **What are my loves?** What do I care about most deeply based on how I use my time, talents, and treasure?
- **What are my loyalties?** Who or what gets the real me? What causes me to commit my time and energies?
- **What are my longings?** Toward what am I aiming my life? What is success? If I continue where I have aimed, where will I end up? What am I thinking about in my private moments?
- **What are my liturgies?** (*Liturgies* is a fancy theological term for the rhythms of life). What do I worship? What are the habits of my life?[5]

Asking these questions, and remembering the disciplines discussed in Chapters 15–16, will help us discern the habits that shape what we love so we can grow in love for God, ourselves, and others.

5. Loving Others

▸ **OBJECTIVE: You will be able to give examples of ways Jesus demonstrated love.**

We have seen that in order to love at all, we must cultivate a loving relationship with God and accept God's love for ourselves. Then, that love can flow freely from us to others.

What does this love look like? It looks like Jesus' *agape* love, characterized by selfless giving and humble sacrifice. Consider a dozen ways Jesus demonstrated love:

- **Jesus spent time with others.** He invested three years of his life with 12 disciples and had close relationships with others (Luke 6:12–16, 8:1–3; John 11:5).
- **Jesus listened.** He paid attention to people and responded to them with compassion (Matthew 15:21–28; Mark 7:24–30, Luke 7:1–10, John 4:1–42).
- **Jesus served others.** He was intent on ministering to the crowds who followed him (Matthew 4:23–25). Washing feet was a job reserved for the lowest of slaves, but Jesus humbly took on this role at the Last Supper (John 13:1–17). Even after he rose from the grave, he made breakfast for his disciples (John 21:9–13).
- **Jesus grieved over human sinfulness and suffering.** He grieved with others and experienced their pain (Matthew 23:37–39, Luke 13:10–13, John 11:33–36).
- **Jesus told the truth.** He didn't lie. He was honest with his fans, foes, friends, family, and heavenly Father (Matthew 26:25, 39; Mark 10:17–22, 15:34; Luke 2:48–51, 8:19–21; John 10:31–32, 21:15–19).
- **Jesus honored women and children.** In a society where women and children were treated as second-class citizens, Jesus persistently valued them (Matthew 18:3, 19:14; Mark 1:30–31, 5:35–43, 14:3–9; Luke 10:38–42; John 8:1–11).
- **Jesus advocated for the poor.** He condemned the neglect and abuse of the poor in society (Luke 11:39–42, 14:12–14, 16:19–25).

- **Jesus treated outsiders** with kindness and respect. He wasn't afraid to talk to prostitutes, social outcasts, tax collectors, or Roman soldiers (Luke 7:1–10, 38–50, 17:11–19, 19:1–10).
- **Jesus gave his life for us.** He suffered the ultimate punishment in our place so that he might bring us into right relationship with God (John 15:12, Philippians 2:8, 1 Peter 3:18).
- **Jesus forgave his enemies.** He was not plotting his revenge on the cross. Instead, he begged mercy for those who sought to kill him (Luke 23:34).
- **Jesus empowered others.** Jesus trained his followers; he also had them put their training to use (Luke 10:1, 16–17). He promised they would do great works for God's glory and commissioned them to be his witnesses (John 14:12, Acts 1:8).
- **Jesus prayed for others.** He prayed constantly. He prayed for the apostles and also for those who would believe in him later (John 17:20). He is still praying for us (Romans 8:34, Hebrews 7:25).

When we consider the many ways Jesus loved others, we see just how tall an order he gave us: "This is my commandment, that you love one another as I have loved you" (John 15:12). God's *agape* has been "poured into our hearts through the Holy Spirit who has been given to us" (Romans 5:5), so we are empowered to love and to "consider how to stir up one another to love and good works" (Hebrews 10:24).

6. Who Is My Neighbor?

▸ **OBJECTIVE: You will be able to summarize what loving your neighbor means.**

According to Scripture, loving our neighbors is not optional. It is expected of God's people. In Leviticus, God spells out the responsibilities that the people of Israel had toward one another (emphasis added):

> You shall not oppress your *neighbor* or rob him. The wages of a hired worker shall not remain with you all night until the morning. You shall not curse the deaf or put a stumbling block before the blind, but you shall fear your God: I am the Lord.
>
> You shall do no injustice in court. You shall not be partial to the poor or defer to the great, but in righteousness shall you judge your *neighbor*. You shall not go around as a slanderer among your people, and you shall not stand up against the life of your *neighbor*: I am the Lord.
>
> You shall not hate your brother in your heart, but you shall reason frankly with your *neighbor*, lest you incur sin because of him. 18 You shall not take vengeance or bear a grudge against the sons of your own people, but you shall love your *neighbor* as yourself: I am the Lord. –Leviticus 19:13–18

"And who is my neighbor?" This is a question that Jesus was once asked by a self-righteous lawyer. Jesus' answer became known as *the parable of the Good Samaritan* (Luke 10:25–37). In the story, a Jewish man was beaten, robbed, and left for dead. A priest and another Jewish man both passed by the wounded man without giving him a thought. Then, along came a Samaritan (recall that the Jews and Samaritans were bitter enemies). He stopped, cared for the man's wounds, and took him to an inn so that he could recover. After relating this story, Jesus asked the lawyer, "'Which of these three do you think was a neighbor to the man who fell into the hands of robbers?' The expert in the law replied, 'The one who had mercy on him.' Jesus told him, 'Go and do likewise.'" (Luke 10:36–37)

Jesus made it clear that neighborliness extended beyond the Israelites to Samaritans, Romans, and other Gentiles. Neighborliness goes beyond family and tribe, beyond the circles in which we feel most comfortable. Every person is our neighbor because we all share a common humanity. So, every person should be an object of our love. This kind of radical love is neither easy or comfortable. As one Bible commentary points out, there are risks:

The Samaritan takes on an extraordinary degree of risk to help this stranger. He risks getting jumped by the same bandits when he stoops to see what has happened to the man. He risks being cheated by the innkeeper. He risks being saddled by the expense and emotional weight of caring for someone who has become chronically ill. But he takes on these risks because he acts as if his own life were the one in question.[6]

Jesus also addressed what it means to be a good neighbor in the Sermon on the Mount (Matthew 5–7), teaching that we are to seek peace, resolve disputes, be honest, resist retaliation, love our enemies, and give to those in need. Jesus' sermon shows us how to treat others based on God's goodness, love, and justice. Despite the risks, this is what we are called to.

7. Neighborliness and Community

▸ **OBJECTIVE: You will be able to express how Christians can contribute to building healthy communities.**

One way to love our neighbors is by pursuing *shalom* in our local communities. Recall that shalom is a state of peace, harmony, wholeness, prosperity, welfare, and tranquility. Shalom grows out of the "community aspect" of creation. Genesis 2:24 says, "Therefore a man shall leave his father and his mother and hold fast to his wife, and they shall become one flesh." (The term meaning *flesh* in Hebrew is *basar*, which also implies the idea of "clan.") Adam and Eve became one family. Their family ultimately expanded to include the whole human race—from those who live next door to those who live halfway around the world (Acts 17:26).

Many Christians follow Martin Luther's teaching and believe that God ordained three principal institutions: the family, the church, and the government.[7] Christians love their neighbors by pursuing *shalom* in these institutions, as well as by working together to build the "intermediary institutions" that make for healthy societies, such as schools, hospitals, and other organizations offering service to the community.

The well-being of our community is not something we can ignore. The prophet Jeremiah wrote to the Israelite captives in Babylon and instructed them to "seek the welfare of the city where I have sent you into exile, and pray to the Lord on its behalf, for in its welfare you will find your welfare" (Jeremiah 29:7). Loving our communities means caring about the well-being of everyone in them, whether they share our faith or not.

So, how do we build strong communities? John Stonestreet, quoted earlier, frequently asks four questions to help people identify how they can participate in this task:

- What's good that we can protect, promote, and celebrate?
- What's broken that we can fix or restore?
- What's evil that we can stop?
- What's missing that we can contribute?[8]

Answering these questions may lead us to volunteer with the local fire department or public school, preserve historic buildings, actively fight against the use of drugs and pornography, or build safe parks for children. These are just a few of the many ways we can contribute to building healthy communities.

Cooperating with others (both Christians and non-Christians) is necessary for getting things done effectively and efficiently, but it is also good in and of itself. By working together with others, we demonstrate God's love. Conflicts may arise about the best way to promote the well-being of the community. Because of our sin nature and differing perspectives, we may disagree over how to pursue our goals, who gets credit for what, who should be in charge, whether someone is abusing power, and an endless array of other concerns. As Christians, we must remember that all people are God's image-bearers and are worthy of respect. With this in mind, we can and should ask God, who owns everything (Psalm 24:1), to help us to work together with others.

8. Neighborliness and Citizenship

▸ **OBJECTIVE: You will be able to explain the concept of Christian dual citizenship and our responsibilities as citizens of God's kingdom.**

The Christian calling to love our neighbors also impacts the way we behave as citizens of the nation in which we live. A citizen of a community, city, or nation is someone who, by birth or naturalization, has the right to be protected by the community or state, and the responsibility to contribute to its welfare and safety. The US Declaration of Independence says that God gave all people rights, including "life, liberty, and the pursuit of happiness."[9] So, US citizens expect their country will protect those rights. They also recognize that, as citizens, they have the responsibility to vote, pay taxes, and obey the law.

Christians have dual citizenship. We are first and foremost citizens of God's kingdom—that is, citizens of heaven. However, this does not free us from being good citizens on Earth (Philippians 3:20, Titus 3:1–2). The rights and responsibilities of citizens vary from one nation to another. Because of this, believers in diverse times and places, with different types of governments, have had to discern what being a good citizen means in their respective contexts.

One responsibility as citizens of God's kingdom is to live peaceably with others as much as possible (Romans 12:18). This includes obeying laws, respecting and praying for local authorities, and paying taxes, while giving our ultimate allegiance to God (Matthew 22:21, Romans 13:1–7, Acts 5:29, 1 Peter 2:13–15, 1 Timothy 2:1–2).

Another of our responsibilities as citizens is to seek justice. God told his people to "seek justice, correct oppression, bring justice to the fatherless, [and] plead the widow's cause" (Isaiah 1:17). Other prophets preached the same message (Hosea 12:6, Amos 5:24, Micah 6:8, Zechariah 7:9). They were recalling the principles of fairness and justice that were built into God's Law from the beginning (for example, see the Ten Commandments, Exodus 20:1–17).

Being a good citizen of God's kingdom can also mean getting involved in local and national government, whether through supporting candidates, running for office, proposing or opposing legislation, or implementing or resisting policy. The Old Testament stories of heroes like Joseph, Esther, Daniel, and others are instructive for us today. Our motivation for getting involved should be to love our neighbors by bringing justice and truth into the realms of power (Luke 6:31).

Christian citizenship requires that we live faithfully and in obedience to Jesus, even under corrupt governments or persecution. There will be times when authorities command us to do what is evil, and when those times come, Christians must say *no.* But these kinds of choices require prayer and discernment, especially with other believers.

A good example of faithful Christian citizenship is John Woolman, a Quaker farmer in the 1700s who came to realize that owning slaves was wrong. He freed his slaves and set about trying to persuade his Quaker neighbors to do the same. Woolman didn't lecture or preach to them. Instead, he asked questions: What does it mean to be a person? What does it mean to own a person? What does it mean to will a person to your descendants as a piece of property? By the time Woolman finished his campaign, all the Quakers in America had released their slaves, and a good number had joined the abolitionist cause.[10]

Woolman, through simple persuasion, played the part of a caring neighbor and brought freedom to thousands. In the same way, Christian citizens today should look for creative ways to love their nation through promoting justice.

9. Love Your Enemies

▸ **OBJECTIVE: You will be able to apply five principles for loving enemies.**

It's all good and well to say, "Love your neighbor," but what if your neighbors aren't very neighborly? What if they don't like you? What if you don't like them? What if they seek to do you harm? How our neighbors treat us doesn't change how we are to treat them. This is the radical teaching of Jesus:

"You have heard that it was said, 'You shall love your neighbor and hate your enemy.' But I say to you, Love your enemies and pray for those who persecute you, so that you may be sons of your Father who is in heaven. For he makes his sun rise on the evil and on the good, and sends rain on the just and on the unjust." –Matthew 5:43–45

As one writer put it, "We don't love those who hate us to get what we want or to manipulate a situation. We do it because that's what children of heaven do."[11]

The idea of treating our enemies like God does is repeated in Luke's gospel (Luke 6:27–36). This response goes counter to how we naturally want to respond to those who despise and abuse us. But loving our enemies isn't optional for Christians. It's an important part of following Jesus' example, as Peter reminds believers facing persecution (1 Peter 2:21–23). It is a way of participating in the life of God.

Martin Luther King Jr., 1964 Nobel Foundation

In his sermon titled "Loving Your Enemies," Dr. Martin Luther King Jr. gave practical advice on how to go about this task:

- **Start by looking at yourself.** Some people might not like you due to jealousy or some other reason. But others might dislike you because you did something that aroused their hate. On this point, King quoted Jesus: "Why do you see the speck that is in your brother's eye, but do not notice the log that is in your own eye?" (Matthew 7:3)
- **Look for the good in others**. "The person who hates you most has some good in him; even the nation that hates you most has some good in it; even the race that hates you most has some good in it," said King. "See God's image there . . . and you will take a new attitude."
- **Choose love rather than hate.** "[Returning] hate for hate only intensifies the existence of hate and evil in the universe. If I hit you and you hit me and I hit you back and go on. . . . It just never ends. Somewhere somebody must have a little sense, and that's the strong person. The strong person is the person who can cut off the chain of hate, the chain of evil. . . . And you do that by love."
- **Guard your heart.** "Hate at any point is a cancer that gnaws away at the very vital center of your life and your existence. It is like eroding acid that eats away the best and the objective center of your life. So, Jesus says love, because hate destroys the hater as well as the hated."
- **Persevere.** King affirmed, "As I look into your eyes, and into the eyes of all of my brothers [and sisters] in Alabama and all over America and over the world, I say to you, 'I love you. I would rather die than hate you.' And I'm foolish enough to believe that through the power of this love somewhere, men [people] of the most recalcitrant bent will be transformed."[12]

The love of Jesus flowing through us to our enemies has the power to break the bonds of hatred and division, transforming not only our enemies, but ourselves as well.

10. Conclusion

Throughout this chapter, we explored what love is and what it looks like to love. We have seen that God's love is *agape*, totally selfless, giving, and for our good. We saw that the most important commandment is to love God and that the second is to love your neighbor as yourself (Matthew 22:37–39). This teaching is so important that it also appears in Mark 12:29–31 and in Luke 10:27. And the gospel of John uses the word "love" 57 times—more than the other three gospels combined.[13] The command to love your neighbor is also repeated in the epistles (Romans 13:9, James 2:8). Clearly, love was central to who Jesus was and what he came to do. It was also central to Jesus' earliest followers. Indeed, for Christians, love is our primary calling and our greatest joy.

Becoming a person who loves like God is the work of the Holy Spirit within us, transforming our desires, reordering our loves, and helping us to receive God's love for ourselves so that it can flow freely to others. Cultivating a life of love begins with looking to Jesus' example. It also means expanding our view of who our neighbor actually is and practicing habits that teach us how to love well. Love demands not just words, but action (1 John 3:18, Matthew 25:34–40), in our local communities and our nation. God's love stretches us even further by challenging us to love our enemies.

Love is the defining mark of a Christian. Francis Schaeffer, an American theologian and philosopher, wrote:

> We as Christians are called upon to love all people as neighbors, loving them as ourselves [and] to love all true Christians in a way that the world may observe. . . . Love—and the unity it attests to—is the mark Christ gave Christians to wear before the world. Only with this mark may the world know that Christians are indeed Christians and that Jesus was sent by the Father.[14]

It is through God's love that we experience salvation, freedom from sin, and everlasting joy. It is through God's love that we become the people he calls us to be. And God's love compels us to share the gospel with others so that they, too, can delight in relationship with the Father, Son, and Holy Spirit. This is what Christianity is all about.

ENDNOTES

[1]Loren Cunningham, *The Book that Transforms Nations: The Power of the Bible to Change Any Country* (Seattle, WA: YWAM, 2007), 44–45.

[2]"Love and the Hebrew Language," The Messianic Prophecy Bible Project, https://free.messianicbible.com/feature/love-and-the-hebrew-language/.

[3]C. S. Lewis in a letter to Mrs. Johnson, dated Feb. 19, 1954. *The Collected Letters of C. S. Lewis: Books, Broadcasts, and the War, 1931–1949*, vol. III, ed. Walter Hooper (New York: HarperCollins, 2004), 428–29; also cited in https://www.cslewis.com/lewis-on-love.

[4]Rick Warren, "We Love Because God Loves Us," Daily Hope with Rick Warren, April 7, 2019, https://www.oneplace.com/ministries/daily-hope/read/devotionals/daily-hope-with-rick-warren/we-love-because-god-loves-us-daily-hope-with-rick-warren-april-7-2019-11807422.html.

[5]John Stonestreet, cited by Jeff Myers, "What is the 'Good Life'?," Summit Ministries, November 5, 2013, https://www.summit.org/resources/articles/what-is-the-good-life/.

[6]"The Good Samaritan at Work—Loving Your Neighbor As Yourself (Luke-10:25–37)," Theology of Work Project, revised June 30, 2017, https://www.theologyofwork.org/new-testament/luke/gods-provision-luke/the-good-samaritan-at-work-loving-your-neighbor-as-yourself-luke-1025-37.

[7]Church and State section under "Lutheranism," *Encyclopaedia Britannica*, https://www.britannica.com/topic/Lutheranism/Church-and-state.

[8]John Stonestreet, cited by Nick Eicher, "Avoiding the Political Illusion," *World Magazine*, November 14, 2014, https://world.wng.org/2014/11/avoiding_the_political_illusion.

[9]"Declaration of Independence: A Transcription," National Archives, https://www.archives.gov/founding-docs/declaration-transcript.

[10]Robert Greenleaf, *Servant Leadership: A Journey into the Nature of Legitimate Power and Greatness*, ed. Larry C. Spears, (Mahwah, NJ: Paulist Press, 2002), 43–44.

[11]"What's So Important About Loving Your Enemies?," Jesus Film Project, June 24, 2019, https://www.jesusfilm.org/blog/important-loving-your-enemies/.

[12]Martin Luther King, Jr., "Loving Your Enemies," The Martin Luther King Jr. Research and Education Institute, Stanford University, https://kinginstitute.stanford.edu/king-papers/documents/loving-your-enemies-sermon-delivered-dexter-avenue-baptist-church.

[13]Robert L. Deffinbaugh, "47. What Is This Thing Called Love? (John 21:1–25)," in *That You Might Believe: Study on the Gospel of John,* Bible.org, August 20, 2009, https://bible.org/seriespage/47-what-thing-called-love-john-211-25, end note 211.

[14]Francis A. Schaeffer, *The Mark of a Christian* (Wheaton, IL: InterVarsity Press, 1970), 59.

18
Conclusion

1. Encountering Scripture

▸ **OBJECTIVE: You will be able to list the steps to reading the Bible well and to summarize the biblical metanarrative.**

For the last 17 chapters, we've been exploring the Christian worldview—what it is, what it means for our lives, and how we get involved in it. In this final chapter, we'll briefly review what we've learned and then consider how Christianity provides meaningful answers to some of life's biggest questions. We'll conclude with a few thoughts about how to share the good news of Christianity with others.

Let's start with review. We've spent a lot of time talking about the Bible, which is inspired by God, rooted in history, and trustworthy in everything it teaches. In it, God reveals himself to us so that we can know him personally and enter into relationship with him. The Bible tells the true story of God's world, and in so telling, it reveals our purpose and how we can participate in God's mission. The Bible is like a compass; it points us in the right direction and guides us in wise living.[1]

Throughout history, the Bible has been carefully copied, preserved, and translated. Many biblical events, places, and characters have been verified in historical and archeological studies, affirming the trustworthiness and reliability of the Bible. However, the evidence does not establish the Bible's authority. The authority of Scripture comes from God himself. It is his message, and if we are to understand and apply it, we must learn to read Scripture well. This involves (1) choosing a good translation; (2) paying attention to the content; (3) understanding its historical context and (4) the literary context; (5) looking for relationships; (6) using Bible helps; and (7) courageously pursuing a response.

God invites us to encounter him in the grand storyline of the Bible. The Bible reveals a metanarrative that is comprehensive, coherent, and normative for our lives. The Bible's story can be told in six acts:

- **Act 1: Creation**—God created a good world where humans could dwell in harmony with him, themselves, others, and creation. Humans are made in God's image and given the task of ruling the earth wisely.
- **Act 2: The Fall**—The first human pair rebelled against God and brought sin into the world, leading to violence, the breakdown of relationships, and death.
- **Act 3: Redemption Initiated**—Despite the catastrophe of sin, God refused to give up on his world. He chose the family of Abraham out of grace, rescued Abraham's descendants (Israel) from slavery, and called them to be a kingdom of priests so that through them all people would be blessed.
- **Interlude: Second Temple Period**—After their failure to be faithful to God and long years spent in exile, Israel looked for a messiah who would rescue them and establish God's kingdom.
- **Act 4: Redemption Accomplished**—Jesus entered the world as the God-incarnate Messiah. He announced the kingdom of God had arrived. Living a fully human and sinless life, Jesus died on the cross, then rose again in order to defeat sin and death.
- **Act 5: Restoration Initiated**—Following Jesus' ascension to heaven, the Holy Spirit came to empower the church to share the good news and to be agents of restoration and reconciliation.

- **Act 6: Restoration Accomplished**—When Jesus returns to Earth, he will bring final judgment on evil and fully establish God's kingdom in the new heavens and new earth.

In reading this great story, we come to know God; we see what he has done, is doing, and will do. We find the meaning of our individual stories by joining them with God's story.

2. Growing in the Life of Faith

▸ **OBJECTIVE: You will be able to name at least 15 attributes of God.**

▸ **OBJECTIVE: You will be able to explain how to grow in relationship with God and how to become more like Christ.**

From our survey of the metanarrative of Scripture, we pressed on to discover who God is, who we are, the goal of the Christian life, and the practices that help us grow to be more like Christ. Let's review those topics.

In order to get a true understanding of God, we must look at how God reveals himself through the metanarrative and individual stories in Scripture. From these we see that God is self-existent, yet he desires to share life with others. He is the Creator, yet he does not stand aloof from his creation. He is personal. He is Spirit, yet he was incarnate in Jesus. God is eternal, all-knowing, all-powerful, everywhere present, unchanging, holy, wise, and righteous. Above all, God is love. God is the most powerful being in the universe, yet he exercises his power through, *agape*, self-giving love, which he displayed most clearly in Jesus.[2] God's loving nature makes sense in light of the fact that God is a Trinity—one Being in three Persons: Father, Son, and Holy Spirit.

God also tells us about us, humans. We were created by God out of love, made in his image, and given responsibility to love, steward, and rule wisely in God's world. However, each person is broken and corrupted by sin. Through his death and resurrection, Jesus saved us from the curse of sin. By trusting in him, we are redeemed from the bondage of sin, are united to Christ, and await our future glorification. In the meantime, Jesus calls us to imitate and follow him. Following Jesus means becoming a servant, picking up our cross, being willing to suffer, living in hope, and glorifying God in all that we do. In becoming like Christ, we become the people that God intended for us to be.

However, this transformation doesn't happen automatically or all at once. We get to cooperate with the Spirit so we can be remade. One of the ways we do this is through practicing spiritual disciplines: solitude, self-examination, prayer, worship, meditating on Scripture, fasting, giving, stewardship, and more. We don't practice these disciplines to earn God's favor but rather to cooperate with the work God wants to do in us. Furthermore, we can't become like Christ all by ourselves. We are always called to follow Jesus in community with other believers. Our individual spiritual practices shape and enable us for life in community. Together, believers worship and exercise their spiritual gifts in order to challenge, encourage, and build one another up. Christian community provides a place for confession and repentance, for celebrating God's work in baptism and communion, for studying Scripture, and for serving one another through love.

Together, we learn to follow Jesus' greatest commandments: love God and love your neighbor (Matthew 22:36–40). The kind of love Jesus calls us to is *agape*—a totally selfless, self-giving love. To love God in this way is to reject all forms of idolatry that lead us astray. It is to be in loving relationship with him, worshipping him as Lord. As we receive God's generous love for ourselves, we come to love him, and this leads us to love our neighbors—our friends, family, and even our enemies. Ultimately, this love becomes a witness for the gospel, which has the power to transform society.

Growing in the life of faith is a lifelong process of listening, trusting, and obeying the Holy Spirit's voice in our hearts and in Scripture. Following Jesus together with others in our community, we become like him.

3. Putting It All Together–Part 1

▸ **OBJECTIVE:** You will be able to articulate how Christianity answers five of life's biggest questions.

At the beginning of this book, we talked about how every worldview claims to offer guidance for life and provide meaningful answers to life's biggest questions. We believe that Christianity provides answers that best fit with the way the world actually is and helps us live in it with meaning and purpose. Let's look briefly at the answers Christianity can give to ten different questions.

Where did I come from? One of the most popular ideas about origins is that humans are the product of a long process of random chance and natural selection, so we are, essentially, an accident. Christianity offers a different answer. It teaches that we are the creation of the Trinitarian God, who is defined by love and who longs to share that love with us. We are not meaningless accidents of nature. We are the product of God's creative love.[3]

Who am I? In the search for identity, many people come to define themselves by what they own, what they can accomplish, or what others say about them.[2] Yet all of these things fail to provide a satisfactory basis for identity. It seems we can never own enough, do enough, or make everyone like us. The Christian story, however, begins by grounding our identity in God. We are God's image-bearers, endowed with dignity and value from our first moment. Nothing can ever change that. We are deeply loved by God and invited to claim our identity as his beloved sons and daughters.

Where am I? How we view the world influences the way we live in it. Is this world a meaningless product of chance, a place we are ultimately free to exploit? Or is the world a material prison, a bad place that will be discarded and from which we will one day escape? The Christian worldview says *no* to both these views. It says that the world is purposeful and valuable because it is God's good creation. Sadly, God's world has been corrupted by sin. One day, however, God will restore all things, allowing creation to flourish again. In the meantime, we have a responsibility to wisely steward the world and its resources.

Is there a God, and if so, what is God like? Some believe that God is an impersonal force; others, that he is a personal Being who is evil or tyrannical; and still others, that he is like a benevolent great granddad in the sky. Some believe that creation and God are the same thing, while others deny the existence of God. The Bible affirms that God's existence is fundamental. He is the uncreated Creator, and he holds the universe together. The Bible also affirms that God is personal, showing self-giving love, goodness, and justice. Though sin separated us from God, he is not distant. He desires to be known and to share his love with us. He reveals himself to us through the Scriptures that point to Christ as our Savior.

Is there any such thing as truth? In the modern West, the idea of truth has largely been abandoned. For many, truth is simply whatever you make it: "You have your truth, I have mine, and both of us are equally right." However, in such a world, there can be no right or wrong, good or evil—anything goes. Christianity makes a bold claim to teaching the truth about God, ourselves, and the world. In addition to encouraging us to use reason, evidence, and argument in pursuit of truth, it invites us to get to know a person—Jesus, who is himself the way, the truth, and the life.

4. Putting It All Together—Part 2

▸ **OBJECTIVE: You will be able to describe how Christianity answers five more of life's biggest questions.**

Whom can I trust? As we have seen, everyone submits to some kind of authority. Without trust, we wouldn't be able to get far in the world. Yet those we trust may let us down, leaving us with feelings of anger and abandonment. Christianity invites us to put our trust in Jesus, the one who never fails. To be sure, God doesn't always do what we want him to, nor does trusting Jesus mean that we will escape suffering. Yet Scripture shows us that God has been faithful in the past, even giving his own life for us, which gives us confidence that we can trust him with the future.

Why am I here? We all want our lives to count for something, to make a difference in the world; but sometimes, even our best efforts fail. It's tempting to throw up our hands, conclude that everything is meaningless, and bury ourselves in entertainment. But Christianity says that we are here because God loves us and wants us to know him, and that our lives have meaning in his great story. As his image-bearers and beloved children, we find purpose as we participate with him in the work of bringing light into darkness until the ultimate restoration.

How should I live? Many people believe that life is all about the pursuit of personal pleasure—that money, fame, power, sex, or something else will bring them happiness. They think the best way to live is to get all you can while you can. Christianity calls us to something totally different. God isn't against pleasure; however, we are not simply free to do as we please, regardless of the consequences. We are called to take our cue from Jesus and participate in God's mission through acts of self-giving love. In following Jesus, we find true joy and satisfaction in life.

How can I know right from wrong? Modern Western culture tells us that there is no such thing as right and wrong, that humans are free from any standard of morality; but time and again, when right and wrong are supposedly erased, right is defined by whoever has the most power. In contrast, for Christians, God is the standard of morality. We are called to imitate God's good character in our lives and decision-making. What is right and wrong is not always crystal clear. But wisdom, discernment, prayer, and careful reflection on Scripture, can lead us to Christlike and just actions.

What happens after I die? Some people think that this life is all there is. Others imagine multiple opportunities at life, conceive of an afterlife where they merge with the universe, or dream of paradise. The Christian worldview teaches that this life is not the end. One day, those who have trusted Christ will rise to be with him in the new creation, where they will be given new bodies, freedom from evil, and the ability to live freely as the people God created them to be. Those who reject Christ will spend eternity away from God's presence. Christians have hope that death is not final, because in his resurrection, Jesus proved himself to be stronger than death.

Here we only briefly sketch the answers that Christianity provides to ten questions, but each answer could be expanded. In addition, there are many more questions to be asked, for example: Why is there pain and suffering? Are there many paths to God? How should we interact with nature? For now, hopefully you are beginning to see how Christianity can provide meaningful and satisfying answers to our biggest questions.

5. Sharing the Good News

▸ **OBJECTIVE: You will be able to deduce that evangelism and apologetics are part of living out the Christian faith.**

Christians have all been commissioned to share the good news of forgiveness from sins and new life in Christ. At the end of the Gospel of Matthew, Jesus instructed the disciples to spread the gospel, teach, disciple, and baptize people in the name of the Father, Son, and Holy Spirit. This is the work of evangelism.

Evangelism is about inviting people to hear the good news of Jesus, put their trust in him, and receive forgiveness and new life. Evangelism is best done in personal conversations. You can start by sharing your own story about what God has done for you, and then inviting others to meet Jesus for themselves and experience the power of his transforming love. Essential to evangelism is verbally sharing the gospel—that Jesus "died for our sins in accordance with the Scriptures, that he was buried, that he was raised on the third day" (1 Corinthians 15:3–4); that Jesus has defeated sin and death; and that Jesus is King over all creation. Ultimately, evangelism is inviting people to become participants in God's story.

We also evangelize by living out the implications of the gospel. James warned believers that faith without works is dead (James 2:14–26). That does not mean we work to earn our salvation. It means we are saved by grace to then do good works (Ephesians 2:8–10). What James is saying, and what Paul teaches in Ephesians, is that true faith in Jesus will transform the way we live. If we do not follow Jesus in our actions, the world will see that our faith is dead and meaningless. That's why, as Christians, we need to regularly ask ourselves: Do our actions align with the teaching of Jesus? Do we love like he does? Do we value and treat people as God's image-bearers? Do we practice forgiveness, mercy, and compassion, even for our enemies? Are we a people defined by justice, healing, and hope? These types of behavior are the signposts pointing to the reality that in Jesus, God's kingdom has truly come into the world.

Some people will be ready and willing to receive the gospel message when they hear it, but others will have doubts or other barriers to belief. This is where apologetics comes in. Apologetics is the art of defending, commending, and translating the Christian faith.[4] It is about demonstrating the wonder and beauty of Christianity to those who have not yet experienced it. Think of apologetics as clearing the way for evangelism. Apologetics helps address questions and objections that people have to Christianity that keep them from accepting the gospel message and following Jesus.[4] Apologists often address questions like: How could a good God allow suffering? Can science and Christianity coexist? What evidence is there that Jesus actually rose from the dead? Are miracles possible? Does God send people to hell? and so on. Good apologetics helps people see how Christianity is reasonable, relevant, and desirable.[5]

In the next volume of this series, we'll spend a lot more time discussing evangelism and apologetics. Along the way, we'll grow deeper in our understanding of the Christian worldview by seeing how it stands up to criticism. We hope that this volume—*Foundations*—has deepened your understanding of the Christian faith and encouraged you on your journey with Jesus. But this is only the beginning. There is so much more to explore!

ENDNOTES

[1]For more discussion on how to read the Bible see Dan Kimball, *How (Not) to Read the Bible* (Grand Rapids: MI: Zondervan, 2020) or see Gordon D. Fee and Douglas Stuart, *How to Read the Bible for All Its Worth* (Grand Rapids, MI: Zondervan Academic, 2014).

[2]Henry Nouwen, "Being the Beloved (Full)," YouTube, https://www.youtube.com/watch?v=v8U4V4aaNWk.

[3]Alister E. McGrath, *Mere Apologetics: How to Help Seekers & Skeptics Find Faith* (Grand Rapids, MI: Baker, 2012), 17.

[4]McGrath, *Mere Apologetics*, 17–23.

[5]Paul M. Gould, *Cultural Apologetics: Renewing the Christian Voice, Conscience, and Imagination in a Disenchanted World* (Grand Rapids, MI: Zondervan, 2019), 24–25.

Appendices

Apostles Creed

[We] believe in God,
the Father almighty,
creator of heaven and earth.

[We] believe in Jesus Christ,
God's only Son, our Lord,
who was conceived by the Holy Spirit,
born of the Virgin Mary,
suffered under Pontius Pilate,
was crucified, died, and was buried;
he descended to the dead.
On the third day he rose again;
he ascended into heaven,
he is seated at the right hand of the Father,
and he will come again to judge the living and the dead.

[We] believe in the Holy Spirit,
the holy catholic [universal] church,
the communion of saints,
the forgiveness of sins,
the resurrection of the body,
and the life everlasting. AMEN.

Recommended Reading

CHRISTIANITY

C. S. Lewis, *Mere Christianity* (New York, NY: HarperCollins, 1952). Helpful for both Christians and skeptics alike, this now-classic explanation and defense of basic Christian beliefs also makes a bold case for the relevance of Christianity in contemporary society.

N. T. Wright, *Simply Christian: Why Christianity Makes Sense* (New York, NY: HarperCollins, 2006). In the tradition of Mere Christianity, New Testament scholar, N. T. Wright, shows how Christianity makes sense of our world by walking readers through key Christian topics—God, Israel, Jesus, the Spirit, worship, prayer, the Bible and many more.

Michael Reeves, *Delighting in the Trinity: An Introduction to the Christian Faith* (Downers Grove, IL: InterVarsity Press, 2012). A surprisingly accessible and lively introduction to Christianity through the lens of the Trinity. With obvious joy and delight, Reeves shows how the Trinity is at the heart of the Christian faith.

W. Gary Phillips, William E. Brown, and John Stonestreet, *Making Sense of Your World: A Biblical Worldview* (Salem, WI: Sheffield Publishing Company, 2008). Written from a distinctly worldviewish perspective, this book explores the fundamentals of the Christian worldview and shows how it offers a compelling vision for all of life.

Alister E. McGrath, *Christianity: An Introduction* (Malden, MA: Blackwell Publishing, 2015). A textbook introduction to Christianity, which, in addition to covering topics like Jesus and the Bible, also looks at Christian creeds, history, and denominations.

SCRIPTURE

Gordon D. Fee and Douglas Stuart, *How to Read the Bible for All Its Worth* (Grand Rapids, MI: Zondervan, 2014). A classic introduction to reading the Bible, this book provides helpful guidance for reading every major genre of biblical literature—from poetry and narrative, to prophecy and parable.

Michael W. Goheen and Craig G. Bartholomew, *The True Story of the Whole World: Finding Your Place in the Biblical Drama* (Grand Rapids, MI: Brazos Press, 2020). One of the best and most accessible explorations of the biblical metanarrative. The previous edition of Goheen and Bartholomew's book provided the outline and template for the six acts of the biblical story described in chapters 6–12 of this textbook.

Eugene H. Peterson, *Eat This Book: A Conversation in the Art of Spiritual Reading* (Grand Rapids, MI: Eerdmans, 2006). Using an ancient method of reading Scripture, *Lectio Divina*, Peterson demonstrates how Scripture is not just to be read, but lived. He also explains how seeing Scripture as a story changes everything.

Lesslie Newbigin, *A Walk Through the Bible* (Louisville, KY: Westminster John Knox Press, 1999). A short, fly-by overview of the biblical story, which includes Newbigin's dynamite conclusion about the uniqueness of the Christian story.

JESUS AND THE GOSPEL

Jeannine K. Brown, *The Gospels as Stories: A Narrative Approach to Matthew, Mark, Luke, and John* (Grand Rapids, MI: Baker Academic, 2020). An introduction to reading and interpreting the gospels using the lens of narrative criticism. Jeannine Brown helps readers see the individual episodes in each gospel as part of the larger story.

Scot McKnight, *The King Jesus Gospel: The Original Good News Revisited* (Grand Rapids, MI: Zondervan, 2011). In this important book, Scot McKnight argues that the gospel is more than just the plan of salvation. It is about Jesus as the completion of the story of Israel.

Richard Bauckham, *Jesus: A Very Short Introduction* (Oxford, England: Oxford University Press, 2011). A small little book written from a scholarly perspective, which introduces Jesus in his historical context and explores his identity and public ministry.

John Stott, *The Cross of Christ* (Downer's Grove, IL: InterVarsity Press, 2021). John Stott's classic masterpiece is the definitive evangelical book on the cross. Stott surveys theories of atonement, examining the meaning and relevance of Jesus' death.

Frederick Buechner, *Telling the Truth: The Gospel as Tragedy, Comedy, and Fairy Tale* (New York, NY: HarperCollins, 1977). Written for preachers but applicable to all, Telling the Truth approaches the gospel from a literary and artistic perspective using examples from King Lear, The Wizard of Oz, and other classic tales to illuminate the truth of the gospel.

DISCIPLESHIP AND SPIRITUAL FORMATION

Jamin Goggin and Kyle Strobel, *Beloved Dust: Drawing Close to God by Discovering the Truth About Yourself* (Nashville, TN: Nelson Books, 2014). Pastor Jamin Goggin and scholar Kyle Strobel explain why self-help strategies for the spiritual life always fail. They encourage readers to see themselves as "beloved dust" and in so doing open themselves up to God's transforming work.

Richard J. Foster, *Celebration of Discipline: The Path to Spiritual Growth* (New York, NY: HarperCollins, 1998). One of the 20th century's landmark texts on the practice of spiritual disciplines and spiritual growth, including discussion of both private and corporate disciplines.

Dietrich Bonhoeffer, *Life Together* (New York, NY: HarperCollins, 1954). Drawn from Bonhoeffer's personal experience of living in community in an underground seminary during World War II, this short work demonstrates the need for, and possibility of, true Christian fellowship.

C. S. Lewis, *The Four Loves* (New York, NY: HarperCollins, 1960). Lewis' classic exposition of the four Greek words for love: *storge* (affection), *philia* (friendship), *eros* (romantic love), and *agape* (self-giving love).

Image Credits

CHAPTER 1

1.5 | Abraham en portrait.jpg | Credit: Octave 444 | https://creativecommons.org/licenses/by-sa/4.0/legalcode

CHAPTER 2

2.6 | City of Carthage.jpg | Credit: Faresbenrayana | https://creativecommons.org/licenses/by-sa/4.0/legalcode

CHAPTER 3

3.5 | Church_of_Saint_George_in_Kurbinovo,_Church_Fathers_in_the_apse.jpg (3.5) | Credit: Tiffany Ziegler | https://creativecommons.org/licenses/by-sa/4.0/legalcode

CHAPTER 4

4.2 | AMR Kirche - Fresko 2.jpg | Credit: Wolfgang Sauber | https://creativecommons.org/licenses/by-sa/3.0/legalcode

4.7 | Keil-Delitzsch.JPG | Credit: Jonund | https://creativecommons.org/licenses/by-sa/4.0/legalcode

CHAPTER 5

5.3 | SDCC 2012 - Iron Man (7573663440).jpg | Credit: Pat Loika | https://creativecommons.org/licenses/by/2.0/legalcode

5.4 | Jean-Francois Lyotard cropped.jpg | Credit: Bracha L. Ettinger | https://creativecommons.org/licenses/by-sa/2.5/legalcode

CHAPTER 6

6.1 | God Enlil, seated, from Nippur, Iraq. 1800-1600 BCE. Iraq Museum.jpg | Credit: Osama Shukir Muhammed Amin | https://creativecommons.org/licenses/by-sa/4.0/legalcode

6.2 | Weener - Bahnhofstraße - Erlöserkirche in 06 ies.jpg | Credit: Frank Vincentz | https://creativecommons.org/licenses/by-sa/3.0/legalcode

6.3 | The Creation Of Adam And Eve.jpg | Credit: Ariel Chavarro Avila |https://creativecommons.org/licenses/by-sa/4.0/legalcode

6.6 | Tilman Riemenschneider schuf (1492-93) die Statuen von Adam und Eva. 2.jpg | Credit: Holger Uwe Schmitt|https://creativecommons.org/licenses/by-sa/4.0/legalcode

6.6 | Tilman Riemenschneider schuf (1492-93) die Statuen von Adam und Eva. 11.jpg | Credit: Holger Uwe Schmitt|https://creativecommons.org/licenses/by-sa/4.0/legalcode

6.9 | Creation Museum, Kentucky-3.jpg | Credit: David Berkowitz |https://creativecommons.org/licenses/by/2.0/legalcode

CHAPTER 7

7.3 | Eva og slangen.jpg | Credit: Villy Fink Isaksen | https://creativecommons.org/licenses/by-sa/3.0/legalcode

7.6 | Adam und Eva im Spitalhof Schwäbisch Gmünd. 01.jpg| Credit: Holger Uwe Schmitt| https://creativecommons.org/licenses/by-sa/4.0/legalcode

7.7 | Wrocław, Ostrów Tumski statua Matki Boskiej z Dzieciątkiem(1).jpg | Credit: Aw58 | https://creativecommons.org/licenses/by-sa/3.0/legalcode

CHAPTER 8

8.5 | Prophet and King David (Orthodox Christian icon).png | Credit: Отрок 12 |https://creativecommons.org/licenses/by-sa/4.0/legalcode

CHAPTER 9

9.8 | The Apocrypha Revised Standard version.jpg | Credit: Xrayguy1969 | https://creativecommons.org/licenses/by-sa/4.0/legalcode

CHAPTER 10

10.5 | Holy Land 2016 P0944 St. Lazarus Roman Catholic Church Resurrection of Lazarus fresco.jpg | Credit: Fallaner | https://creativecommons.org/licenses/by-sa/4.0/legalcode

CHAPTER 11

11.2 | Painting of Pentecost in Coimbra.jpg (Section 2) | Credit: Jose Goncalves | https://creativecommons.org/licenses/by-sa/4.0/legalcode

CHAPTER 12

12.2 | PMa ANG002 F Angers.jpg | Credit: Paul M.R. Maeyaert | https://creativecommons.org/licenses/by-sa/4.0/legalcode

12.5 | Detalje fra gravsted Lie Kirkegård.JPG | Credit: Orf3us | https://creativecommons.org/licenses/by-sa/3.0/legalcode

CHAPTER 13

13.2 | Anselm von canterbury.jpg | Credit: Andreas Faessler | https://creativecommons.org/licenses/by-sa/4.0/legalcode

CHAPTER 15

15.9 | 1640_Francisco-de-Zurbaran_Saint-Anthony-the-Abbot.jpg | Credit: Hakjosef | https://creativecommons.org/licenses/by-sa/4.0/legalcode

15.9 | Eugene Peterson.jpg | Credit: Clappstar | https://creativecommons.org/licenses/by/3.0/legalcode

CHAPTER 16

16.6 | Baptism at Eastside Christian Church2018.jpg | Credit: Eastside Christian Church | https://creativecommons.org/licenses/by/2.0/legalcode

16.9 | Annie Chikhwaza with orphaned twins.jpg | Credit: MediaWatch | https://creativecommons.org/licenses/by-sa/4.0/legalcode

16.9 | Emanuel AME Charleston, South Carolina.jpg | Credit: Kellyjeanne9 | https://creativecommons.org/licenses/by-sa/4.0/legalcode

Indexes

Word Index

Items in **bold** are key terms. Items in *italics* are titles of works or denote foreign words.

A

B

C

D

E

F

G

H

I

J

K

L

M

S

T

U

V

W

X

Y

Z

Scripture Index

Verses in blue are key verses.

JOHN

ACTS

ROMANS

1 CORINTHIANS

2 CORINTHIANS